REASON AND CONDUCT IN HUME
AND HIS PREDECESSORS

REASON AND CONDUCT IN HUME
AND HIS PREDECESSORS

by

STANLEY TWEYMAN

MARTINUS NIJHOFF / THE HAGUE / 1974

To my daughter Justine Susan

ISBN 90 247 1582 2

PRINTED IN BELGIUM

TABLE OF CONTENTS

PREFACE

Can reason play a significant role in making moral distinctions and in generating moral precepts? In this book I attempt to provide Hume's answers to these questions in the light of his employment of the 'Experimental Method', his doctrine of perceptions, and his analysis of reason. In addition to this, attention is paid to some of Hume's rationalist predecessors – most notably, Samuel Clarke and William Wollaston – in order to assess Hume's critique of the rationalists.

Regarding the preparation of this book I wish to thank Professor Ronald J. Butler who introduced me to Hume's writings. Professors W. J. Huggett, R. F. McRae, and F. E. Sparshott each read the original draft of this book and provided me with extremely valuable comments and criticisms. My wife Barbara Tweyman and my mother Fay Tweyman provided me with constant support throughout the time I was preparing this book, and for this, as well as for many other things, I will always be grateful. My father-in-law, the late Joseph Millstone, a man I dearly loved and respected, also provided me with support during the time I was working on this book. His death is for me an incalculable loss, and his memory is something I will always cherish.

Because there is considerable shifting of the textual references in the case of Hume's *Treatise of Human Nature* and the two *Enquiries*, for the convenience of the reader I should like to point out that all such references are to the Selby-Bigge editions, and that within these editions the following main divisions in terms of the pages they occupy are : *Treatise*, Book I, p. 1-274; *Treatise*, Book II, p. 275-454; *Treatise*, Book III, p. 455-621; *Enquiry Concerning Human Understanding*, p. 5-165; *Enquiry Concerning the Principles of Morals*, p. 169-323.

INTRODUCTION

Hume's *Treatise of Human Nature* and his *Enquiry Concerning the Principles of Morals* both show that he holds that his views on morality are to be understood through the application of his Experimental Method, his theory of perceptions, and his analysis of reason to the positions held by his rationalist predecessors. In this way Hume held that the untenability of the rationalists' positions [1] would be exposed, and this in turn would pave the way for the acceptance of his own ethical theory which has its foundation in feeling, this being the only alternative Hume considers to rationalism in ethics.

My aim in this book is to follow Hume through this task he has set for himself, a task noted by some but not yet carried through.[2] Accordingly, in the first four chapters attention is paid to those ingredients the interaction of which Hume believes will be able to establish the truth of his own ethical views. Chapter one examines Hume as an 'anatomist' of human nature, and attempts to provide a rationale for adopting the Experimental Method as the only method of inquiry. Any question which Hume raises and any answer he provides are couched in terms of his theory of perceptions. To fully understand both his questions and answers, therefore, an adequate understanding of his doctrine of impressions and ideas is required. In the second chapter, an attempt is made to show what Hume regards as the distinguishing features of these two kinds of perceptions, and what he means when he employs these terms. This analysis will permeate most of what follows in the succeeding chapters. The third chapter, for example, will avail itself of the findings in the second in examining Hume's

---

[1] I say 'positions' since we shall find that there is much diversity in the views held by the rationalists.

[2] See, for example, Henry D. Aiken, *Hume's Moral and Political* (Hafner Publishing Company, New York, 1948). Reprinted: Hafner Publishing Company, New York 1966, p. xxvii.

concept of reason. In addition, the third chapter will disclose that Hume actually has three senses of reason – demonstrative, causal, and distinctions of reason – rather than two (demonstrative and causal). Our study in this chapter will help us both in making clear the manner in which Hume employs the term 'reason' and in trying to make clear the roles which Hume assigns to reason in morality. Significantly, all three senses of reason will be seen to play a vital role.

The fourth chapter will be concerned with those aspects of the moral theories of Hume's rationalist predecessors which are relevant to our study in this work. In this regard I have confined myself primarily to Samuel Clarke and William Wollaston inasmuch as it is usually supposed that Hume is attacking their ethical theories.[3]

Chapter five is devoted entirely to Book III, Part I, Section i of the *Treatise* in which Hume raises the opening question of his inquiry into morality, namely, 'Whether 'tis by means of our ideas or impressions we distinguish betwixt vice and virtue, and pronounce an action blameable or praise-worthy?' and where he seeks to refute his rationalist predecessors. In the light of my discussion in the first three chapters the meaning of Hume's question is provided. And by means of my discussion in the first four chapters I will attempt to show that Hume is unable to refute the moral theories of Clarke and Wollaston : Hume has failed to see that much of what he accepts Wollaston and/or Clarke also regard as true; that certain parts of his attack on Walloston and Clarke are based on a misunderstanding of their views; and that some central areas of disagreement between Hume on the one hand and Wollaston and Clarke on the other are not attended to by Hume at all.

In addition to his attack on the rationalists in the first section of the third book of the *Treatise*, Hume also attacks rationalism in the second book of the *Treatise* (Book II, Part III, Section ii, 'Of the Influencing Motives of the Will') by attempting to establish that reason cannot yield rules of action in opposition to the dictates of passion. In my sixth chapter each of Hume's arguments will be examined especially as they apply to Samuel Clarke's view of the opposition of reason and passion, and I will argue that here again Hume's attack on rationalism in ethics fails : Hume is not able to show that reason cannot dictate actions. The section in the *Treatise* under examination in this chapter also gives us some insight into Hume's views on the relationship between conduct and demonstrative and

---

[3] See for example, John Laird, *Hume's Philosophy of Human Nature* (Methuen: London, 1932). Reprinted: Archon Books, 1967, p. 214.

causal reasoning. This will also be examined, and certain confusions regarding the relationship between causal reasoning and conduct will be cleared up.

Since Hume holds that reason is incapable of yielding practical judgments alone he concludes that the practical judgments of morality cannot be derived from reason. The aim of my seventh chapter is to determine exactly how Hume argues such judgments are obtained and to establish the various roles which Hume assigns to reason with regard to moral conduct.

My concluding chapter will offer a critical appraisal of Hume's approach to morality with particular emphasis on his use of the Experimental Method in an effort to establish the untenability of the moral theories of Wollaston and Clarke.

CHAPTER I

MORAL PHILOSOPHY AND ITS METHOD

I. AIM OF MORAL PHILOSOPHY

In his *Treatise of Human Nature* [1] and in the two later *Enquiries*[2], Hume's concern is with moral philosophy, an area he also labels the science of human nature.[3] This realm of enquiry he distinguishes from natural philosophy which had made remarkable advances under Newton. Moral philosophy itself is divided by Hume into the "easy and obvious philosophy" and the "accurate and abstruse".[4] People engaged in the latter are referred to as 'anatomists',[5] while those in the former are spoken of as 'painters'[6]. The easy and obvious philosophy treats men as being born chiefly for action [7] and as being influenced by taste and sentiment. As such, what is thought to be most desirable is painted in the most complimentary fashion, employing poetry and eloquence wherever necessary, and in general "treating their subject in an easy and obvious manner, and such as is best fitted to please the imagination, and engage the affections".[8] The accurate and abstruse philosophy considers man as a reasonable rather

---

[1] All references to the *Treatise of Human Nature* are taken from the Selby-Bigge edition, Oxford: Clarendon Press (1888), heieafter cited as T. followed by the page number.

[2] All references to the *Enquiries* are taken from the Selby-Bigge edition, Oxford: Clarendon Press (1902), hereafter cited as E. followed by the page number.

[3] E. 5.

[4] E. 6.

[5] See for example E. 10, T. 621.

[6] See for example E. 5, T. 621.

[7] E. 6.

[8] E. 5. The effectiveness of this type of philosophy is also noted by Hume. For example, in one passage he writes : "Tis difficult for us to withhold our assent from what is pointed out to us in all the colours of eloquence... We are hurried away by the lively imagination of our author or companion; and even he himself is often a victim of his own fire and genius." (T. 123) See also E. 6-7.

than as an active being and regards human nature as a subject of study.[9]

Both branches of moral philosophy are seen by Hume as being both didactic and remedial so far as human behaviour is concerned.[10] Nevertheless, the accurate and abstruse philosophy, which Hume also labels metaphysics,[11] is incapable of having this influence on its own.

... the abstruse philosophy, being founded on a turn of mind, which cannot enter into business and action, vanishes when the philosopher leaves the shade, and comes into open day; nor can its principles easily retain any influence over the conduct and behaviour. The feelings of our heart, the agitation of our passions, the vehemence of our affections, dissipate all its conclusions, and reduce the profound philosopher to a mere plebian".[12]

How, then, can the abstruse philosophy have a reference to human behaviour? Hume's answer is that it can do so through its ability to advise the painter :

The anatomist ought never to emulate the painter ... An anatomist, however, is admirably fitt'd to give advice to a painter; and 'tis even impractical to excel in the latter art, without the assistance of the former. We must have an exact knowledge of the parts, their situation and connexion, before we can design with any elegance or correctness. And thus the most abstract speculations concerning human nature, however cold and unentertaining, become subservient to *practical morality*; and may render this latter science more correct in its precepts, and more persuasive in its exhortations".[13]

Accordingly, although speculative in nature, metaphysics is practical in its goal :

Indulge your passion for science ... but let your science be human, and such as may have a direct reference to action and society".[14]

---

[9] E. 6.

[10] "Moral philosophy... may be treated after two manners; each of which has its peculiar merit, and may contribute to the entertainment, instruction, and reformation of mankind." (E. 5)

[11] E. 11.

[12] E. 7.

[13] T. 620-621. See also E. 9-10.

[14] E. 9. In addition, Hume maintains that metaphysics cannot be ignored since "there is no question of importance whose decision is not comprised in the science of man : and there is none, which can be decided with any certainty, before we become acquainted with that science (T. xx). The subjects most intimately connected with metaphysics or human nature are logic, morals and criticism, and politics since in each of these it is an aspect of man which is being studied : "The sole end of logic is to explain the principles and operations of our reasoning faculty, and the nature of our ideas : morals and criticism regard our tastes and sentiments : and politics consider men as united in society, and dependent on each other." (T. xix). Mathematics, natural philosophy, and

Hume points out that metaphysics has not yet attained the status of a science.[15] As a result he conceives his task in the *Treatise* and *Enquiry* to be that of trying to render metaphysics into a science.[16]

II. METHOD

How then are we to begin our investigation of human nature? That is, by what means does Hume intend to construct this new foundation for the sciences? His answer is that we must have recourse to observation and experience :

And as the science of man is the only solid foundation for the other sciences, so the only solid foundation we can give to this science itself must be laid on experience and observation.[17]

Hence the subtitle of the *Treatise* – "An attempt to introduce the experimental Method of Reasoning into Moral Subjects". Hume's point here is not that there exists a variety of methods out of which he has chosen one. His point is rather that the Experimental Method is the only method available. Problems raised by such a bold claim will be examined presently.

The pivotal role of experience has led many commentators to hold that for Hume reports of immediate experience are infallible. For example, N. K. Smith writes : "Immediate experience, in his [Hume's] view, yields an absolute certainty. As a mode of face to face awareness, it reveals impressions and ideas exactly as they are".[18] Certain passages in the text can be cited to substantiate this position. For example :

---

natural religion also have some connection with human nature since "they lie under the cognizance of men, and are judged by their powers and faculties." (T. xix).

[15] "Here indeed lies the justest and most plausible objection against a considerable part of methaphysics, that they are not properly a science... ." (E. 11).

See also T. xvii, T. 273.

[16] "Here then is the only expedient, from which we can hope for success in our philosophical researches, to leave the tedious lingring method, which we have hitherto followed, and instead of taking now and then a castle or village on the frontier, to march up directly to the capitol or center of these sciences, to human nature itself; which being once masters of, we may everywhere else hope for an easy victory." (T. xx).

See also T. 273.

In the *Enquiry* Hume writes : "The only method of freeing learning... is to enquire seriously into the nature of human understanding..." (E. 12).

[17] T. xx.

[18] N. K. Smith, *The Philosophy of David Hume* (Macmillan, London, 1941). Reprinted : Macmillan and Co. Ltd., St. Martin's Press, New York, 1960, p. 113. Later in the book Kemp Smith reiterates this position : "Immediate consciousness... is an *infal-*

Consciousness never deceives.[19]
... this belief, I say, arises immediately, without any new operation of the reason or imagination. Of this I can be certain, because I am never conscious of any such operation.[20]
... all sensations are felt by the mind, such as they really are ...[21]
For since all actions and sensations of the mind are known to us by consciousness, they must necessarily appear in every particular what they are, and be what they appear. Every thing that enters the mind, being in *reality* as the perception, 'tis impossible any thing shou'd to *feeling* appear different. This were to suppose, that even where we are most intimately conscious, we might be mistaken.[22]

However, what has not been noticed is that certain passages indicate a view opposed to that above :

The chief obstacle ... to our improvement in the moral or metaphysical sciences is the obscurity of the ideas, and ambiguity of the terms.[23]
For it being usual, after the frequent use of terms, which are really significant and intelligible, to omit the idea, which we would express by them, and to preserve only the custom, by which we recall the idea at pleasure; so it naturally happens, that after the frequent use of terms, which are wholly insignificant and unintelligible, we fancy them to be on the same footing with the precedent, and to have a secret meaning, which we might discover by reflection. The resemblance of their appearance deceives the mind ...[24]

If we can clear up this difficulty then I submit that in addition to removing the inconsistency we shall gain greater insight into Hume's full method.

By closely examining the second set of passages we can see that the obscurity in what is presented to consciousness concerns our languid perceptions or ideas, and those operations of the mind which strike the mind in a manner similar to ideas; whereas in those passages in which Hume speaks of the non-deceptive nature of what presents itself to consciousness he is speaking of our sensations, or as he refers to them, our more lively perceptions or impressions.[25] Hume sometimes speaks of the employment

---

lible mode of apprehension. This is a position to which Hume holds consistently from start to finish of the *Treatise.*" (p. 455). See also p. 125.

[19] T. 66.
[20] T. 102.
[21] T. 189.
[22] T. 190. See also T. 366.
[23] E. 61. See also E. 13, 60.
[24] T. 224. See also T. 33, 65, 205 (n), 267.
[25] "These impressions are all strong and sensible. They admit not of ambiguity." (E. 62). "An idea is by its very nature weaker and fainter than an impression... its weakness render(s) it obscure." (T. 73).
A more detailed examination of impressions and ideas will be presented in the next

of "experience and observation" [26] and sometimes of "careful and exact experiments"[27]. And the text bears out that when Hume speaks of 'experience and observation' as the 'only solid foundation' we can give to the science of human nature, he usually has in mind the apprehension of our impressions. In addition, his move from "experience and observation" to the more precise formulation "careful and exact experiments, and the observation of those particular effects, which result from its (i.e. the mind's different circumstances and situations" appears to indicate that his concern is with our ideas—their origin, nature, or reality or with those operations of the mind which strike the mind in a manner similar to ideas.[28] Nevertheless, the employment of "experience and observation" and "careful and exact experiments" complement one another inasmuch as for Hume no idea can be understood until we examine the impression from which it is derived :

'Tis impossible to reason justly, without understanding perfectly the idea concerning which we reason; and 'tis impossible perfectly to understand any idea without tracing it up to its origin, and examining that primary impression from which it arises. The examination of the impression bestows a clearness on the idea; and the examination of the idea bestows a like clearness on all our reasoning.[29]

Accordingly, Hume conceives of himself as providing moral philosophy with a microscope, so to speak, in order to enable it to carry out its program :

These impressions are all strong and sensible. They admit not of ambiguity. They ... may throw light on their correspondent ideas which lie in obscurity. And by this means we may, perhaps, attain a new microscope or species of optics, by which, in the moral sciences, the most minute, and most simple ideas may be so enlarged as to fall readily under our apprehension, and be equally known with the grossest and most sensible ideas, that can be the object of our inquiry.[30]

----

chapter. Nevertheless, as I will now go on to show, even the Introduction to the *Treatise* already presupposes some insight into the distinction between impressions and ideas.

[26] T. xx.

[27] T. xxi. An ecxellent example of Hume's employment of careful and exact experiments occurs when Hume is concerned with the idea of necessary connection. (T. 74ff., E. 25ff,. A. 11ff.).

[28] "It is remarkable concerning the operations of the mind, that, though most intimately present to us, yet, whenever they become the object of reflection, they seem involved in obscurity; nor can the eye readily find those lines and boundaries, which discriminate and distinguish them. The objects are too fine to remain long in the same aspect or situation... " (E. 13).

For examples of the point I am now making see T. 61, 203ff., 253ff.

[29] T. 74-75.

[30] E. 62.

Although this last quotation has received much attention in the literature, it is an error to think that this is Hume's final word on the subject. For Hume points out that certain impressions are also subject to the ambiguities found in ideas :

The confusion, in which impressions are sometimes involv'd, proceeds only from their faintness and unsteadiness ...[31]

Whenever this occurs, careful and exact experiments must again be employed; only in such cases these experiments are needed to throw light upon our impressions.[32] When Hume speaks of the confusion in which impressions are sometimes involved, we shall see that he has in mind confusing an impression with an idea or confusing the feeling attached to certain impressions with the feeling attached to the operation of certain faculties. Most of Hume's moral theory is directed toward establishing that both types of confusion have misled his rationalist predecessors. In the case of certain impressions then our approach is similar to that employed regarding ideas : "An idea is by its very nature weaker and fainter than an impression; – If its weakness render it obscure, 'tis our business to remedy that defect, as much as possible, by keeping the idea steady and precise ..." [33] Careful and exact experiments performed where our impressions are weak are, I submit, directed toward the same end. The obscurity in which, as we now see, both impressions and ideas can be involved, has its source in us and is not an intrinsic part of any perception : "... since all impressions are clear and precise, the ideas, which are copy'd from them, must be of the same nature, and can never, but from our fault, contain any thing so dark and intricate".[34] More specifically, the obscurity in any perception is a function of the weak hold which the mind has of it.[35]

Summing up the situation as so far uncovered we find the following : Our impressions are usually vivid with a consequent clarity which enables us to employ them in order to shed light on our ideas or weaker perceptions.

---

[31] T. 19.

[32] One passage makes this matter especially clear. At one point in Book II of the *Treatise* we find Hume maintaining that all perceptions are conjoined with emotion, although most of the time these emotions are languid and go unnoticed. Nevertheless, he holds that "however custom may make us insensible of this sensation, and cause us to confound it with the object or idea, 'twill be easy, by careful and exact experiments, to separate and distinguish them." (T. 373).

[33] T. 73.

[34] T. 72-73.

[35] "... its weakness render(s) it obscure... " See also Hume's analysis of belief, *Treatise*, Bk. I, Pt. III.

If an impression is weak and languid, we can employ careful and exact experiments to put the impression in a clearer light, that is, to enable the mind to get a better hold on it, and in this way gain a greater understanding of our ideas.

Those passages enjoining a reliance on our impressions because of their clarity have a characteristic Cartesian ring to them [36] and can lead to the belief that Hume holds that it is the mere clarity of our impressions which ensures the success of metaphysics. In fact, however, the clarity found in most impressions is but a necessary condition of the success of metaphysics, and is not considered by Hume to be sufficient or necessary and sufficient for the success of metaphysics. For concerning clarity, Hume has two things to say. In the first place, as we have seen, the clarity of the impression bestows a similar clarity on the correspondent idea which enables a fuller understanding of it. And secondly, the clarity of the idea establishes that what is being thought is entirely consistent :

How any clear, distinct idea can contain circumstances, contradictory to itself ... is absolutely incomprehensible; and is, perhaps, as absurd as any proposition, which can be formed.[37]

Nevertheless, the reliance on the clarity of impressions presupposes that there is an impression corresponding to every idea, and it also presupposes that the reliance on experience is somehow justified. A full discussion of the former point will be postponed until the next chapter, although the latter point can be dealt with here.

III. JUSTIFICATION OF THE METHOD

An effective discussion of the problems involved in adopting a standpoint in philosophy (and elsewhere) is presented by Oliver Johnson in an article entitled *Begging the Question*,[38] and for our purposes it will be convenient to approach this topic through this article. Johnson points out that when two people are arguing a philosophical question and the discussion reaches an ultimate principle or set of principles held by one of the disputants, his opponent can then raise the problem of how he knows that his principles are true, and Johnson adds, at this point there can be no meaningful argument between the two people.

[36] T. 72-73.
[37] E. 157-158.
[38] *Dialogue*, Vol. VI, 1967, No. 2. This article is not being discussed *in toto*, and consequently most of Johnson's positive comments are being omitted.

... it is impossible to argue the most fundamental of philosophical issues – those concerned with ultimate principles – for the disputants in any such argument would have either to agree in their principles and then the argument would be concerned simply with matters of logical implications that follow from these principles or they would have to disagree in their principles and then they would turn out to be, strictly speaking, unable to talk to each other.[39]

In addition, Johnson holds that from the fact that disputes about ultimate principles are not possible, it follows that all attempts at philosophical arguments are question-begging against one's opponent since the principles held by the other person cannot be ruled out as untenable. Applying this to Hume, Johnson writes :

Over and over again Hume dismisses positions in metaphysics, ethics, theology, and other fields by arguments that rest finally on an appeal to his empiricist theory of knowledge. Once again, all these arguments beg the question against philosophers who reject empiricism.[40]

Addressing himself to empiricists generally, he asserts :

Your claim to know rests on the assumption that the appeal to empirical evidence provides a legitimate criterion of knowledge. But how would you justify that assumption? ... as long as he remains an empiricist, the appeal to empirical evidence as a criterion of knowledge must remain for him the end of the road. It is used to support every knowledge claim he makes but is itself supported by nothing. To appeal to it, therefore, in the face of a possibility of other, incompatible knowledge criteria is to beg the question against these criteria.[41]

To beg the question Johnson maintains that a theory must satisfy two conditions [42] : (a) a theory maintaining the denial of the original theory must be logically possible, i.e. the theory must be free from contradiction, and (b) the conflicting theory must be ruled out on the grounds that it is incompatible with the ultimate principles of the original theory. It is the first of the two conditions mentioned which Johnson holds to be the more important. Accordingly, it is only if there is no alternative to a given theory, that a theory can be taken as true and no question is begged.[43]

---

[39] *Ibid.*, 136-137.
[40] *Ibid.*, 138.
[41] *Ibid.*, 140.
[42] *Ibid.*, 142.
[43] From all that has been said Johnson concludes that the only ultimate principle which does not beg the question in his sense is the appeal to logical nessity : "... logical necessity itself is a legitimate knowledge criterion and... therefore, we can with complete justification claim to know any proposition to be true if we can demonstrate that

The exposition of Johnson's article presented above has brought out two main points : (a) concerning ultimate principles we either agree or disagree; (b) Hume dismisses his opponents by having recourse to his empiricist theory of knowledge : hence, he begs the question. I now propose to turn to Hume to see whether a reply to these points can be reconstructed.

Hume begins the *Treatise* by calling attention to the fact that previous thinkers have, among other things, accepted principles on trust,[44] and as a result they have generated the multitude of opinions present in Metaphysics. And yet there are passages in which Hume also claims to be accepting his principles on the same basis :

... we can give no reason for our most general and most refined principles, beside our experience of their reality ...[45]

In this passage Hume is stating explicitly that the reliance on experience is not argued for, but merely accepted. On the other hand we find him saying that Metaphysics must begin with self-evident principles :

To begin with clear and self-evident principles ... [is] ... the only method(s), by which we can hope to reach truth, and attain a proper stability and certainty in our determinations.[46]

It seems then that Hume is maintaining two positions in regard to his empiricist standpoint, namely, that it is taken upon trust, and secondly that the standpoint is self-evident. If the former is true, then it appears that Johnson's first and second points about ultimate principles apply to Hume since Hume would be conceding that no arguments about ultimate principles are possible. However, if the adoption of the Experimental Method as an ultimate principle is viewed by Hume as self-evident, then Hume could be interpreted as maintaining that the denial of his position is self-contradictory, in which case he appears to be in accordance with

---

the denial of that proposition involves a contradiction... it [i.e. logical necessity] avoids begging the question for the simple reason that in its case there is no question to be begged. When we claim to know something on the grounds that it is logically self-evident, we are implying that the denial of what we assert involves a contradiction, hence is logically impossible. so cannot be." (p. 143-144). My own analysis will not require that attention be given to this point.

[44] "Principles taken upon trust... are everywhere to be met with in the systems of the most eminent philosophers, and seem to have drawn disgrace upon philosophy itself." (T. xvii).

[45] T. xxii.

[46] E. 150.

Johnson's criterion (mentioned in footnote 43) for an acceptable ultimate principle (although we may want to debate whether in fact Hume's ultimate principles are self-evident).

A better understanding of this whole situation can be obtained by determining against whom Hume thinks he must defend his method and how he sets out to defend it. Clearly, it is not the vulgar, for he holds that his method is only an improvement on the vulgar approach.[47] It is other philosophers against whom he is arguing, and they fall into two groups – Pyrrhonians or extreme sceptics, and non-empiricists.

Concerning Pyrrhonism [48] or the sceptical objections to moral evidence or reasonings concerning matters of fact Hume admits that the arguments of the sceptic carry some conviction with them while we attend to them, and it takes great effort to refute them, although full refutation is not always possible.[49] Hume also admits that dogmatism is a liability in philosophy.[50] Nevertheless, he holds that a verbal refutation of excessive scepticism is in no wise necessary since these arguments cannot have a lasting influence upon us. Nature or Instinct, not argumentation, breaks the force of excessive scepticism : "... no thing can be more serviceable, than to be once thoroughly convinced of the force of Pyrrhonian doubt, and of the impossibility, that anything but the strong power of natural instinct, could free us from it".[51] Of course, even the sceptic is unable to maintain his principles once he leaves his study.[52]

If, while confronted by the excessive sceptic we seek to criticize him, then, Hume asserts, we have two courses of action. In the first place we can point out that it lacks any value : "... no durable good can ever result from it; while it remains in its full force and vigour".[53] Secondly, we can

[47] "... philosophical decisions are nothing but the reflections of common life, methodised and corrected." (E. 162).

[48] Hume's fullest treatment of this topic appears in Section XII of the first *Enquiry*.

[49] "These principles may flourish and triumph in the schools; where it is, indeed, difficult, if not impossible, to refute them." (E. 159).

[50] "In general, there is a degree of doubt, and caution, and modesty, which... ought for ever to accompany a just reasoner." (E. 152).

[51] E. 162.

[52] "And though a Pyrrhonian may throw himself or others into a momentary amazement and confusion... the first and most trivial event in life will put to flight all his doubts and scruples... When he awakes from his dream, he will be the first to join in the laugh against himself, and to confess, that all his objections are mere amusement." (E. 160, see also *Dialogues Concerning Natural Religion*, Oxford, the Clarendon Press, 1935. Reprinted : Library of Liberal Arts, New York, 1943 p. 132).

[53] E. 159.

challenge the sceptic : "We need only ask such a sceptic, *What his meaning is? And what he proposes by all these curious researches?* He is immediately at a loss, and knows not what to answer".[54] Accordingly, Hume would point out to the sceptic that nothing the sceptic has said can threaten the reliance on experience since this destructive type of Pyrrhonism [55] cannot have a lasting influence on us and to yield to it (were it able to have a lasting influence upon us) would be disastrous.[56]

Accordingly, destructive Pyrrhonism cannot destroy Empiricism since it is experience which destroys destructive Pyrrhonism.[57] Nevertheless, it is a non sequitur to conclude that because destructive scepticism cannot be maintained in the face of experience that therefore Hume's Experimental Method is the only method for philosophy. It is important then to determine just how Hume carries out his attack on rival philosophers.

One tactic which cannot be used is to show one's opponent that his views cannot have a lasting effect on us; that is, the approach cannot be similar to that employed against the Pyrrhonian, since in various places Hume concedes that his own philosophical views based on the experimental method also can have no great impact on the vulgar consciousness.[58] Nevertheless, our inability to maintain Pyrrhonism in the face of experience provides Hume with a strategy against rival philosophers.

Hume's quest is for principles of human nature. He believes such principles can be uncovered through careful and exact experiments. Now, as the discussion of destructive Pyrrhonism has shown, all empirical evidence cannot be rejected when dealing with questions of fact. It follows then that if a rival philosopher rejects any aspect of Hume's experiments, he must show what he believes to be faulty or defective. The one thing he cannot do, however, is reject all empirical evidence : to do so would be

---

[54] E. 159-160.

[55] I call it *destructive* in order to be able to contrast it later with a benefical or constructive type of scepticism. Hence, it must not be thought that Hume sees no value in scepticism.

[56] "... he must acknowledge, if he will acknowledge anything, that all human life must perish, were his principles universally and steadily to prevail. All discourse, all action would immediately cease; and men remain in total lethargy... " (E. 160).

[57] "The great subverter of *Pyrrhonism* or the excessive principles of scepticism, is action, and employment, and the occupations of common life." (E. 158-159).

[58] For example, summing up his investigation of the source of moral distinctions, and noticing its similarity to the result of his inquiry into the idea of necessary connection Hume remarks : "... and this discovery in morals, like that other in physics, is to be regarded as a considerable advancement of the speculative sciences; tho, like that too, it has little or no influence on practice." (T. 469).

tantamount to becoming a destructive sceptic. Therefore, if Hume is to be criticized, the criticism must, in the first instant, be directed against the experiments he undertakes.

From this discussion a reply to Johnson on Hume's behalf is possible. Concerning Johnson's first point that regarding ultimate principles we either agree or disagree Hume would say that it is possible to argue with an opponent while retaining the appeal to experience as an ultimate principle by showing the latter our inability to reject all empirical evidence on questions of fact; hence, he must concede a role for the Experimental Method when dealing with matters of fact. Inasmuch as all such evidence cannot be ruled out of court, Hume's point is that discussion about what to count as evidence and what to reject is also possible :

These sceptical topics [e.g. the crooked appearance of an oar in water] indeed, are only sufficient to prove, that the senses alone are not implicitly to be depended on; but that we must correct their evidence by reason, and by considerations, derived from the nature of the medium, the distance of the object, and the disposition of the organ, in order to render them, within their sphere, the proper *criteria*, of truth and falsehood.[59]

In short, since it is not possible to reject or distrust all beliefs based on experience, any philosophy (such as Johnson's) which seeks to do so is unrealistic and unacceptable. Beyond this, in the case of those – especially the rationalists – who persist in their claim that experience can be augmented or perhaps replaced by a rival faculty, Hume's procedure is to undertake an examination of the faculty in question, and to show that it is not fitted to perform the function alleged in its behalf. Since the capacities of our various faculties are subject to introspective analysis, Hume asserts that here too the reliance on experience cannot be abandoned. Accordingly, there cannot be an empiricist *bias* when dealing with these faculties.

Johnson's second point that Hume's empiricism begs the question against all other alleged knowledge criteria is also without force. For even if the denial of the Experimental Method is logically possible, and hence even if the Experimental Method begs the question in Johnson's sense, Hume could maintain that Johnson's objection – and all others like it – is insufficient to destroy the force of empirical evidence. Since the alternative to experience when dealing with matters of fact is Pyrrhonism, and since the principles of human understanding are matters of fact,[60] Hume argues

[59] E. 151.
[60] E. 13.

that there can be no justification for a different method in Metaphysics. To the claim that Metaphysics can go beyond the Experimental Method because it can deal with matters such as substance which are not perceivable, Hume objects on the ground that no meaning can be given to such notions,[61] and claims that it is incumbent on his opponent to prove otherwise. In addition, whenever such claims arise, Hume seeks to show that that position and the belief attending it are traceable to certain principles of human nature, and that they are usually generated when the mind is unable to reconcile or reject contrary principles.[62] Accordingly, the belief in matters which are unobservable is largely a method of pacification whereby the mind is able to set itself at ease. (This, of course, is consistent with such notions having no meaning if Hume can show that the belief that such notions have meaning or are intelligible is illusory.)[63] What is important here, however, is that since no one can seriously deny the relevance of empirical evidence when dealing with matters of fact, Hume could request that his opponent show what is defective with the evidence he presents in accounting for his opponent's position. Put in this light, the charge that Hume's Experimental Method begs the question in Johnson's sense appears insignificant.

The last point to be discussed is the conflict pointed out earlier between Hume's claim that his position is taken upon trust, and his claim that the position, if it is to provide a proper standpoint for philosophy, must be self-evident. The matters taken up in the last few pages leave no doubt that Hume is serious about his trust claim, since we are led instinctively to rely on our senses when dealing with questions of fact. At no time did we encounter anything approaching the position that the reliance on experience is self-evident, and so far as I can see, no other passage in the

[61] See, for example, T. 72, T. 224.

[62] The most important passages bearing on this point are at T. 224-226. have These little bearing on what follows and consequently will not be dealt with in detail.

[63] See, for example T. 224, where Hume discusses how some philosophers are misled when they are unable to find a perceivable connection between a cause and its effect. Or again, in speaking of our attempts to reconcile the identity of an object with the succesion of related but different perceptions of that object which are presented to us Hume writes : "In order to justify to ourselves this absurdity, we often feign some new and unintelligible principle, that connects the objects together, and prevents their interruption or variation. Thus we feign... the notion of a *soul*, and *self* and *substance*, to disguise the variation... where we do not give use to such a fiction, our propension to confound identity with relation is so great, that we are apt to imagine something unknow and mysterious connecting the parts, beside their relation; and this I take to be the case with regard to the identity we ascribe to plants and vegetables." (T. 254-255).

Humean corpus does so either. There is, however, one passage in which Hume apologizes for ever having said that something is evident, certain, or undeniable :

... we are apt not only to forget our scepticism, but even our modesty too; and make use of such terms as these, *'tis evident, 'tis certain, 'tis undeniable*; which a due deference to the public ought, perhaps, to prevent. I may have fallen into this fault after the example of others; but I here enter a *caveat* against any objections, which may be offer'd on that head; and declare that such expressions were extorted from me by the present view of the object, and imply no dogmatical spirit, nor conceited idea of my own judgment, which are sentiments that I am sensible can become no body, and a sceptic still less than any other.[64]

Hume's position is therefore that the reliance on experience is based exclusively on trust; but it is a trust to which each of us must give our assent when dealing with questions of fact. Thus, we are again brought to see that "philosophical decisions are nothing but the reflections of common life, methodized and corrected"[65]; and we are brought to see that only through this method will true metaphysics replace the false philosophies.

We must therefore glean up our experiments in this science from a cautious observation of human life, and take them as they appear in the common course of the world ... Where experiments of this kind are judiciously collected and compared, we may hope to establish on them a science, which will not be inferior in certainty, and will be much superior in utility to any other of human comprehension.[66]

[64] T. 273-274.
[65] E. 162.
[66] T. xxiii.

CHAPTER II

IMPRESSIONS AND IDEAS

I. IMPRESSIONS AND IDEAS DIFFER IN KIND

We have seen that for Hume the true portal to metaphysics is through the sometimes laborious task of mental anatomy, and that the beginning of the latter is through an examination of our manifold states of consciousness.

To begin with, Hume refers to whatever presents itself to consciousness as a perception.[1] He then goes on to divide all our perceptions into impressions and ideas : "All the perceptions of the human mind resolve themselves into two distinct kinds, which I shall call impressions and ideas".[2] Although Hume believes that the distinction made above is readily comprehensible,[3] it has given rise to much confusion and a great divergence of opinion on the part of Hume's commentators. This section, therefore, will be devoted to the resolution of some of these difficulties.

The passage quoted above maintains that impressions and ideas differ in kind.[4] However, the bulk of Hume's ensuing comments seems to

[1] "When I turn my reflection on *myself*, I can never perceive this *self* without some one or more perceptions; nor can I ever perceive anything but the perceptions." (T. 634).

"The annihilation, which some people suppose to follow upon death, and which entirely destroys the self, is nothing but an extinction of all particular perceptions... " (T. 634-635).

"Our author begins with some definitions. He calls a *perception* whatever can be present to the mind, whether we employ our senses, or are actuated with passion, or exercise our thought and reflection." (A. 8).

[2] T. 1.

[3] "I believe it will not be very necessary to employ many words in explaining this distinction." (T. 1)

[4] Early in Bk. III (p. 456) Hume again asserts this position : "Now... perceptions resolve themselves into two kinds, viz. *impressions* and *ideas*... " Similarly, in the *Enquiry* (p. 18) we find : "Here therefore we may divide all the perceptions of the mind into two classes or species... "

substantiate the claim that impressions and ideas can differ in but one respect, and that this difference is merely one of degree. He tells us that different perceptions present themselves to consciousness differently : some enter forcefully and others enter less forcefully and in a less lively manner. Forceful perceptions are called impressions; languid perceptions are called ideas :

Those perceptions, which enter with most force and violence, we may name *impressions*; and under this name I comprehend all our sensations, passions and emotions, as they make their first appearance in the soul. By *ideas* I mean the faint images of these in thinking and reasoning ...[5]

Accordingly, ideas are exact copies of impressions and differ from the latter only in the way they present themselves to consciousness. Impressions and ideas, we are told, do not even differ in nature :

That idea of red, which we form in the dark, and that impression, which strikes our eyes in sunshine, differ only in degree, not in nature.[6]

We find then that Hume appears to be offering two different accounts of the distinction between impressions and ideas.

Norman Kemp Smith has noticed this dichotomy in Hume and claims that the two accounts are inconsistent, and that in the case of certain passages the criterion of force and vivacity breaks down, and gives way to Hume's treatment of impressions and ideas as types of perceptions which stand in contrast to each other :

There remains for consideration the one other main tenet which Hume propounds in the first section of the *Treatise* ... it is ambiguously formulated and ... it is by no means held to, in unmodified form, in the latter stages of the argument. I refer to the contention ... that the difference between impressions and ideas consists in force and liveliness. What renders Hume's statements obscure and bewildering is the twofold manner in which the difference is formulated, as being at once a difference of *kind* and yet also a difference that admits of *degree*. The two ways of regarding it, so little compatible with one another, are almost equally emphasized.[7]

In Books II and III of the *Treatise* there are a number of passages in which ... ideas and impressions are set in *contrast* to one another in a manner by no means in keeping with the teaching of Book I. [For example] in Book III of the *Treatise* there are passages in which ideas and impressions ... are again definitely contrasted, and that in ways to which mere force and liveliness are not really relevant.
   'Now as perceptions resolve themselves into two kinds, viz. *impressions* and

[5] T. 1.
[6] T. 3.
[7] Smith, p. 209-210.

ideas, this distinction gives rise to a question, with which we shall open our present inquiry concerning morals, *Whether 'tis by means of our* ideas *or* impressions *we distinguish betwixt vice and virtue, and* pronounce an action blameable or praiseworthy? ...'
In the answer which Hume eventually gives to this question the *contrast* between impressions and ideas ... [is] ... maintained.[8]

What is not immediately clear is why the different degrees of force and vivacity cannot provide the contrast of which Kemp Smith speaks and which would enable Hume to make a distinction in kind between impressions and ideas. Hume could be holding that all perceptions possessing a certain vivacity or less are ideas, whereas those possessing any greater vivacity are impressions. In this way, then, the contrast of which Kemp Smith speaks could perhaps be upheld through the criterion of force and vivacity. In addition, assuming Hume did abandon the criterion of force and vivacity, it is not evident what replaced it, nor why it was replaced. In order to arrive at an answer to these various questions I shall begin by seeking to establish what Hume holds constitutes a distinction in kind.

II. DISTINCTIONS IN KIND

There is one passage in which Hume provides a criterion for determining whether a distinction in kind is warranted. It appears at the end of his discussion of the seven different philosophical relations wherein he raises the question whether 'difference' should be included as an eighth philosophical relation. And he answers that 'difference' rather than being a relation is a "negation of relation".[9] Hume continues : "Difference is of two kinds as opposed either to identity or resemblance. The first is called a difference of *number*; the other of *kind*".[10]

It is, of course, the latter type of difference that we are interested in here. But the passage quoted raises certain questions which must be answered here if the passage itself is to be understood. To understand why difference is a negation of relation we shall have to inquire into what Hume means by a relation and what is required before one can be said to exist.

Hume points out that the word 'relation' has two meanings :

The word RELATION is commonly used in two senses considerably different from each other. Either for that quality, by which two ideas are connected together in the imagination, and the one naturally introduces the other ... or for

---

[8] *Ibid.,* p. 281-283.
[9] T. 15.
[10] T. 15.

that particular circumstance, in which even upon the arbitrary union of two ideas in the fancy, we may think proper to compare them.[11]

Now, although at this point we are primarily concerned with Hume's remarks concerning the second sense of relation – since it is here that he has introduced the notion of a difference of kind – it will be necessary to discuss both senses of relation since, as will become evident as we proceed, the second sense of relation – which Hume calls philosophical – is fully comprehensible only in the light of his discussion of the first type of relation, the natural relations.[12]

Hume asserts that although the imagination can possess no ideas not received through either our external or internal senses, nevertheless "it has an unlimited power of mixing, compounding, separating, and dividing these ideas, in all the varieties of fiction and vision".[13] But did the imagination not possess "principles which are permanent, irresistible, and universal" [14] which guide it, its influence in connecting or associating ideas would be left to chance. If there were no natural principles of association, our simple ideas would rarely be found in the same combinations. Since ideas are commonly found in similar groupings, it follows that there is "some bond of union among them, some associating quality, by which one idea naturally introduces another".[15] This type of association of ideas is called 'natural' since it is done unreflectively.[16] And it is founded upon "three principles of connection among ideas, namely, *resemblance, contiguity* in time or place, and *cause and effect*".[17]

---

[11] T. 13.

[12] There is a passage in the *Abstract* in which Hume emphasizes the importance of the natural relations so far as all the operations of the mind are concerned : "Thro' this whole book, there are pretensions to new discoveries in philosophy; but if any thing can intitle the author to so glorious a name as that of an inventor, 'tis the use he makes of the principle of the association of ideas, which enters into most of his philosophy... all the operations of the mind must, in a great measure, depend on them." *An Abstract of a Treatise of Human Nature.* Reprinted (from the 1740 copy) with an Introduction by J. M. Keynes and P. Sraffa, Archon Books, Hamden, Connecticut, 1965, p. 31-32. Reprint of the 1740 copy owned by J. M. Keynes was first published in 1938 by the Cambridge University Press. Hereafter this book will be referred to as A. followed by the appropriate page number.

[13] E. 47, see also T. 10, 623-624.

[14] T. 225.

[15] T. 10.

[16] "... certain relations... make us pass from and object to another, even though there be no reason to determine us to that transition... The Principles of union among ideas I have reduc'd to three general ones... " (T. 92).

[17] E. 25. See also T. 11.

Hume does not develop his discussion in any great detail since he accepts what he has said as being very clear, decisive, and capable of little argumentation. Consequently, of resemblance he merely states :

'Tis plain, that in the course of our thinking, and in the constant revolution of our ideas, our imagination runs easily from one idea to any other that *resembles* it, and that this quality alone is to the fancy a sufficient bond and association.[18]

Similarly, of contiguity he asserts :

'Tis likewise evident, that as the senses in changing their objects, are necessitated to change them regularly, and take them as they lie *contiguous* to each other, the imagination must by long custom acquire the same method of thinking, and run along the parts of space and time, in conceiving its objects.[19]

Since cause and effect will receive a comprehensive discussion later in the *Treatise*, Hume merely states here : " 'Tis sufficient to observe that there is no relation, which produces a stronger connexion in the fancy, and makes one idea more readily recall another, then the relation of cause and effect betwixt objects".[20]

As is well known, Hume's solution to the problem of causal inference centers around the habit or custom which the mind acquires of connecting those ideas in thought when it has found the impressions of these ideas to be constantly conjoined in experience. As such, the explanation of causality as a natural relation parallels the explanation Hume offers in the case of the natural relation of contiguity. In both cases, repeated observations accustom the mind to relate what was found to be related before. But this need not necessarily be the case with respect to resembling objects, and as a result Kemp Smith questions Hume's inclusion of resemblance in the list of natural relations :

... how far can resemblance be viewed as a 'natural relation' on all fours in this particular respect with contiguity in time and place. That in a certain proportion of the instances of recall the ideas concerned in the recall are found *on comparison* to resemble one another, cannot, of course, be questioned ... But Hume, we cannot help noting, does not give any reason for holding that it is owing to this *resemblance*, that they have this power of recall. They may never have been experienced together in the past, and since, on recall, they are not together in consciousness until after the association has operated, it cannot be by any *awareness* of the resemblance that the operation has been determined. Yet if there be no awareness of the resemblance, what grounds have we for assuming that it is a principle of association co-ordinate with that of contiguity in time and place? [21]

[18] T. 11.
[19] T. 11.
[20] T. 11.
[21] Smith, p. 241-242.

The difficulty with Kemp Smith's analysis is that it fails to emphasize those aspects of the natural relations which Hume holds to be of primary importance. Hume has nowhere said that there must be an awareness of any of these uniting qualities in order for the association to take place.[22] It does not follow that because the natural relations of contiguity and causality are contingent upon what we observe through our outer senses that the association takes place because we are now aware of the relations we have observed. In fact, it is this very point which Hume repeatedly plays down : " 'Tis evident, that the association of ideas operates in so silent and imperceptible a manner, that we are scarce sensible of it and discover it more by its effects ..." [23] Thus there need be no awareness of the relations of contiguity and cause and effect in order for the appropriate association of ideas to take place. Indeed, if such an awareness were required, it is difficult to see what Hume could mean by calling such relations 'natural'. If this awareness were necessary before the association of ideas takes place, it would also be difficult to comprehend Hume's assertion that the uniting principles are "a gentle force which commonly prevails ... nature in a manner pointing out to everyone those simple ideas which are most proper to be united ...",[24] and that they constitute "a kind of *attraction* ... in the mental world".[25]

All the natural relations then are characterized not by any conscious awareness of the qualities involved in the association of ideas but rather by the association or transition itself : "The very nature and essence of relation is to connect our ideas with each other, and upon the appearance of one to facilitate the transition to its correlative".[26] Hence, in response to the quotation from Kemp Smith we can say that resemblance is a principle of association co-ordinate with that of contiguity insofar as it produces an association of ideas.

[22] In fact, Hume denies that we can ever understand the underlying causes of this association : The effects of the association of ideas "are everywhere conspicacous; but as to its causes, they are mostly unknown, and must be resolv'd into *original* qualities of human nature, which I pretend not to explain." (T. 13). It is true that Hume later offers us a physiological explanation of the association of ideas. (T. 60). However, that he does not commit himself to it is evidenced by the fact that he refers to the explanation itself as "specious and plausible" and merely claims to have "recourse" to it, as opposed to accepting it. It is merely a device which he employs "in order to account for the mistakes that arise from these relations."

[23] T. 305.
[24] T. 10-11.
[25] T. 12.
[26] T. 204.

At the conclusion of his discussion of the natural relations, Hume points out that one of the effects of this union or association of ideas is the emergence of the complex idea of 'relations',[27] and the context makes it clear that this sense of relations applies to Part I, Section V where he introduces the seven philosophical relations. As such it seems that Hume intends the philosophical relations to be parasitic upon the natural relations. But that this is not always the case he is careful to point out in at least two passages. In the first he says that the complex idea of relations "*generally* arise(s) from some principle of union among our simple ideas",[28] and in the second passage we are told that such relations can arise "even upon the arbitrary union of two ideas in the fancy".[29]

The text further reveals that in the case of the philosophical relations what is being emphasized in addition to the association of ideas is the notion of comparison, and the need for a common quality to form the basis of the comparison. Thus, once ideas have been associated in the fancy, the complex ideas of relations are arrived at by "the comparing of objects",[30] and at one point he defines a philosophical relation as "any particular subject of comparison" [31] even though it lacks a connecting principle. Even if a connecting principle (i.e. one or more of the natural relations) is not present, " 'tis impossible to found a relation but on some common quality".[32] Therefore, resemblance is again brought into prominence : "no objects will admit of comparison, but what have some degree of resemblance".[33] Besides resemblance, Hume mentions six more sources of philosophical relations : identity, relations of time and space, proportions in quantity or number, degrees in any quality, contrariety, and causation.

When discussing Hume's treatment of the philosophical relations, Huxley maintains the following concerning the relation of co-existence (a species

[27] T. 13. The other complex ideas which he mentions here are those of 'modes' and 'substances', but they will not concern us here.

[28] T. 13, my italics.

[29] T. 13. This is just as we would expect inasmuch as Hume has already asserted that the imagination can separate and unite all the ideas it possesses. (T. 10).

[30] T. 14.

[31] T. 14.

[32] T. 236.

[33] T. 14. In a second passage akin to this one Hume asserts that resemblance is not only the source of philosophical relations, but is the foundation of all relations : "... *no relation of any kind can subsist without some degree of resemblance.*" (T. 15). Accordingly, all relations- both natural and philosophical- are parasitic upon resemblance. What this shows is that all the natural and philosophical relations are merely different manifestations of resemblance acting either as that which associates ideas in the fancy or as that which allows us to compare ideas which are associated in the fancy.

of the relation in time) : "Suppose two flashes of red to occur together, then a third feeling might arise ... which we call co-existence ... [It is] no more capable of being described than sensations are ... [It is] as little susceptible of analysis into simpler elements. Like simple tastes and smells, or feelings of pleasure and pain, [it is an] ultimate irresolvable fact of conscious experience ... Though devoid of the slightest resemblance to the other impressions, [it is], in a manner, generated by them".[34] Now, Huxley is mistaken in holding that the perception which arises is indescribable since it cannot be analyzed into simpler elements, the reason being that the idea of the relation of co-existence according to Hume is a complex idea. As such, it must be analyzable into simpler elements. What has misled Huxley, I believe, is his other claim that the perception which arises does not resemble the other two impressions, for if this is the case, the new perception will have a content which is entirely different from the others. Now Huxley is correct in holding that the perception which arises is devoid of the slightest resemblance to the other impressions, if by that he means that its content is different from the content of the other impressions. That is, the perception arising is not a perception of a red flash. Although the perception bears no resemblance to the content of the other two perceptions, it must – if Hume's emphasis on resemblance is to be seriously upheld - utilize some resemblance which the other two perceptions bear to each other. And the resemblance in this case can be nothing else but the time in which both flashes appeared. As a result of a comparison of the two flashes of red with respect to the time in which they appeared, we are made aware of the similarity which the one flash bears to the other, that is, we are made to see that they co-exist. The perception which is generated, therefore, contains the awareness of this similarity.

The preceding is not, of course, intended as a full account of Hume's theory of the philosophical relations – that task must be postponed until the next chapter – but it does give us some indication of how the perception of a relation arises, and what it is we can be aware of when we are aware of a relation. In addition, it sheds light upon Hume's claim cited earlier that the idea of a relation is a complex idea. Since the perception of a relation arises through comparing two objects which share a common property, the perception of a relation can be meaningful only when the related objects are also comprehended. In other words, to comprehend a philosophical relation, the relata must be known and they must be united

[34] T.H. Huxley, *Hume with Helps to the Study of Berkeley* (Macmillan, London, 1886). Reprinted : Greenwood Press, New York, 1968, p. 81.

in the imagination. (Hence Hume's emphasis on the natural relations when discussing the philosophical relations since they unite perceptions in the mind and provide a common quality which can be the source of the comparison.) In this sense then the perception of a relation can be regarded as complex inasmuch as it always depends upon the other perceptions.[35] This account also shows that Huxley is mistaken in the passage cited earlier since the perception which arises is unintelligible without the other two perceptions thereby distinguishing it from perceptions of tastes, smells or feelings of pleasure and pain. In the case in question the new perception contains the awareness of the equality of the two other perceptions with regard to time of existence. Accordingly, what we are aware of is describable in a way in which the perception of a smell or taste is not.

III. THE CRITERION OF FORCE AND VIVACITY

Our discussion to this point will enable us to answer the first question raised earlier, namely, why the different degrees of force and vivacity do not appear able to provide the contrast Hume requires to draw a distinction in kind between impressions and ideas even though in certain passages Hume claims that the differences in force and vivacity can provide the basis for such a distinction.[36] A relation for Hume – that is, a philosophical relation – can be said to exist when upon the comparison of ideas, a new perception arises in the mind as a result of some resemblance between the perceptions or ideas we are comparing. Since a difference in kind is equivalent to a negation of relation, Hume's meaning must then be that a difference in kind exists if this new perception is not generated when we attempt to compare two perceptions in a certain respect, that is, if the perceptions are found not to be resembling in that respect.

On this account, two reasons can be given for denying that force and vivacity can provide the contrast to which Hume often draws attention

---

[35] There are two further passages which corroborate this interpretation. Before offering us his list of philosophical relations in Section V, Part I, Hume writes : „It may perhaps be esteemed an endless task to enumerate all those qualities which make objects admit of comparison, and by which the ideas of *philosophical* relations are produced." (T. 14). We are here clearly told that upon comparing the two ideas a new perception or idea – that of a philosophical relation – is generated. Several lines earlier than the passage quoted above we are told : "Thus distance will be allowed by the philosophers to be a true relation, because we acquire an idea of it by the comparing of objects... "

[36] E. 18. See also T. 2.

when discussing impressions and ideas. The first reason is that Hume specifically allows the degrees in any quality to be a source of philosophical relation :

When any two objects possess the same *quality* in common, the *degrees* in which they possess it, form a fifth species of relation.[37]

Secondly, Hume admits that at times impressions and ideas are indistinguishable with respect to their force and vivacity since there are occasions when impressions become as languid as ideas and occassions when ideas become as vivacious as impressions :

The common degrees of these (i.e. impressions and ideas) are easily distinguished; tho' it is not impossible but in particular instances they may very nearly approach to each other. Thus in sleep, in a fever, in madness, or in any violent emotions of the soul, our ideas may approach to our impressions : As on the other hand it sometimes happens, that our impressions are so faint and low that we cannot distinguish them from our ideas.[38]

Many commentators [39] have seen the consequence which follows from the last passage : It is a legitimate question to ask for the criterion Hume

[37] T. 15.

[38] T. 2. Elsewhere, Hume makes the same point : "... a lively imagination very often degenerates into madness or folly... When the imagination from any extraordinary ferment of the blood and spirits acquires such a vivacity as disorders all its powers and faculties... every chimera of the brain is as vivid and intense as any of these inferences, which we formely dignify'd with the name of conclusions concerning matters of fact, and sometimes as the present impressions of the senses." (T. 123).
    This passage definitely shows that Hume holds that at times ideas do approach to the level of vivacity possessed by impressions, and the last part of the passage quoted from T. 2 above shows Hume holds that impressions may possess the degree of vivacity usually held by an idea. Accordingly, Hume is not arguing that impressions and ideas always have their own separate spheres of force and vivacity and may at times *approximate* that of the other.

[39] For example, D. G. C. Macnabb, *David Hume : His Theory of Knowledge and Morality* (Hutchinson's University Library, London, 1951). Reprinted : Basil Blackwell, Oxford, 1966, p. 23-24. See also Smith p. 209-210.
    One commentator who refuses to concede that the criterion of force and vivacity breaks down is Huxley. He writes : "Hume has been criticized for making the distinction of impressions and ideas depend upon their relative strength or vivacity. Yet it would be hard to point out any other character by which the things signified can be distinguished. Anyone who has paid attention to the curious subject of what are called 'subjective sensations' will be familiar with examples of the extreme difficulty which sometimes attends the discrimination of ideas of sensation from impressions of sensations, when the ideas are very vivid, or the impressions are faint." Huxley, p. 77.
    Huxley fails to note that were the different degrees of force and vivacity the sole criterion for distinguishing impressions from ideas, then all strong perceptions should

is employing when he classifies as an impression the perception that is as weak and languid as those he calls ideas. Were a difference in degree of force and vivacity the only criterion for distinguishing impressions and ideas there could never be any confusion or mistaking one for the other : *all* our more lively perceptions would, by the mere fact of their liveliness, be classified as impressions, and *all* our weaker perceptions would be classified as ideas. The fact that we can at times be led into error when attending solely to force and vivacity, therefore, makes it clear that Hume means to distinguish impressions from ideas in some other manner. Nevertheless, what has not been noticed is that an explanation is in order as to why Hume thinks he can move between this other criterion and force and vivacity. Accordingly, a solution to this problem will be attempted once the second manner in which Hume distinguishes impressions from ideas is found. Also, what has not been seen is that even if Hume does not always want to hold that impressions can become as languid as ideas, or ideas as vivacious as impressions, but only that they can approach each other's vivacity, his theory of relations would prevent force and vivacity from providing the basis for a distinction in kind.

IV. THE CRITERION OF SUBSTANTIAL EXISTENCE

Perhaps, the basic distinction between impressions and ideas is the distinction between that which is a substance and that which is not. The only definition of substance which Hume considers is that offered by Descartes, namely, a substance is "something which may exist by itself".[40] But were we to accept this definition of substance, then Hume argues, it would apply to whatever is conceivable, and not solely to impressions :

Whatever is clearly conceiv'd may exist; and whatever is clearly conceiv'd, after any manner, may exist after the same manner. This is one principle ... Again, every thing, which is different, is distinguishable, and every thing which is distinguishable, is separable by the imagination. This is another principle. My conclusion from both is, that since all our perceptions are different from each other, and from everything else in the universe, they are also distinct and

---

be treated as impressions and all languid ones as ideas. In other words, the confusion he raises could never arise given this criterion.

John B. Stewart, *The Moral and Political Philosophy of David Hume* (Columbia University Press, New York and London, 1963) fails to note that Hume maintains that impressions and ideas can be confounded. See p. 26 ff.

[40] T. 233.

separable ... and may exist separably, and have no need of anything else to
support their existence. They are, therefore, substances, as far as this definition
explains a substance.[41]

V. IMPRESSIONS ARE PARADIGMATIC; IDEAS ARE DERIVATIVE

Hume wishes to maintain that certain perceptions are temporally posterior
to other perceptions and are caused by the latter. Perceptions, for Hume,
may be divided into those which are simple and those which are complex.
Simple perceptions "are such as admit of no distinction or separation".
"The complex are the contrary of these and may be distinguished into
parts".[42] The point to be established does not necessarily apply to our
complex ideas :

I observe, that many of our complex ideas never had impressions, that correspond
to them ... I can imagine to myself such a city as the *New Jerusalem*, whose
pavement is gold and walls are rubies, tho' I never saw any such.[43]

However, with respect to simple ideas there are very few instances of ideas
appearing before their correspondent impressions :[44]

I consider the order of their *first appearance*; and find by constant experience,
that the simple impressions always take the precedence of their correspondent
ideas, but never appear in the contrary order.[45]

What Hume believes this discussion terminates is the long dispute concerning
innate ideas :

... the present question concerning the precedency of our impressions or ideas,
is the same with what has made so much noise in other terms, when it has been
disputed whether there be any *innate ideas*, or whether all ideas be derived from
sensation and reflexion.[46]

What is not at all clear is how significant Hume's remarks are, or whether,
in fact, what he is saying is at all significant. It appears from the above
passage that Hume believes the doctrine of innate ideas can be ruled out
by establishing that in the order of time a simple impression must precede
a simple idea. However, since every perception presenting itself to con-

---

[41] T. 233. See also T. 207, 244, 245, 259.
[42] T. 2.
[43] T. 3.
[44] The only one which Hume admits is the case of the missing shade of blue. See
T. 5, E. 20-21. It will be discussed toward the end of this chapter.
[45] T. 5.
[46] T. 7.

sciousness must have a first appearance (this is analytically true), and since a perception in its first appearance is called an impression ("Those perceptions ... we may name *impressions* ... as they make their first appearance in the soul."[47]) it follows that for every perception there is an impression. Further, since no perception in its first appearance is called an idea, it follows that every idea is preceded by an impression. If this is Hume's meaning, the doctrine of innate ideas appears to be ruled out by a definition of 'impression' and an analytic statement, and the refutation of innate ideas appears trivial.

Nevertheless, the above argument does not adequately capture Hume's meaning. Curiously enough, what Hume does mean can be ascertained in part through attending to a footnote which appears in the first *Enquiry*.[48] In this footnote Hume raises the question of the sense of 'innate'. Three possible senses are discussed. Firstly, if by innate is meant natural, that is, the opposite of uncommon, artificial, or miraculous, then Hume asserts that all perceptions are natural. Secondly, if by innate is meant contemporaneous with birth then he thinks the dispute about innate ideas is frivolous since it is not important to decide whether thinking begins before, at, or after birth. However, if in the third place, we take innate to mean "what is original or copied from no precedent perception, then may we assert that all our impressions are innate and our ideas not innate". Hume's refutation of innate ideas, therefore, centres around the fact that certain of our perceptions have no paradigm anywhere, and it is these paradigmatic perceptions or impressions which are temporally prior to our ideas and cause the latter.

The experiments which Hume undertakes to prove this thesis seek to establish that impressions are both sufficient and necessary conditions for the occurrence of their correspondent ideas :

(a) To give a child an idea of scarlet or orange, of sweet or bitter, I present the objects, or in other words, convey to him these impressions; but proceed not so absurdly, as to endeavour to produce the impressions by exciting the ideas.[49]

(b) ... where-ever by any accident the faculties, which give rise to any impressions, are obstructed in their operations, as when one is born blind or deaf; not only the impressions are lost, but also their correspondent ideas; so that there never appear in the mind the least traces of either of them. Nor is this only true, where the organs of sensation are entirely destroy'd, but likewise where they have never been put in action to produce a particular impression. We cannot form to

[47] T. 1.
[48] E. 22.
[49] T. 5.

ourselves a just idea of the taste of pine-apple, without having actually tasted it.[50]

(a) above establishes impressions as the sufficient condition of ideas on inductive grounds; (b) establishes impressions as the necessary condition of ideas on inductive grounds. Combining (a) and (b) then we get impressions as the necessary and sufficient condition for the appearance of ideas. But, further, the experiments cited above do not show impressions as the necessary and sufficient conditions for *any* ideas, but only for those ideas which, in content, are exactly like the impression in question. Accordingly, Hume's experiments, if accepted, establish both that the doctrine of innate ideas is false and that impressions precede *their* ideas or that every idea is a copy of a precedent impression.[51] One further point remains : It must somehow be established that impressions or perceptions in their first appearance are paradigmatic. In favour of this thesis Hume relies on two different sources of evidence. He argues firstly that since we are never presented with anything but impressions and ideas, therefore we are unable to make any statement concerning the causes of our perceptions in their first appearance :

It is a question of fact whether the perceptions of the senses be produced by external objects, resembling them : how shall this question be determined? By experience surely; as all other questions of a like nature. But here experience is, and must be entirely silent. The mind has never anything present to it but the perceptions, and cannot possibly reach any experience of their connexion with objects. The supposition of such a connexion is, therefore, without any foundation in reasoning.[52] See also T. 84, T. 275.

This argument, however, does not establish that impressions are paradigmatic : It only shows that we can never know whether they are paradigmatic or merely copies of objects, and, strictly speaking, this is the thesis Hume wants to defend.

[50] T. 5.

[51] No commentator to my knowledge has ever seen that Hume regards his experiments as establishing these two points, and not simply the first. It is usually thought that the resemblance between an idea and an impression is established simply by citing particular instances of such resemblances and then challenging anyone to find an idea which does not resemble an impression. (See T. 3-4.) Smith, for example, adopts this position. See p. 207-208. However, before citing the two experiments mentioned above, Hume explicitly states that two points are going to be established : "... we shall here content ourselves with establishing one general proposition, *That all our simple ideas in their first appearence are deriv'd from simple impressions, which are correspondent to them, and which they exactly represent.*" (T. 4).

[52] E. 153.

As to those *impressions*, which arise from the *senses*, their ultimate cause is, in my opinion, perfectly inexplicable by human reason, and 'twill always be impossible to decide with certainty, whether they arise immediately from the object, or are produc'd by the creative power of the mind, or are deriv'd from the author of our being.[53]

For us, perceptions on their first appearance are paradigmatic since they cannot be traced beyond themselves; and this limitation in philosophy accords entirely with the trust the vulgar are naturally disposed to place in their senses.

... however philosophers may distinguish betwixt the objects and perceptions of the senses; which they suppose co-existent and resembling; yet this is a distinction, which is not comprehended by the generality of mankind, who as they perceive only one being, can never assent to the opinion of a double existence and representation. Those very sensations, which enter by the eye or ear, are with them the true objects, nor can they readily conceive that this pen or paper, which is immediately perceiv'd, represents another, which is different from, but resembling it.[54]

Hume's point then is that true philosophy and the vulgar concur in holding that upon their first appearance to consciousness perceptions or impressions are to be regarded as paradigmatic since no paradigm for them can ever be found nor do our natural instincts lead us to seek for such a paradigm. It is this which leads Hume to say that for the vulgar their impressions are their only objects,[55] and which provides the justification for Hume's frequent interchanging of the term 'impression' and 'object'.[56]

But not all impressions are such that no adequate causal account can be given of them. Impressions are divided by Hume into those of sensation and those of reflection. Thus far we have spoken only of impressions of sensation : "Original impressions or impressions of sensation are such as without any antecedent perception arise in the soul ..."[57] On the other

[53] T. 84.

[54] T. 202.

[55] "... the vulgar confound perceptions and objects, and attribute a distinct continu'd existence, to the very things they feel or see." (T. 193).

[56] For example, he says as we saw earlier "to give a child an idea of scarlet or orange, of sweet or bitter, I present the objects, or in other words, convey to him these impressions... " (T. 5). Or again, "... 'tis confest, that no object can appear to the senses, or in other words, that no impression can become present to the mind, without being determin'd in its degrees both of quantity and quality." (T. 19). Hume also wants to argue that the fact that our impressions are our only objects and that the causes of our impressions of sensation cannot be ascertained by us presents no problem : "We may draw inferences from the coherence of our perceptions, whether they be true or false; whether they represent nature justly, or be mere illusions of the senses." (T. 84).

[57] T. 275.

hand, "secondary or reflective impressions are such as proceed from some of these original ones, either immediately or by the interposition of its idea".[58] Impressions of reflection constitute "our passions, desires, and emotions".[59] That Hume does not spend much time analyzing our impressions of sensation is due to the fact that they are not the proper subject matter of metaphysics or human nature, but of anatomy and natural philosophy :

'Tis certain that the mind, in its perceptions, must begin some where; and that since the impressions precede their correspondent ideas, there must be some impressions, which without any introduction make their appearance in the soul. As these depend upon natural and physical causes, the examination of them wou'd lead me too far from my present subject into the sciences of anatomy and natural philosophy.[60]

The study of human nature will confine itself to impressions of reflection :

I shall here confine myself to those other impressions, which I have call'd secondary and reflective, as arising either from the original impressions, or from their ideas.[61]

In fact, as can be seen from the two preceding quotations, whether something belongs to natural philosophy or moral philosophy depends upon whether the specific concern is with impressions of sensation or impressions of reflection. Hume's concern with impressions of reflection is largely that of accounting for them causally. Thus in the early pages of the *Treatise* he writes : "Let us consider how they stand with regard to their existence, and which of the impressions and ideas are causes, and which effects. The *full* examination of this question is the subject of the present treatise ..." [62] The text shows – and this we will see at least in part as we proceed – that the distinguishing feature of an impression of reflection, including the impression of reflection in causality, is that although caused, its content is not a copy of the content of those perceptions which caused it to come into existence. Here, therefore, in the case of impressions of reflection Hume holds that a causal account can be given wherein the paradigmatic character of our impressions can be clearly seen.

Whatever perceptions are paradigmatic for us, Hume holds, are always an object of feeling, whereas those whose content is derivable from other

[58] T. 275.
[59] T. 8.
[60] T. 275-276.
[61] T. 275-276.
[62] T. 4.

perceptions are always an object of thought. Accordingly, the distinction between impressions and ideas can be made in terms of the objects of feeling and thinking :

... all our ideas are nothing but copies of our impressions, or in other words, ... it is impossible for us *to think* of anything, which we have not antecedently *felt*, either by our external or internal senses.[63]

If we combine the points made above, the true distinction between impressions and ideas will be forthcoming. Being paradigmatic for us and associated with the faculty of feeling which whenever actuated generates our assent, impressions when present to consciousness either singly (when they are not associated) or collectively (when they are associated into complex impressions) constitute our facts, or as Hume sometimes puts it, our matters of fact.[64] Ideas, being derivative in content must be the object of those faculties which normally treat their objects in this way. In the previously quoted passage Hume maintains that the faculty which does so is thought. The text bears out that Hume wishes to place three faculties under the general heading of thought based on the fact that all three mental operations have recourse to ideas. These three faculties are reasoning, remembering, and imagining. Accordingly, an idea is best spoken of as that by means of which we are able to reason, remember, or imagine.[65]

---

[63] E. 62. (See also T. 1-2, A. 9).

[64] Thus, for example, after establishing that moral distinctions are not derived from reason but from impressions Hume asserts : "Here is a matter of fact; but 'tis the object of feeling, not of reason." (T. 169). In the case of those impressions which are languid and therefore confounded with ideas, Hume is maintaining that the philosopher can take on a normative role, and prescribe how we are to regard such perceptions. Such prescriptions have little effect on our everyday lives but are important, as we shall see, for the philosopher.

[65] In a rarely quoted footnote, Hume distinguishes these three faculties by contrasting the imagination with memory and reason : "In general we may observe, that as our assent to all probable reasonings is founded on the vivacity of ideas, it resembles many of those whimsies and prejudices, which are rejected under the opprobrious character of being the offspring of the imagination. By this expression it appears that the word, imagination, is commonly us'd in two different senses; and tho' nothing be more contrary to true philosophy, than this inaccuray, yet in the following reasonings I have often been obliged to fall into it . When I oppose the imagination to the memory, I mean the faculty, by which we form our fainter ideas. When I oppose it to reason, I mean the same faculty, excluding only our demonstrative and probable reasonings. When I oppose it to neither, 'tis indifferent whether it be taken in the larger or more limited sense, or at least the context will sufficiently explain the meaning." (T. 117-118). (See also T. 8-10, 84-85, 108.)

The analysis presented above provides reasons as to why Hume had to abandon force and vivacity as the distinguishing feature between impressions and ideas. The material presented in the first few pages of the *Treatise* is intended – among other things – to terminate once and for all the problem of innate ideas. If force and vivacity were viewed by Hume as a sufficient distinction between impressions and ideas then the problem of innateness would be resurrected and would lead Hume to the following position. Some languid perceptions are not copies of anything we can apprehend empirically and some lively perceptions are copies of other perceptions. Now, given the notion of innateness with which Hume is working, namely, what is original or copied from no precedent perception, and force and vivacity as the distinguishing characteristic between impressions and ideas, Hume would be led to conclude that some impressions are not innate and some ideas are innate. However, since this is precisely what he wants to deny it follows that force and vivacity must be dropped as the distinguishing feature of impressions and ideas.

Our analysis of the distinguishing feature between impressions and ideas also provides sufficient grounds for making a distinction in kind between impressions and ideas – a distinction, which as we have seen, Hume repeatedly maintains he wants to make. A distinction in kind was seen to exist when, upon comparing perceptions, they were found not to be resembling in a certain respect. Now the paradigmatic nature of some perceptions and the derivative nature of the content of others amply provide the basis for a distinction in kind. Impressions and ideas correspond exactly in content so that in this respect a distinction in kind is not possible. The degrees of force and vivacity, rather than providing a source for contrasting perceptions, enable one to compare them. Amidst this similarity, however, we do find the contrast required to draw a distinction in kind since impressions are paradigmatic and ideas never are. I submit, therefore, that on the basis of what Hume has to say about distinctions in kind and his discussion of innateness that the distinction Hume makes between impressions and ideas is in terms of those perceptions which are paradigmatic and those which are not.

VI. THE ROLE OF FORCE AND VIVACITY

Earlier I raised the question as to why Hume thinks he can move between the criterion discussed above and force and vivacity as a means of distinguishing impressions from ideas. We are now in a position to answer this question.

The first reason for this interchange is due to the fact that in most cases our livelier perceptions are our paradigmatic perceptions and our weaker perceptions are our derivatives ones :

Those perceptions, which enter with most force and violence, we may name impressions; and under this name I comprehend all our sensations, passions, and emotions, as they make their first appearance in the soul. By *ideas*, I mean the faint images of these in thinking and reasoning.[66]

There are certain instances, however, when Hume appears to emphasize force and vivacity and neglect the criterion discussed above. This occurs primarily in Hume's theory of sympathy to which we will devote more attention later. Nevertheless, even at this point it is important to anticipate remarks such as :

... an idea of a sentiment or passion may ... be so enliven'd as to become the very sentiment or passion.[67]

To account for this it is necessary to see that the quality of being paradigmatic or being derivative is not a feature of a perception which can be apprehended when the perception alone is presented to consciousness. Accordingly, force and vivacity, being features of our perceptions which are apprehended whenever the perception in question is perceived can lead the mind into mistaking impressions and ideas :

When the imagination, from any extraordinary ferment of the blood and spirits, acquires such a vivacity as disorders all its powers and faculties, there is no means of distinguishing betwixt truth and falsehood ... Every chimera of the brain is as vivid and intense as any of those inferences, which we formerly dignify'd, with the name of conclusions concerning matters of fact, and sometimes as the present impressions of the senses.[68]

Ideas, therefore, can *imitate* impressions if their liveliness is increased :

Wherever we can make an idea approach the impressions in force and vivacity, it will likewise imitate them in its influence on the mind; and *vice versa*, where it imitates them in that influence ... this must proceed from its approaching them in force and vivacity.[69]

Even in the case of sympathy Hume is very careful to point out when it is first introduced that it is *the idea* of the sentiments of others which is being entertained, although it is being done in an extremely forceful manner :

[66] T. 1.
[67] T. 319
[68] T. 123. See also T. 265.
[69] T. 119.

All these relations [viz. causality, contiguity, resemblance] when united together, convey the impression or consciousness of our own person to the idea of the sentiments or passions of others, and makes us conceive them in the strongest and most lively manner.[70]

When Hume moves from this type of expression – the strict philosophical type – to speaking of the conversion of ideas of sentiments into impressions this is due to the fact that he wants to accommodate himself to the vulgar notion of what is taking place, and, of course, in the case of sympathy the vulgar confound intense ideas for the impressions themselves.[71] Therefore, Hume does not abandon the criterion for distinguishing impressions from ideas discussed earlier. Rather, he simply takes note of the fact that ideas can sometimes affect us as impressions usually affect us, and in some cases, sympathy for example, this is more important than the true distinction between impressions and ideas.

VII. FURTHER CONFIRMATION PROVIDED BY THE MISSING SHADE OF BLUE

Other commentators have emphasized the pivotal role which the copy nature of ideas plays in Hume's philosophy. For example, Huxley writes : "The fundamental proposition of all Hume's philosophy is that ideas are copied from impressions".[72] Nevertheless, no commentator to my knowledge has ever attempted to argue that this is the only criterion which Hume employs to distinguish impressions from ideas. Thus, although Huxley makes the claim cited above, he elsewhere argues that force and vivacity provides the means of distinguishing impressions from ideas.[73] N. Capaldi [74] also emphasizes the copy theory of ideas in various places but never seeks to show that only this criterion is employed by Hume to characterize an idea. In one place he writes : "Hume distinguishes impressions from ideas in several ways, but for our purposes the distinction is either one of vivacity, with impressions possessing a greater degree of

---

[70] T. 318.

[71] Another instant wherein Hume seeks to conform his language to vulgar notions appears when Hume recognizes that the vulgar confound perceptions and objects : "In order, therefore, to accommodate myself to their notions, I shall at first suppose; that there is only a single existence, which I shall call indifferently *object* or perception, according as it shall seem best to suit my purpose... " (T. 202).

[72] Huxley, p. 140.

[73] *Ibid.*, p. 77.

[74] N. Capaldi, *Judgment and Sentiment in Hume's Moral Theory* (University Microfilms, A Xerox Company, Ann Arbor, Michigan, 1965).

vivacity than ideas, or one of reference, where impressions are non-referential and ideas are referential ..." [75]

Capaldi's claim that Hume uses either of the two criteria he mentions in order to distinguish between impressions and ideas encounters difficulties when we come to Hume's discussion of the missing shade of blue.[76] The missing shade of blue is introduced by Hume to show that "there is one contradictory phenomenon, which may prove, that 'tis not absolutely impossible for ideas to go before their correspondent impressions". The problem with Hume's analysis is to determine why the perception which appears is classified as an idea rather than an impression. But neither of the two criteria suggested by Capaldi can assist us here. The criterion of reference is of no use for there may not be an impression of the missing shade of blue anywhere in nature, giving rise to the view that the perception which arises is non-referential, that is, on Capaldi's view it is an impression. In other words, on Capaldi's interpretation the perception which arises would be classified as an impression if there is no impression to which the perception of the missing shade can have reference, or an idea if there is such an impression. Hume, however, insists that the perception of the missing shade is an idea, thereby indicating that the perception is regarded as an idea independently of whether there is another perception of this shade of blue which is itself non-referential. The criterion of force and vivacity is also of no assistance here in understanding why the perception of the missing shade is an idea, since as we have already seen, Hume allows that some impressions are not very vivacious or forceful, and some ideas are. Hence, merely inspecting the perception of the missing shade of blue with respect to its force or vivacity cannot really help to decide whether the perception is an impression or an idea, and yet Hume regards this perception as an idea.

My own analysis of the distinguishing feature between impressions and ideas does provide an explanation for why the perception of the missing shade of blue is an idea rather than an impression. Hume does not intend that the mind could have this perception even if we were not aware of the other shades. That is, the perception or presence of the other shades is a necessary condition for obtaining the perception of the missing shade. Now Hume does not indicate how the mind actually provides itself with the perception in question, and for the point I am now going to make it is not necessary to speculate on how it is that the idea arises beyond maintaining

---

[75] *Ibid.*, p. 14.
[76] T. 5-6, E. 20-21.

that to have the idea of the missing shade of blue we require an awareness of the other shades in the series and one or more mental operations to enable us to construct this idea from our awareness of the shades in the rest of the series. (My own opinion is that the idea is provided relationally, so that we are made aware that the missing shade is darker than the shade to one side of where it is supposed to be and lighter than the shade to the other side). In other words, the perception of the missing shade of blue is called an idea by Hume because its content is traceable to the contents of other perceptions with the aid of one or more mental operations. It is then the derivative character of the perception in question which renders it an idea.

A perception for Hume is an impression if the content of that perception is not traceable to the content of any other perceptions, even if it is caused by other perceptions (impressions and/or ideas). In short, a perception is an impression if there is no paradigm for it. On the other hand, a perception is an idea if the content of that perception is traceable to the content of one or more other perceptions (impressions and/or ideas). Thus, the perception of the missing shade of blue is an idea because the content of the perception is derivable from the contents of other ideas in the series through one or more mental operations. The reason why Capaldi missed this point is that he interprets the notion of derivation only in the sense of being caused. Thus he writes : "Hume makes a second distinction between impressions and ideas by calling attention to the derived character of ideas. Ideas are derived from impressions or are temporally posterior to impressions. Even this distinction is not definitive. Impressions of reflection ... are derived from ideas".[77] The point which Capaldi misses is that there is an additional sense of derivation which is crucial to Hume's doctrine of impressions and ideas, namely, that in which the content of a perception is derived from the content of one or more other perceptions. Impressions are distinguished from ideas in terms of how the content of the perception stands to the content of the perceptions which cause the perception in question.

[77] Capaldi, p. 114.

CHAPTER III

HUME'S ANALYSIS OF REASON

I. THREE SENSES OF REASON

With the completion of our discussion of Hume's justification for the adoption of the Experimental Method in moral philosophy and our discussion of the basic elements of experience, we can now turn to Hume's analysis of reason. I argued in the last chapter that by the term 'impression' Hume intends to convey the notion of fact, and by 'idea' he means whatever is the object of thought, namely, that by which we reason, remember, or imagine. Hume's analysis of reason takes advantage of this two-fold distinction of our perceptions, for we are told that although all our reasoning employs ideas, in our reasonings we can either be concerned with matters of fact (or impressions) or with ideas :

... the operations of human understanding divide themselves into two kinds, the comparing of ideas, and the inferring of matters of fact ...[1]

Corresponding to these two operations of the understanding, there are two kinds of truth :

Truth or falsehood consists in an agreement or disagreement either to the *real* relations of ideas, or to *real* existence and matter of fact.[2]

Since truth, for Hume, is discernible only through reasoning, he refers to reason as being "the discovery of truth or falsehood" [3] and as "a kind of cause, of which truth is the natural effect".[4] What is true or false, however, is judgments since they alone have a reference to truth or reason :

---

[1] T. 463.
[2] T. 458. See also T. 448.
[3] T. 458.
[4] T. 180.

... nothing can be contrary to truth and reason, except what has a reference to it, and ... the judgments of our understanding only have this reference ...[5]

The theory of truth to which Hume is committed then is a correspondence theory in which a judgmrnt is true if (a) it states a relationship which actually obtains between certain ideas or (b) if it states that something exists (or has existed or will exist) which does exist (has existed or will exist).

Scholarship on Hume's analysis of reason suffers from two serious shortcomings. Firstly, very early in the *Treatise*,[6] Hume indicates that the matters discussed in Part I of Book I form "the elements of this philosophy" and although the topic of 'distinctions of reason' is discussed in the above mentioned part of the text, its importance in Hume's philosophy is usually overlooked.[7] In fact, to the best of my knowledge the expression 'distinctions of reason' is employed by Hume in only four passages [8] – all of them being in the *Treatise* – and in these the pivotal role of such distinctions is never enunciated. It is my contention that Hume was correct in introducing this topic as an 'element' in his philosophy, and I shall attempt to show as we proceed that distinctions of reason play an important role both in Hume's moral theory, and in his account of reason as the comparison of ideas. Secondly, very little work has actually been done on reason as that faculty which compares ideas. And yet much of Hume's moral theory rests upon a proper understanding of this kind of reasoning. In this chapter part of this neglect will be remedied : Distinctions of reason and reason as the comparison of ideas will be discussed in detail along with causal reasoning which has received the bulk of attention in the literature. As such Hume will be regarded as holding that there are three senses of reason – reason as a comparison of ideas, distinctions of reason and causal reasoning.

II. CAUSAL REASONING

Although there are numerous difficulties in Hume's views on causal reasoning, for our purposes the majority of our attention can be devoted

---

[5] T. 415-416.

[6] T. 13.

[7] The one exception to this with which I am familiar is Professor Ronald J. Butler who first brought the doctrine of distinctions of reason in Hume's philosophy to my attention.

[8] T. 25, T. 43, T. 67, T. 245.

to reason as a comparison of ideas and distinctions of reason. Hume's views on causal reasoning do not greatly influence the interpretation one places on his moral theory, and as a result, this kind of reasoning is not exceptionally problematic to the extent that we are seeking to understand what Hume means. For now then, with regard to causal reasoning and necessity, it will suffice to point out that Hume remarks that in the absence of our knowledge of powers or connections between objects, causal necessity depends upon constant conjunction and the habit which the mind develops to pass from one perception to another :

> If objects had not an uniform and regular conjunction with each other, we shou'd never arrive at any idea of cause and effect; and even after all, the necessity, which enters into that idea, is nothing but determination of the mind to pass from one object to its usual attendant, and infer the existence of one from that of the other. Here then are two particulars, which we are to consider as essential to necessity, viz. the constant *union* and the inference of the mind; and wherever we discover these we must acknowledge a necessity.[9]

Additional points concerning causal reasoning will be introduced whenever it is appropriate to do so.

III. DISTINCTIONS OF REASON

Among the distinctions which Hume introduces very early in the *Treatise* is that between simple and complex perceptions. Simple perceptions are those which admit of no distinction nor separation,[10] whereas those which are complex can be distinguished into the simple perceptions of which they are composed,[11] through the power which the imagination possesses of producing a separation wherever it perceives a difference.[12] A simple perception, therefore, is a perceptual primitive which is not reducible into parts, that is, into other more basic perceptions.

Hume argues that although simple perceptions are not amenable to further distinctions in terms of parts, they are still susceptible to distinctions of reason. As examples of this distinction, Hume speaks of "figure and the body figur'd", "motion and the body mov'd",[13] "length and breadth",[14]

---

[9] T. 400.

[10] T. 2.

[11] "Complex ideas may, perhaps, be well known by definition, which is nothing but an enumeration of those parts or simple ideas, that compose them." (E. 62).

[12] "Wherever the imagination perceives a difference among ideas. it can easily produce a separation." (T. 10).

[13] T. 24.

[14] T. 43.

and "an action and its substance".[15] The actual example employed in his discussion is the distinction between the colour and the figure in a globe of white marble. Hume points out that when presented with a globe of white marble the colour is inseparable and indistinguishable from the form or figure. However, if we also observe a globe of black marble and a cube of white marble, and compare it with the globe of white marble we will be able to distinguish the colour and figure of the latter through the resemblances it has with the other two objects. That is, the colour of the globe resembles the colour of the cube, and the figure of the globe resembles the figure of the black marble. The awareness of these resemblances Hume refers to as a "kind of reflection" or comparison,[16] and that to which we are attending – in this case the colour of the figure – he refers to as an "aspect".[17] Thus, although simple perceptions lack parts, they do possess aspects – aspects which are discovered through finding resemblances between the perception in question and others :

... we consider the figure and color together, since they are in effect the same and indistinguishable; but still view them in different aspects, according to the resemblances, of which they are susceptible.[18]

The fact that Hume offers a separate name for the operation under discussion makes it appear as though it is a separate operation of the mind not yet covered in his discussion. A close look at matters discussed earlier, however, shows that this is not the case. Since distinctions of reason are made through comparing an idea with other ideas in order to determine certain resemblances between them, and since all comparisons between ideas are essentially an attempt to establish philosophical relations between them, it follows that distinctions of reason are nothing but the determination of philosophical relations between a certain idea and others.

Further refinements on Hume's view are now in order. In the first place, Hume is extremely misleading in holding that at least two different objects are required for a distinction of reason. Quite clearly, a comparison could take place even if one object were involved so long as some particular change occurred within it, and we were able to retain in memory the original appearance of the object. For example, if the globe of white marble of which Hume speaks were to be painted black, a comparison would still be possible between the object as it was formerly, and as it is

15 T. 245.
16 T. 25.
17 T. 25.
18 T. 25.

now. In such an instance, we could still find a resemblance in shape between the object at two different times. But even this analysis of the matter is misleading, since it lends support to the view that before the philosophical relation required for a distinction of reason is uncovered there must be some qualitative difference between the objects or perceptions involved. In point of fact, however, this need not always be the case. Let us suppose that I acquired a globe of white marble shortly before I left my study yesterday evening, and that I stationed this globe on my desk. Upon returning to my study this morning I see an object on my desk and remark that this is the globe which I received yesterday and that no perceptible change has occurred in it since that time. It is clear that in this case I can distinguish the figure from the colour – I know there has been no change in the colour *and* I know there has been no change in the shape – even though no qualitative contrast is present. In fact, in this case it is precisely because there is no qualitative change in the object that we say the object has remained unaltered. For a distinction of reason to take place, therefore, what is required is the awareness of a resemblance which a simple perception bears to some other perception, or to itself at some other time. The contrast which Hume emphasizes is a necessary condition for a distinction of reason when learning how to make such distinctions. However, once this has been learned, the contrast ceases to be necessary.

Up to now I have been assuming that Hume is correct in holding that a distinction of reason is applicable only in the case of simple ideas : "... the *distinction* of ideas without any real *difference* ... is founded on the different resemblances which the same simple idea may have to several different ideas".[19] Our preceding discussion, however, has already shown that distinctions of reason do occur with respect to complex ideas in the sense of complex idea discussed earlier.[20] Since philosophical relations exist between complex ideas, and since all distinctions of reason are nothing but the establishment of philosophical relations, it follows that distinctions of reason can occur with respect to complex ideas. Nevertheless, this argument is misleading in itself since it obfuscates the very special role which distinctions of reason play. The problem here then is one of determining when in fact a special label is warranted when we are involved with the comparison of ideas. This analysis will complete my discussion of distinctions of reason.

The notion of a simple idea discussed earlier presupposes that there be

[19] T. 67.
[20] See footnote 11.

some limit to the separations possible within an idea. And Hume holds
that there are such limits :

... the idea, which we form of any finite quality is not infinitely divisible, but
that by proper distinctions and separations we may run up this idea to inferior
ones, which will be perfectly simple and indivisible. In rejecting the infinite
capacity of the mind, we suppose it may arrive at an end in the division of its
ideas ... the imagination reaches a *minimum*, and may raise up to itself an idea,
of which it cannot conceive any subdivision, and which cannot be diminished
without a total annihilation.[21]

In the light of this passage it is clear that the very examples which Hume
has employed when introducing the notion of distinction of reason, namely,
the globe of black marble and the cube of white marble, cannot be considered examples involving simple ideas : it is possible to imagine, for
example that the globe is split into two equal parts. Therefore, not only
are distinctions of reason possible in the case of complex ideas, but Hume's
own discussion of the matter employs complex ideas.

The equivocation involved in the term 'simple idea' can now be made
explicit. On the one hand, by a simple idea Hume means one which is
such that *no* distinction or separation is possible with respect to it. The
example Hume uses is the idea of a grain of sand :

When you tell me of the thousandth and ten thousandth part of a grain of sand,
I have a distinct idea of these numbers and of their different proportions : but
the images, which I form in my mind to represent the things themselves, are
nothing different from each other, nor inferior to that image, by which I represent
the grain of sand itself, which is supposed to vastly exceed them ... the idea of
a grain of sand is not distinguishable, nor separable into twenty, much less into
a thousand, ten thousand, or an infinite number of different ideas.[22]

On the other hand, the discussion offered on distinctions of reason points
out that Hume is also prepared to call any idea 'simple' when considered
from the point of view of qualities it possesses which we find to be
inseparable from each other. That is, since colour and figure are always
found together, any idea viewed solely in terms of these attributes can be
called a simple idea. The important point brought out then is that because
of the second sense of simple idea uncovered, Hume is committed to the
view that distinctions of reason are possible in the case of complex ideas,
when this term is taken as the opposite of simple idea in the first sense.
Putting the matter generally, we can say that distinctions of reason are
possible in the case of *all* our ideas with respect to those features of our

[21] T. 27.
[22] T. 27.

ideas such as colour and figure which are not separable by the imagination alone. Further, although all philosophical relations are *based* [23] on some resemblance between ideas, distinctions of reason are employed solely *to establish* a resemblance between a simple idea (in the second sense discussed) and some other idea so that an inseparable aspect of the simple idea can be discerned. Accordingly, of the seven different philosophical relations discussed by Hume [24] distinctions of reason employ only resemblance, and resemblance is employed in order to isolate aspects of simple ideas.

IV. REASON AS THE COMPARISON OF IDEAS

(A) Not all relations yield knowledge in the strict sense [25]

Hume begins his discussion by reminding us that there are seven different kinds of philosophical relations – resemblance, identity, relations of time and place, proportions in quantity or number, degrees in any quality, contrariety, and causation. But now we are told that these relations can be divided into two classes, namely, those which remain unalterable so long as the ideas compared remain the same,[26] and those which can be changed without any change in the idea. The contrast between the two kinds of relations is illustrated as follows. The equality existing between the three angles of a triangle and two right angles is discovered from the idea of a triangle and this relation of equality is invariable so long as the idea remains unaltered, that is, so long as what is being contemplated is a triangle. On the other hand, the relations of contiguity and distance between two objects can be altered simply by changing their location, even though the objects themselves and their correspondent ideas remain unchanged. Hence, the relations of contiguity and distance between two objects are not discernible merely through a comparison of their correspondent ideas. Similarly, even though two objects are perfectly resembling, and appear in the same place at different times, they may be numerically different; and since causal powers or forces are never discoverable merely from contemplating the ideas of objects, it follows that the relation of cause and effect is one which can be changed without any change in the ideas we have of objects. Accordingly, of the seven relations mentioned,

[23] Just what more is involved will be seen later in the chapter.
[24] T. 14-15.
[25] Hume's fullest discussion of this topic appears in Bk. I, Pt. III, Section i of the *Treatise*.
[26] T. 69, 70.

three – relations of time and place, identity, and causation – do not depend solely on the content of the ideas involved and are not 'constant'.[27] Since knowledge is nothing but the assurance arising from the comparison of ideas,[28] and since this assurance is not possible in the case of these relations, it follows that the above mentioned relations do not yield knowledge. In fact, in the case of identity and relations of time and place, Hume wants to say that the term 'reasoning' is inappropriate and should be replaced by 'perception' :

All kinds of reasoning consist in nothing but a *comparison*, and a discovery of those relations, either constant or inconstant, which two or more objects bear to each other. This comparison we may make, either when both the objects are present to the senses, or when neither of them is present, or when only one. When both the objects are present to the senses along with the relation, we call *this* perception rather than reasoning ... According to this way of thinking, we ought not to receive as reasoning any of the observations we may make concerning identity, and the relations of time and place; since in none of them the mind can go beyond what is immediately present to the senses ..." [29]

Only in the case of causation is the term reasoning appropriate for of the three relations mentioned only causation provides us with an assurance which goes beyond the present testimony of the senses : " 'Tis only *causation*, which produces such a connexion, as to give us assurance from the existence or action of one object, that 'twas followed or preceded by any other existence or action ..." [30] In short, then, in the case of the relations of identity, time and place, and causation, the relations are independent of what is thought, and consequently these three relations do not yield knowledge in the strict sense. Further, since all three types of relations depend upon observation, statements concerning these relations must be empirical or *a posteriori*.

The four remaining relations, on the other hand, are entirely dependent on what is thought, and therefore are discernible *a priori*. These relations Hume refers to as 'infallible' [31] and the necessity involved he calls 'absolute'.[32] Three of these relations – resemblance, contrariety, degrees in quality – are discoverable without a chain of reasoning, and therefore are apprehended through intuition rather than demonstration.[33] At times the

[27] T. 73.
[28] T. 124.
[29] T. 73.
[30] T. 73-74.
[31] T. 79.
[32] T. 95.
[33] "Three of these relations are discoverable at first sight, and fall more properly

same is the case with proportions in quantity or number "especially where the difference is very great and remarkable".[34] In all other cases, Hume points out that we must settle the proportions with some liberty (i.e. do away with precision) or proceed in a more artificial manner, (i.e. employ a demonstration).

(B) Three conflicting views on those relations yielding knowledge

The analysis of knowledge as so far stated, although seemingly clear, is permeated with difficulties. For example, both N. K. Smith [35] and R. F. Anderson [36] hold that Hume's view of knowledge requires that the term idea be used equivocally. Smith writes :

It is when he proceeds to expound the character and grounds of the difference between the two classes of relations, that his argument becomes evasive and obscure ... When Hume is describing the four relations that make *knowledge* possible, 'idea' tends to be taken in the sense of 'ideal' *content* apprehended. In the case of the other three relations it is ideas as *existents*, i.e. as *objects*, which alone come under consideration.

R. F. Anderson writes :

Now it may appear odd, at this juncture, that Hume is affirming that there are necessary or essential relationships discoverable among distinct ideas, as in his example of the triangle, while he regularly denies that there are any such relationships among distinct existences. For we recall that according to Hume's doctrine (T. 258) every distinct perception is a distinct existence, and is thus, we may suppose, as much a matter of fact as is any external object ... There is another possible view ... which may ... relieve the apparent contradiction in Hume's holding that there are necessary relationships among distinct ideas, although there are no necessary relationships among distinct existences, some of which are ideas. It appears possible that in granting there are necessary relationships which may be traced among ideas, Hume is employing "idea" in a some-

---

under the province of intuition than demonstration. When any objects resemble each other, the resemblance will at first strike the eye, or rather mind; and seldom requires a second examination. The case is the same with *contrariety* and with the *degrees* of any *quality*." (T. 70).

[34] T. 70.
[35] Smith, p. 350.
[36] R.F. Anderson, *Hume's First Principles*, (University of Nebraska Press), p. 59-62.
   In another passage later in the same book, p. 172-173, Anderson similarly writes "... the wholly certain demonstrative reasoning... would appear to be possible if the ideas involved are not existences; for it is only among distinct existences that Hume has denied there are such discernible necessary connections as would permit inference of one from another."

what different sense than elsewhere. Certain remarks suggest that ideas are to be understood not as the natural products and images of impressions, but rather, in a more traditional sense, as mere forms or essences.

By ideas regarded as forms or essences Anderson means ideas "as we might regard them apart from their possible or actual existence".[37]

There are three passages which Anderson uses to support this thesis. The first is the passage on the two kinds of truth quoted earlier in this chapter in which the first kind of truth is said to involve the properties of ideas "consider'd as such" and Anderson suggests that by this phrase Hume may intend that ideas are taken as forms or essences. Secondly, he cites a passage in the first *Enquiry* [38] in which we are told that discovering relations between ideas is independent of any existent. And here again Anderson claims that this remark is intelligible only if our thought is concerned with ideas which are mere forms or essences, for "if our thought must involve existent ideas, the images of our impressions, then obviously there could not be any such certain propositions discoverable independently of existence".[39] The last passage noted is one in which Hume asserts that demonstrative reasoning is concerned with "the abstract relations of our ideas",[40] and that its proper province is "the world of ideas" as opposed to the world of "realities". Anderson reacts to this passage by saying that here ideas are treated as forms or essences occupying an ideal realm sharply distinguished from the existent world.[41]

The point raised by both commentators is most important since it has implications which go well beyond the alleged equivocation on the term 'idea'. In the first place, relying upon his basic distinction between impressions and ideas wherein ideas are copies of impressions, Hume infers that

... wherever ideas are adequate representations of objects [or impressions] the relations, contradictions, and agreements of the ideas are all applicable to the objects; and this we may in general observe to be the foundation of all human knowledge.[42]

[37] *Ibid.*, p. 65.

[38] "All the objects of human reason or enquiry may naturally be divided into two kinds, to wit, *Relations of Ideas*, and *Matters of Fact*. Of the first kind are... every affirmation which is either intuitively or demonstratively certain... Propositions of this kind are discoverable by the mere operation of thought, without dependence on what is anywhere existent in the universe." (E. 25).

[39] Anderson, p. 67.

[40] T. 413.

[41] Anderson, p. 12.

[42] T. 29.

Accordingly, whatever relations are uncovered through the comparison of ideas are applicable to the correspondent impressions or objects. Nevertheless, in Hume's writings we find remarks such as

... matter of fact and external existence are evidently incapable of demonstration. Whatever *is* may *not be*. No negation of a fact can involve a contradiction.[43]

leading to the belief that Hume cannot permit the conclusions arrived at by the comparison of ideas to be applicable to impressions or objects. If this is so, then, the basic distinction between ideas and impressions breaks down since it is no longer true that whatever holds of ideas also holds of the correspondent impressions. It is this interpretation of the matter which led Anderson to maintain that Hume is treating ideas involved in demonstrations as forms or essences without regard to their possible or actual existence.

A third position is also derivable from the text : the last passage quoted above argues that matters of fact and existences cannot be demonstrated, and in numerous passages throughout the text we find remarks which show that Hume regards *all* perceptions to be existences. For example, in one place he writes :

There is no impression nor idea of any kind, of which we have any consciousness or memory, that is not conceiv'd as existent ... we never remember any idea or impression without attributing existence to it ...[44]

What follows from these two passages is the view that Hume must give up the position that necessary relations can be apprehended even among ideas. Anderson [45] remarks on this interpretation that it is apparently because of this concession that Hume sometimes argues that there can be no certainty in demonstration but only probability (see especially *Of Scepticism with Regard to Reason*) that the demonstrative sciences must therefore decline to the level of the moral sciences, and be learned from repeated experiences as we behave regarding causes and effects.

Our problem then is considerable. For we must now decide which of these three views Hume actually held. Since no one of these views is consistent with any other, it is clear that Hume should not be holding to more than one of them.

(C) Steps toward resolving the conflict

In an effort to resolve this problem I believe it to be best to begin with a careful analysis of how Hume thinks a comparison of ideas takes place

[43] E. 163-164.
[44] T. 66. See also T. 94.
[45] Anderson, p. 172-175.

in the case of the four relations yielding knowledge in the strict sense.

Now, the first matter which we should attempt to understand is just what Hume means by the understanding being concerned in a comparison of ideas with the proportions of ideas considered as such [46] or the abstract relations of our ideas.[47] Concerning this view Anderson writes : "Now we may recall that Hume has very firmly said that we have no abstract ideas because all our ideas are individual and particular. This would seem to rule out also any knowledge, on our part, of any abstract relations among ideas. If we do indeed have knowledge of abstract relations of any ideas, therefore, I suggest that these ideas are not the existent images of our impressions but are instead mere forms or essences".[48] I believe Anderson to be wrong in this passage, especially in so far as he interprets Hume to be holding that we have no abstract ideas if ideas are taken as copies of impressions, but that we can have such abstract ideas if ideas are forms or essences.

That Anderson's view is mistaken can be seen from the following considerations. Firstly, in the discussion of abstract ideas [49] Hume is not concerned with denying that we *employ* ideas abstractly; he is simply trying to decide whether an idea so employed is general or particular. And he concludes that such ideas are particular since (1) we cannot abstract the precise degree of a quality from the quality itself, (2) ideas possess the characteristics of impressions, being derived from impressions, and all impressions are particular, and (3) we cannot conceive of an object which lacks a precise degree of quality and quantity. As Hume himself says : "Abstract ideas are therefore in themselves individual, *however they may become general in their representation*".[50] As to their becoming general in their representation he means that they become general by being annex'd to a general term, "that is, to a term, which from a customary conjunction has a relation to many other particular ideas, and readily recalls them in the imagination [if they are needed]".[51] Accordingly, Hume is not denying that we have abstract ideas : his study is only concerned

---

[46] T. 89, T. 448.

[47] T. 69, T. 413. Since Hume does not seem to want to macke any distinction between these expressions, I will not distinguish between them at this point.

[48] Anderson, p. 62.

[49] T. 17-24, E. 158n.

[50] T. 20, my italics.

[51] T. 22. Hume gives the following example : "Thus shou'd we mention the word triangle, and form the idea of a particular equilateral one to correspond to it, and shou'd we afterwards assert, *that the three angles of a triangle are equal to each other*, the other individuals of a scalenum and isosceles, which we overlook'd at first, immediately crowd

to determine what we can mean by such an idea. Given this analysis, it can be seen that Hume can accept knowledge of the abstract relations of ideas without equivocating on the term idea, provided that the analysis is consistent with the doctrine of abstract ideas. To assist us in explicating this matter let us use the relation of degrees in a quality.

Assume that the air temperature is 68° F. and that the air emanating from the furnace duct is 89° F. Hume wants to argue that we see immediately (or intuit) that the latter is warmer than the former. Nevertheless, the mind does not stop here for the claim that 89° F. is warmer than 68° F. holds regardless of what it is which is 68° F. and 89° F. For the relation of being warmer than depends solely on the temperature involved and not on what things happen to possess these temperatures. The problem now is to decide how we come to consider the temperatures independently of any particular objects without having to alter the original sense of ideas as being a copy of impressions.

Hume never discusses this matter directly and consequently an answer must be constructed rather than sought in a specific part of the text. A comparison of ideas will seek a generalization : as, for example, in the case we are considering that whenever two different things or the same thing in different respects possess temperatures of 68° F. and 89° F., the latter will always be warmer than the former. Now, Hume's theory of abstract ideas demands that in the consideration of this generalization we consider *particular* objects which can then stand for *all* objects possessing these temperatures. So far, then, no alteration in his original exposition of ideas is necessary. However, this analysis also does not yet do justice to the expressions "abstract relations of ideas", or "the proportions of ideas considered as such" inasmuch as we have not yet shown in what way or in fact in what sense the relation of the ideas is abstract or the proportion of the ideas is considered as such.

Now, I suggest that by the expression "the proportion of ideas considered as such" Hume is expressing the truth that, for example, the relation of being warmer than depends solely on the temperatures involved, and not on what things happen to possess these temperatures. The question remaining then is to decide how we come to consider the temperatures independently of any particular objects. Hume's only solution to this is to employ his analysis of distinctions of reason. Just as we never encounter figure without color, so we never encounter temperature, for example, without

---

in upon us, and make us perceive the falsehood of this proposition, tho' it be true with relation to that idea, which we had form'd."

something possessing this temperature. Accordingly, temperature is inseparable in experience from the thing possessing the temperature. Therefore, to separate the temperature from the thing possessing the temperature a distinction of reason is required whereby a resemblance or philosophical relation is established between the objects being treated.

By the 'abstract relations of ideas' Hume means that the temperatures now being compared must stand for all similar temperatures for we find when we compare these temperatures that so long as our ideas remain the same, the relation abides, and that given the ideas in question the denial of our comparison is inconceivable : that is, in the case under consideration we find that we cannot think that it is false that 89° F. is warmer than 38° F. Since our finding that the one temperature is hotter than the other is meant to cover all such instances, it is clear that the ideas in question, although particular, are being treated abstractly. In this way we can universalize our claim and hold that whenever something is 68° F. and something else is 89° F., the latter is warmer than the former.

To properly distinguish knowledge in the strict sense from an inductive inference, it must be possible to state and justifiably so that the relation in question holds necessarily. Now, as we have seen, Anderson holds that since Hume has denied that necessary relations obtain among distinct existences, Hume can hold that there are necessary relations only if he treats ideas as essences and not as existences. In order to determine the accuracy of Anderson's comment, it will be helpful to examine certain comments which Hume makes on the topic of existence.

Hume himself was aware of the relevance of the topic of 'existence' to his analysis of knowledge for he writes :

It may not be amiss, before we leave this subject [of space and time], to explain the ideas of *existence* and of *external existence*; which have their difficulties, as well as the ideas of space and time. By this means we shall be better prepar'd for the examination of knowledge and probability, when we understand perfectly all those particular ideas which may enter into our reasoning.[52]

The most striking feature of Hume's discussion on the topic of existence is his claim that whatever we conceive, we conceive as existent :

There is no impression nor idea of any kind, of which we have any consciousness or memory, that is not conceiv'd as existent ...[53]

Further, Hume argues that the idea of existence is not a separate idea which attends each perception :

[52] T. 66.
[53] T. 66.

... the idea of existence must either be deriv'd from a distinct impression, conjoin'd with every perception or object of our thought, or must be the very same with the idea of the perception or object ... So far from there being any distinct impression, attending every impression and every idea, that I do not think there are any two distinct impressions, which are inseparably conjoin'd. Tho' certain sensations may at one time be united, we quickly find they admit of a separation, and may be presented apart. And thus, tho' every impression and idea we remember be consider'd as existent, the idea of existence is not deriv'd from any particular impression.

The idea of existence, then, is the very same with the idea of what we conceive to be existent.[54]

The main difficulty with these passages is determining exactly what Hume means by 'existence' and by his claim that whatever we conceive we do so as existing. Determining what he means will be facilitated by considering what has been offered as a criticism to Hume's position. Pears [55] attacks Hume by maintaining that the idea of existence must be a separate idea, since otherwise nobody could have a negative existential thought. Now Hume himself acknowledges that we do have such thoughts. For example, in one place he writes "... that Caesar, or the Angel Gabriel, or any being never existed, may be a false proposition, but still is perfectly conceivable ..." [56]

Pears' solution to Hume's alleged problem of accounting for how we are able to have negative existential thoughts is to claim (along with Hume) that existence is not a separate impression, but to disagree with Hume by maintaining that it may still be a separate idea :

Admittedly it is a peculiar idea, because it adds nothing to anything in the world, and so is not a predicate (an ambiguous thesis), and, no doubt, this peculiarity was one of the things that led Hume to conclude that complete thoughts are single ideas. But we can avoid this conclusion if we treat existence as an idea of a higher order – viz. the idea of an idea's having a correspondent impression or impressions ...[57]

In fact, however, what is overlooked is that Hume does not restrict his discussion to 'existence', for his discussion is two-fold – he speaks of 'existence' and of 'external existence'.[58] The error commentators commit in this regard is to attend to Hume's comments on existence (as we did above)

[54] T. 66.

[55] In *David Hume : A Symposium*, edited by D. F. Pears (Macmillan and Company Ltd., 1963). Reprinted : Macmillan, St. Martin's press, New York, 1966, p. 17.

[56] E. 164.

[57] Pears, p. 18.

[58] See T. 66-68.

and neglect entirely his view on external existence, thereby attributing a view to Hume to which he is not subject. To develop his views on external existence Hume begins by reiterating his basic position that we can be aware only of perceptions (impressions and ideas) :

... 'tis universally allow'd by philosophers, and is besides pretty obvious of itself, that nothing is ever really present to the mind but its perceptions or impressions and ideas ...[59]

Given this, and the fact that all ideas are derived from antecedent impressions, it follows that we cannot even think of an external object which is different from our impressions and ideas :

Let us chace our imagination to the heavens, or to the utmost limits of the universe; we never really advance a step beyond ourselves, nor can conceive any kind of existence, but those perceptions, which have appear'd in that narrow compass.[60]

Therefore, the idea of a perception and of an external existence must be identical.

... as every idea is deriv'd from a preceding perception, 'tis impossible our idea of a perception, and that of an object or external existence can ever represent what are specifically different from each other.[61]

But not all perceptions are thought of as external existences. Accordingly, the problem Hume faces is to account for the manner in which some perceptions come to be thought of as external existences or objects, while yet conceding his point that whatever we conceive we conceive as existing. His solution centers around the fact that a given perception can come to stand in different sets of relations :

Generally speaking we do not suppose them [perception and object] specifically different; but only attribute to them different relations, connexions, and durations.[62]

By the term 'relations' in the above Hume is referring to the relation of identity (since a succession of resembling and interrupted perceptions is regarded as individually the same or identical through a given period of time when perceptions are regarded as objects) and to spatial relations

---

[59] T. 67.

[60] T. 67-68. Similarly at T. 216 Hume says : "We never can conceive any thing but perceptions, and therefore must make everything resemble them."

[61] T. 68. See also T. 216, T. 241, T. 244.

[62] T. 68. See also T. 241, 244. I need not, for our purposes, go into this matter in any great detail. The part of the text which is relevant here, however, is *Of Scepticism with Regard to the Senses* (T. Bk. I, Pt. IV, Sect. II)

(since the perception qua object is regarded as remaining the same in space whereas qua perception it need not be regarded as occupying space at all); by 'connexions' he means that a perception qua object is held to be able to enter into causal relations or connexions which the same perception qua perception could not so enter; and by 'durations' he means that whereas perceptions are 'perishing' existences [63] a perception viewed as an external existence is held to have a continued and independent existence. A perception, therefore, is itself a neutral entity which can be treated simply as a perishing existence and can also be treated as an external object.

With this in mind, some sense can be made out of Hume's concession that we can have negative existential thoughts, for to think that Caesar does not now exist is merely a matter of denying that the impression corresponding to the idea of Caesar can be regarded as possessing the relations mentioned above, that is, what is denied is that the impression of Caesar can be given certain spatial, causal, and temporal relations.

Having now seen that Hume wishes to distinguish 'existence' from 'external existence' and what he means by external existence, we must determine what he means by 'existence' and by the expression that whatever we conceive we conceive as existing. Hume's distinction between existence and external existence is, I submit, included by him in order to allow for different modalities in our reasonings, in this case the distinction between actual and possible existence. We have already seen that the notion of external existence is synonymous with actual existence. And there are at least two passages in which Hume clearly states that by the term 'existence' he intends to convey the notion of possible existence :

Whatever can be conceiv'd by a clear and distinct idea *necessarily* implies the possibility of existence ...[64]

To form a clear idea of any thing, is an undeniable argument for its possibility ...[65]

Accordingly, to say that whatever we conceive we conceive of as existing is tantamount to saying that whatever we conceive may exist, i.e. may have certain spatial, causal, and temporal relations.

Having now seen what Hume means by a comparison of ideas and the sense to be given to the term existence, we have yet to look at the theory of the philosophical relations if we are to adequately assess the positions in Hume discussed earlier.

[63] T. 194.
[64] T. 43.
[65] T. 89. See also T. 32.

In the preceding chapter a detailed discussion was undertaken which sought to establish that the distinction between impressions and ideas for Hume is based on the fact that a perception is an impression if its content is not traceable to any other perceptions even though it may be caused by other perceptions. A perception is an idea, on the other hand, if its content is derivable from other perceptions either directly, as for example where a simple idea is derived from its correspondent simple impression, or indirectly, such as in the case of the perception of the missing shade of blue wherein the perception is obtained from other perceptions with the assistance of one or more mental operations. Further, in the last chapter we saw that the content of the perception of a relation is dependent upon the resemblance obtaining between the ideas compared. In the case of the relation of co-existence, for example, we are thinking of the similarity which the two ideas bear to each other in virtue of their time of existence. The perception of the relation, therefore, makes explicit this equality which obtains between the two flashes of red. In other words, the perception of the relation derives its content from the relata with the assistance of comparison. As such, it must be classified as an idea. Accordingly, it is surprising to see Huxley and others [66] maintain that there are impressions of philosophical relations. Referring to 'succession', 'resemblance', and 'co-existence' Huxley writes "... they must be called *impressions of relation* ... In fact we may regard them as a kind of impressions of impressions ..." [67] Huxley's position can now be seen to be incorrect since the awareness (perception) which constitutes a philosophical relation is nothing but a copy of percedent perceptions (namely, those being compared) in the extended sense of copy introduced in the last chapter when discussing the missing shade of blue. This explains why when Hume first introduces the philosophical relations [68] he refers to them as 'ideas' (or more precisely 'complex ideas', the reason for which was offered in the last chapter) and not as 'impressions'.

In one passage Hume provides a general statement concerning the comparison of ideas :

It seems to me, that the only objects of the abstract science or of demonstration are quantity and number, and that all attempts to extend this more perfect species of knowledge beyond these bounds are mere sophistry and illusion. [1]*As the component parts of quantity and number are entirely similar*, their relations become

[66] See, for example, F. Zabech, *D. Hume, Precursor of Modern Empiricism*, (Martinus Nijhof, The Hague, 1960), p. 99-100.

[67] See Huxley, p. 81-82.

[68] T. 13.

intricate and involved, and nothing can be more curious, as well as useful, than to trace, [2]*by a variety of mediums,* [3]*their equality or inequality,* [4]*through their different appearances.*[69]

The sections of this passage which I have italicized and numbered are most noteworthy for our purposes. The first italicized section shows that philosophical relations for Hume require that what is compared be thought of in terms of parts or units. Section [2] is more difficult to understand, but can be made meaningful if we bear in mind that all philosophical relations presuppose or are based on some resemblance, and that Hume's enumeration of the various kinds of philosophical relations is an attempt to show the different kinds of resemblances there are which allow us to compare ideas. I submit that section [2] above is simply stating this view of Hume's : To speak of "a variety of mediums" is to acknowledge that there are different kinds of resemblances which allow us to compare ideas. If a comparison of ideas is based on some resemblance between two ideas, and if as we saw in section [1] all philosophical relations treat what is being compared as possessing parts or units, then the comparison itself should yield a knowledge of an equality of such units (as in the case of co-existence) or an inequality (as, for example, that 89º F. is warmer than 69º F. – the expression 'is warmer than' being the expression which is appropriate for expressing an inequality between two perceptions with regard to their temperatures). Section [3] above, therefore, is acknowledging the fact that through a comparison of ideas we can only uncover whether an equality or inequality obtains between two perceptions in virtue of a common property. Section [4] must be read in conjunction with section [3] and when this is done it becomes clear that section [4] is referring to the fact that our comparisons may continue and the relations between objects may be changed (hence his reference in section [3] to equality or inequality) through the alterations which are noted in objects through their various appearances to the senses. For example, although one object is warmer than another at t^1, it may at t^2 be found to be the same temperature. In short, then, the passage under examination discloses that all comparisons for Hume, and therefore, all philosophical relations seek to disclose whether or not there is an equality of units between two ideas in virtue of a common property. The four relations which yield knowledge in the strict sense differ from the other three which do not in that in the case of the latter the comparison can be undertaken *a priori* whereas in the case of the other three, the objects or perceptions themselves must be present. In each case,

[69] E. 163, my italics.

however, the resultant perception of the relation must be regarded as an idea since its content is derivable from the relata with the assistance of a comparison.

Through the material discussed in the preceding chapter we have been led to see that the perception which arises when comparing ideas in order to establish a philosophical relation between them must be regarded as an idea. The material discussed in the last chapter can now help us even further. Since impressions have been identified with Hume's use of the terms 'matter of fact' and 'external existence', and since philosophical relations are not impressions, it follows that philosophical relations are not matters of fact or external existences.

We can now begin to assess the difficulties in Hume's analysis of demonstration. In the first place, our analysis has shown that the ideas involved in a comparison of ideas must be regarded minimally as ideas of what may exist, and not, as Anderson has maintained, as essences as we might regard them apart from their possible or actual existence. Now, although the ideas involved are regarded as ideas of what may exist, the necessity involved in a relationship between them is discerned only through an act of thought, and the necessity involved is nothing but an awareness of how a common property is placed in different ideas, that is, whether the ideas contain the property equally or unequally. In other words, that a certain object has a certain property is a matter of fact and that another object also has this property to some extent is also a matter of fact. But that they possess the property 'equally' or 'unequally' is not strictly speaking a fact, but is rather a notion introduced to express the results of a comparison between them, or in other words, to make explicit what is already thought in the ideas themselves. Hence, as Hume states in one place : "... the necessity, which makes two times two equal to four, or the three angles of a triangle equal to two right ones, lies only in the act of the understanding by which we consider and compare these ideas ..." [70] This passage does not mean that the necessity is psychological as opposed to logical. Rather it is an attempt on Hume's part to draw attention to the fact that relations are not matters of fact but are ideas discerned through comparison. Thus Hume is not committed to reducing logical necessity to psychological.

This last point raises the problem of how Hume can allow logical necessity into his system. The answer to this can be gathered from what has been said about the four relations which yield knowledge in the strict

[70] T. 166.

sense : logical necessity is present to the extent that statements concerning these four relations either express identity statements or statements concerning some inequality. For example, in the case of 'degrees in any quality', to say that one object weighs the same as another is, for Hume, to affirm that each possesses the same number of units of weight, whereas to say one object is heavier than another is to say that the number of units of weight in one object exceeds the number of units of weight in the other. It can now also be seen why in the case of these relations the contrary is held to be inconceivable and contradictory. It is inconceivable and contradictory to deny that equals are equal or that unequals are unequal.

Earlier in this chapter mention was made of the fact that Hume speaks of these four philosophical relations as 'infallible' and as possessing 'absolute' necessity. Sense can now be made of their inclusion. These relations are 'infallible' in that once one understands the ideas being compared, it is not possible to err in the comparison, since any error will be a logical contradiction and hence inconceivable. Further, the necessity is 'absolute' since never will it be the case that so long as the content of the ideas remains the same, equals will become unequal or unequals equal.

(D) Resolving the conflict

Our attention can now be directed to the three views of knowledge introduced earlier in this chapter. Our own analysis has yielded the view that Hume is committed to holding that since relations which yield knowledge in the strict sense are mind dependent there can be no relations among external existences or matters of fact since these are not regarded as mind dependent. Relations, therefore, are not themselves matters of fact, and as a result, of the three views examined earlier, it is the second position which comes closest to Hume's actual position, although as I have shown, there is no need for Hume to equivocate on the meaning of the term idea thereby rendering idea as essence in Anderson's sense. As my analysis has shown ideas can be regarded as images of impressions and yet be subject to necessary relations once we understand what Hume means by 'necessity' and by 'relation'.

What, then, is to be said for the other two positions cited earlier, especially since there is some textual support for each? The first view examined, it will be recalled, maintained that wherever ideas adequately represent their objects or impressions, any relations, contradictions, and agreements of the ideas are applicable to the objects or impressions (T. 29). The term to attend to here is 'applicable' for it is noteworthy that Hume is not maintaining that relations 'hold' of objects or impressions as they do of ideas. That they are merely 'applicable' to impressions of objects indicates that this is something we ourselves do, rather than something which we uncover in objects themselves. The frequency of such acts of application is often noted by Hume : For example, when speaking of why we regard causal necessity to be present in objects he says : 'Tis a common observation, that the mind has a great propensity to spread itself on external objects, and to conjoin with them any internal impressions, which they occasion ...''[71] Or again, in another place concerning another matter he writes : "There is a very remarkable inclination in human nature, to bestow on external objects the same emotions, which it observes in itself ..." [72] Now, both these passages indicate that we have a propensity to externalize internal *impressions*. But I have been maintaining that the perceptions giving rise to philosophical relations are *ideas* and that it is these which we are externalizing or applying to objects or impressions. And in one passage Hume concedes that a similar process of externalization is possible in their case as well : "There is a very remarkable inclination in human nature ... to find every where those ideas, which are most present to it".[73] I submit, therefore, that such is the case with the perceptions of relations which, although ideas, are 'spread' over external objects, and to show that this is the case Hume employs the special term 'applicable'. In addition to characterizing this vulgar tendency, however, Hume intends to make an important epistemological point as well, viz. it is through the comparison of ideas that we can determine that which in fact cannot exist. That is, since all philosophical relations are discerned through the units or parts contained in the relata, and since ideas are copies of their correspondent impressions or objects, it follows that if the assertion of a certain relation is found to be inconceivable or contradictory then the correspondent objects or impressions cannot contain the particular number of units or parts simultaneously. An example will be helpful here. In an isosceles triangle, we find that the angles supported by the two equal sides are always equal to each other. Further, we find that in the light of the demonstration employed to prove this, the denial of this proposition is inconceivable. The conclusion which we can draw then is that it cannot be the case in fact that an isosceles triangle should exist in which the number of degrees found in one of the angles supported by one of the equal sides should be either greater or less than the number of degrees found in the angle

[71] T. 167. See also E. 78 footnote.
[72] T. 224.
[73] T. 224.

supported by the other equal side. This is the kind of thing Hume has in mind when he asserts that "... whatever *appears* impossible and contradictory upon the comparison of these ideas, must be *really* impossible and contradictory, without any farther excuse or evasion".[74] Accordingly, the comparison of ideas is seen to be a sufficient condition for determining what (logically) cannot exist.

I turn now to the third position attributed to Hume, viz. the one which maintains that since matters of fact and existences cannot be demonstrated and since in various passages Hume maintains that all perceptions including ideas are existences it follows that necessary relations cannot be demonstrated between ideas. It is further held that Hume then altered his position so that there can be no certainty in demonstration, only probability. The demonstrative sciences then are reduced to the level of the moral sciences, where the emphasis is on constant conjunctions.[75] The evidence which is cited in support of this position is to be found largely in 'Of Scepticism with Regard to Reason'. (T. Bk. I, Pt. IV, Sect. I).

Repeatedly, Hume identifies the necessity involved in propositions to be demonstrated with the necessity in propositions which are intuitively certain.[76] Furthermore, he regards a demonstration as nothing more than a series of intuitions. Accordingly, if the demonstrative sciences are reduced to the level of the moral sciences where the only kind of necessity is psychological and certainty gives way to probability, then even in the case of the philosophical relations which are usually intuitively certain the only necessity involved would be psychological. We can see, therefore, that any alteration in Hume's view regarding the necessity and certainty involved in demonstrative reasoning would similarly affect his views of necessity and certainty in intuition. It follows from this that in the section 'Of Scepticism with Regard to Reason' all the philosophical relations said to yield certainty are actually in view.

I stated that Hume regards a demonstration as nothing more than a series of intuitions and that this in part accounts for why any threat to the former is also a threat to the latter. This point can be elaborated through examining the text. At one point Hume speaks of 'our assurance in a long enumeration' and states that 'none will maintain' that it exceeds probability. However, he continues by arguing that this establishes 'that there scarce is any proposition concerning numbers of which we can have a fuller security' :

[74] T. 29.
[75] Anderson, p. 173.
[76] See, for example, T. 95.

For 'tis easily possible, by gradually diminishing the numbers, to reduce the longest series of addition to the most simple question, which can be formed, to an addition of two single numbers; and upon this supposition we shall find it impracticable to shew the precise limits of knowledge and of probability, or discover that particular number, at which the one ends and the other begins. But knowledge and probability are of such contrary and disagreeing natures, that they cannot well run insensibly into each other ... Besides, if any single addition were certain, every one wou'd be so, and consequently the whole or total sum; unless the whole can be different from all its parts. I had almost said, that this was certain; but I reflect, that it must reduce *itself*, as well as every other reasoning, and from knowledge degenerate into probability.[77]

In this passage Hume is arguing that attempting to reduce a complex problem to a more simple one will not insure the status of intuition, since if this intuition were certain, there is no reason for doubting the successive intuitions in the original formulation of the problem. As a result, the status of intuition is itself suspect. Again, therefore, any threat to the certainty of a demonstration is a threat to the certainty of intuition, and as the same reasoning processes – that is, a comparison of ideas – takes place in all philosophical relations previously spoken of as yielding certainty, it can be seen that all comparative reasoning is being challenged in the section on scepticism with regard to reason. Thus, Hume says that "all knowledge resolves itself into probability ..." [78] and later in the same section raises the question "after what manner the mind ever retains a degree of assurance in any subject?" [79]

Now, we have seen that ideas are not treated by Hume as matters of fact are, for the latter are regarded as *external* or *actual* existences whereas the former are regarded as *possible* existences and therefore as mind dependent. Further, insofar as these latter are mind dependent they are subject to the comparison of ideas, with the resulting idea or relation being nothing but an awareness of an equality or inequality obtaining between these ideas.

Nevertheless, to stop our analysis at this point would be to beg the question for the view of commentators like Anderson is that it is only when Hume treats ideas as 'existences' (i.e. existences on a par with matters of fact) that he denies necessary relations among ideas. Hence, a refutation of this view cannot be undertaken by examining passages in *other* parts of the text. What is required is to examine 'Of Scepticism with Regard to Reason' and attempt to determine whether there is in fact any real change

[77] T. 181.
[78] T. 181.
[79] T. 184.

in Hume's position. I will attempt to establish that there is not, thereby showing that Hume holds an entirely consistent view of the philosophical relations.

The section begins with a statement to the effect that in demonstrative sciences, although the syntactical rules are certain and infallible, we may err in applying them in a problem.

We must, therefore, in every reasoning form a new judgment, as a check or control on our first judgment or belief; and must comprehend a kind of history of all the instances, wherein our understanding has deceiv'd us, compar'd with those, wherein its testimony is just and true ... By this means all knowledge degenerates into probability; and this probability is greater or less, according to the veracity or deceitfulness of our understanding, and according to the simplicity or intricacy of the question.[80]

The material in the preceding paragraph represents the *first* part of Hume's argument in 'Of Scepticism with Regard to Reason' and before proceeding further some explanation should be provided of what lies behind Hume's view. For this, passages will have to be examined from other parts of the text.

The view now under examination actually seems inconsistent with much of what Hume says on other occasions. In one place Hume argues that the belief attending demonstration and intuition is easily accounted for and unproblematic :

... Wherein consists the difference betwixt believing and disbelieving any proposition? The answer is easy with regard to propositions, that are prov'd by intuition or demonstration. In that case, the person, who assents, not only conceives the ideas according to the proposition, but is necessarily determin'd to conceive them in that particular manner, either immediately or by the interposition of other ideas. Whatever is absurd is unintelligible; nor is it possible for the imagination to conceive any thing contrary to a demonstration.[81]

The conclusion of a valid demonstration is irresistible once the demonstration itself is understood just as a proposition is irresistible when apprehended directly through intuition, and further, once it is understood it is not subject to criticisms which can weaken its authority :

But here we may observe, that nothing can be more absurd, than the custom of calling a *difficulty* what pretends to be a *demonstration*, and endeavouring by that means to elude its force and evidence. 'Tis not in demonstrations as in probabilities, that difficulties can take place, and one argument counter-balance another, and diminish its authority. A demonstration, if just, admits of no opposite

[80] T. 180.
[81] T. 95.

difficulty; and if not just, 'tis a mere sophism, and consequently can never be a difficulty. 'Tis either irresistible, or has no manner of force. To talk therefore of objections and replies, and ballancing of arguments in such a question as this, is to confess, either that human reason is nothing but a play of words, or that the person himself, who talks so, has not a capacity equal to such subjects. Demonstrations may be difficult to be comprehended, because of the abstracted-ness of the subject; but can never have any such difficulties as will weaken their authority, when once they are comprehended.[82]

Now, these two passages, when taken alone, seem inconsistent with the position taken in 'Of Scepticism with Regard to Reason'. Nevertheless, when linked with other passages it can be seen how Hume's view of demonstration in these two passages becomes susceptible to the views of the sceptic.

In one of these passages Hume writes :

The principal difficulty in the mathematics is the length of inferences and compass of thought, requisite to the forming of any conclusion.[83]

Besides the length of inference, we are told that the ideas compared are not closely related, that is, the equality or inequality between the ideas is not easily discerned but requires many other ideas to mediate :

If the mind, with greater facility, retains the ideas of geometry clear and determinate, it must carry on a much longer and more intricate chain of reasoning, and compare ideas much wider of each other, in order to reach the abstruser truths of that science.[84]

Accordingly, the connection (equality or inequality) between the ideas in the conclusion of a demonstration cannot be established by a definition. For example, "*That the square of the hypotenuse is equal to the squares of the other two sides,* cannot be known, let the terms be ever so exactly defined, without a train of reasoning and enquiry".[85]

Taking these points together, namely, the inordinate length of many inferences in demonstrative arguments, and the fact that the connection between the terms in the conclusion is not clearly discerned, it is easy to see why even Hume's account of demonstration leads to difficulties which the sceptic seeks to exploit. For the two criteria of inconceivability (that is, that we cannot conceive anything contrary to a valid demonstration) and irresistibility (that is, that a valid demonstration when understood must command our assent) are seen to fall short of perfect assurance

[82] T. 31.
[83] E. 61.
[84] E. 61.
[85] E. 163.

inasmuch as even when we reason incorrectly they appear to be present. (Of course, if the reasoning were perfectly understood they would not be present, but now the question is raised as to how we can determine that the reasoning has been perfectly understood). Inconceivability and irresistibility, therefore, can no longer be regarded as infallible criteria for the validity of a demonstrative argument nor for propositions which are apprehended intuitively since the same criteria are applied to them. Thus begins the problem in "Of Scepticism with Regard to the Reason" for each demonstration now becomes suspect and subject to the control of probability. Thus Hume's insistence on enlarging our view "to comprehend a kind of history of all the instances wherein our understanding has deceiv'd us, compar'd with these, wherein its testimony was just and true". Our analysis to this point, besides unpacking the much needed background to 'Of Scepticism with Regard to Reason' is important since it shows Anderson to be wrong when he maintains that the section in question gains its momentum through its treatment of ideas as existences on a par with matters of fact thereby rendering impossible the discernment of necessary relations even among ideas. Hume is not here saying that there are no necessary relations among ideas; rather he is maintaining that the ones which there are are difficult to discern in the demonstrative sciences.

Nevertheless, although Anderson is wrong in holding that the section is predicated on the notion of ideas as existences on a par with matters of fact as existences, he may still be correct in holding [86] that Hume does obscure the distinction between knowledge and probability thereby reducing knowledge to probability because of the weakness of the human mind. (This is, of course, consistent with the claim that there are necessary relations between ideas). A careful inspection of the remainder of 'Of Scepticism with Regard to Reason' will show that even this is not the case, and that therefore from start to finish Hume holds a consistent view.

Now, given that the force of the argument in 'Of Scepticism with Regard to Reason' has thus far shown that knowledge reduces itself to probability, Hume now asks upon what foundation the latter form of reasoning stands.[87] Just as knowledge claims are subject to the control of probability, so is the latter subject to a further correction since even in the estimation of probability we recall having erred, and realize we have no assurance of not erring in the future :

[86] Anderson, p. 64.

[87] "Since therefore all knowledge resolves itself into probability, and becomes at last of the same nature with that evidence, which we employ in common life, we must

As demonstration is subject to the control of probability, so is probability liable to a new correction by a reflex act of the mind, wherein the nature of our understanding, and our reasoning from the first probability become our objects.[88]

In other words, the problem of error which reduced knowledge to probability is now transferred to probability. Thus the second judgment of probability, rather than strengthening our original claim actually weakens it, since once the possibility of error is allowed in assessing probability, the second judgment of probability is itself suspect and susceptible to a further assessment. Of course, this new judgment is also suspect and subject to the control of an additional probability and so on, "till at last there remain nothing of the original probability, however great we may suppose it to have been, and however small the diminution by every new uncertainty".[89]

Immediately succeeding this argument Hume makes three points. First, the argument just put forward is pyrrhonistic, and is one which neither Hume nor anyone else ever took seriously for long. The second point he makes is "Nature, by an absolute and uncontrollable necessity has determin'd us to judge as well as to breathe and feel"[90], indicating that it is through the influence of nature that the argument of the Pyrrhonian against reason does not have a sustained hold on us *and* that it is through Nature that we resume our reasonings. The third point made by Hume is his reason for putting the argument of the Pyrrhonian forward : "My intention then in displaying so carefully the arguments of the fantastic sect, is only to make the reader sensible of the truth of my hypothesis, *that all our reasonings concerning causes and effects are deriv'd from nothing but custom; and that belief is more properly an act of the sensitive, than of the cogitative part of our natures*".[91] It is this latter claim of Hume's which is usually taken as supporting the view that Hume reduces all reasoning to causal reasoning and all necessity to psychological necessity or custom.

Pyrrhonism, as was pointed out in the opening chapter of this book, need not be entirely destructive, but can be constructive in providing a lesson which is philosophically valuable. Now, if Anderson's view is correct then we can infer that the lesson of Pyrrhonism there is two-fold : (a) that all knowledge reduces to causality or probability, and (b) that

---

now examine this latter species of reasoning, and see on what foundation it stands." (T. 181).

[88] T. 182.
[89] T. 182.
[90] T. 183.
[91] T. 183.

Nature working through custom is the only means through which causal claims and beliefs are prevented from losing their influence on us. In fact, however, this view is not correct, since as I will now attempt to show, Hume does not want to maintain that all knowledge reduces to causality.

The outstanding lesson of Pyrrhonism in this case is that Pyrrhonism is incapable of dealing any blow to our intuitive and demonstrative reasonings and that we need no justification for employing such reasonings. In order to see that this is so we need only examine certain remarks which Hume makes toward the end of 'Of Scepticism with Regard to Reason' and in the conclusion to Book I of the *Treatise*.

After providing the sceptic's argument which seeks to destroy intuitive, demonstrative, and causal reasoning, Hume points out that even though no error occurs in the sceptical reasoning, we still continue to believe; hence, belief is some peculiar manner of conception [92] rather than a rational activity. But now he goes on and asks how it is that even if belief is a matter of conceiving an idea in a certain manner we still retain any belief in the face of the sceptic's argument, since, if the sceptic's argument is founded on a rational basis, then Hume's position simply shows that the sceptic opposes the original belief or manner of conception with an opposing one and again it appears that the mind can be reduced to total uncertainty.[93] In other words, maintaining that belief is a part of the sensitive element of our natures does not seem to rule out the sceptic's influence. Hume's answer to this is that, strictly speaking, the sceptic's argument lacks any influence because a much greater effort of mind is needed for it (since it is an unnatural conception of one's ideas) and the imagination will not be as affected by any conception of ideas it generates as it will be by something which is more natural :

... after the first and second decision; as the action of the mind becomes forc'd and unnatural, and the ideas faint and obscure; tho' the principles of judgment, and the ballancing of opposite causes be the same as at the very beginning; yet their influence on the imagination, and the viguour they add to, or diminish from the thought, is by no means equal. Where the mind reaches not its objects with easiness and facility, the same principles have not the same effect as in a more natural conception of the ideas; nor does the imagination feel a sensation, which holds any proportion with that which arises from its common judgments and opinions.[94]

... the conviction, which arises from a subtile reasoning, diminishes in proportion to the efforts, which the imagination makes to enter the reasoning, and to con-

[92] T. 184.
[93] T. 184.
[94] T. 185.

ceive it in all its parts. Belief, being a lively conception, can never be entire, wheer it is not founded on something natural and easy.[95]

Again, in the conclusion to Book I, we find Hume saying :

... I have already shown [this is a reference to T. 182 ff.] that the understanding, when it acts alone, and according to its most general principles, entirely subverts itself and leave not the lowest degree of evidence in any proposition, either in philosophy or common life. We save ourselves from this total scepticism, only by means of that singular and seemingly trivial property of the fancy, by which we enter with difficulty into remote views of things, and are not able to accompany them with so sensible an impression, as we do those, which are more easy and natural.[96]

Accordingly, Hume maintains that given the lack of influence which the sceptic's argument possesses, demonstrative reasoning remains intact and is neither demolished nor reduced to probability. Thus, at the beginning of the succeeding section he indicates what the lesson of the preceding section was : "Thus the sceptic still continues to reason and believe, even tho' he asserts, that he cannot defend his reason by reason ..." [97] The argument of the sceptic is either totally effective or entirely ineffective. From a logical point of view, Hume argues, it is effective; but not being able to maintain a hold on the mind, it is seen to be entirely ineffective.

It is true that Hume says that he provided the sceptical argument in order 'to make the reader sensible of the truth of my hypothesis, that all our reasonings concerning causes and effects are deriv'd from nothing but custom; and that belief is more properly an act of the sensitive, than of the cogitative part of our natures'.[98] However, to hold that this is *all* Hume sought to establish in this section requires totally disregarding the last four pages of this section where he is intent on showing that the sceptic's argument, while persuasive from a logical point of view, cannot maintain its hold on us at all. But that Hume includes the passage quoted above can be rendered intelligible if we recall that Hume argued that causal or probable reasoning is subject to the sceptic's argument just as much as demonstrative reasoning is. Thus, the fact that we still continue

---

[95] T. 186.

[96] T. 267-268. It should also be pointed out that Hume realizes the consequences of rejecting all 'refined or elaborate' reasonings, and, it should be added, of accepting them. See T. 268-269. A full discussion of this matter is not relevant to this chapter, although it might be pointed out that Hume does hold, consistent with his view that refined reasoning has no influence on us, that his own analysis of causality and the origin of moral distinctions will have no impact on our daily lives. See T. 167, T. 469.

[97] T. 187.

[98] T. 183.

to employ causal reasoning shows that it is something other than a rational faculty which provides the basis for such reasoning, and which leads us to believe in certain causal connections. Probable reasoning, having no standard for certainty in its own pronouncements, would, if derived from a rational faculty, destroy itself. Its non-destruction, therefore, proves that it is not a rational undertaking, but a natural one. The error of certain commentators is to attend to this conclusion and then hold that this somehow constitutes Hume's view on intuitive and demonstrative reasoning.

We can see therefore that no change in Hume's view of intuitive and demonstrative reasoning occurs in 'Of Scepticism with Regard to Reason'.

CHAPTER IV

REASON AND CONDUCT IN HUME'S PREDECESSORS

In the light of the epistemological considerations put forward in the previous chapters, we are now partially prepared to examine Hume's views on the role of reason in morality. Hume's views on this topic are essentially a reaction to the rationalist conception of reason in ethics typified in figures such as Ralph Cudworth, Samuel Clarke and William Wollaston.[1] It is therefore important to examine their views before beginning an analysis of Hume's position.

I. RALPH CUDWORTH

Cudworth begins by trying to establish that moral good and evil and other moral terms "cannot possibly be Arbitrary things made by Will without Nature". The reason given for this is "it is Universally true, that things are what they are, not by Will but by Nature". Two problems immediately arise concerning this account : (a) what does Cudworth mean by 'arbitrary' and (b) what steps does Cudworth take to try to establish the truth of his claim that it is universally true that things are what they are by nature and not by will, since as his argument now stands it begs the question. That is, in trying to show that morality is not arbitrary he has recourse to this universal claim whereas the truth of this universal claim depends on the non-arbitrary character of morality. Hence, to avoid begging the question his universal claim must be substantiated.

In attempting to establish that it is universally true that things are what

---

[1] All references to Cudworth are taken from the two-volume work, *The British Moralists*, edited by Selby-Bigge. All references to Selby-Bigge are taken from the Library of Liberal Arts edition, 1964, and these will be cited by S.B. followed by the appropriate volume and page number. This book was originally published by Oxford at the Clarendon Press, 1877.

they are not by will but by nature Cudworth has recourse to examples. He says that things are white through whiteness, black by blackness, triangular by triangularity. At first this sounds like nothing more than a return to the Platonic theory of Forms but a closer view of Cudworth's doctrine shows this not to be the case. For Cudworth is only concerned with the defining characteristics of a thing or property and not with their being an Ideal World in which things can participate. For example, he writes : "... Omnipotence itself cannot by mere Will make a Body Triangular, without having the Nature and Properties of a Triangle in it; That is, without having three Angles equal to two Right ones".[2] Thus, his claim is that for whatever is there are defining characteristics such that a thing cannot become another thing without taking on the defining characteristics of that other thing. This, of course, prevents essential change through the will alone, either divine or human since the will cannot be a formal cause :

Omnipotent Will cannot make things Like or Equal one to another, without the Natures of Likeness and Equality ... For though the Will of God be the Supreme Efficient Cause of all things, and can produce into Being or Existence, or reduce into Nothing what it pleaseth, yet it is not the Formal Cause of any thing besides itself ...[3]

From this analysis he concludes that since things are what they are in virtue of their defining characteristics (his expression is 'by the Necessity of their own Nature') there is no such thing as an arbitrary essence or relation which can be changed by will or pleasure : An arbitrary essence would be a being without a nature or defining characteristic, which is a contradiction in terms, and hence would be a nonentity. Thus in answer to question (a) raised earlier we can see that Cudworth objects to classifying moral good and evil as arbitrary since to do so for him is to affirm that something exists which is devoid of any defining characteristics. Accordingly, since for whatever is there are defining characteristics which make it what it is, Cudworth applies this analysis to moral good and evil, justice and injustice, and maintains that they "cannot be Arbitrarious Things, that may be Applicable by Will indifferently to any Actions and Dispositions Whatsoever. For the Modes of all Subsistent Beings, and the Relations of things to one another, are immutably and necessarily what they and not Arbitrary, being not by will but by Nature".[4]

---

[2] S. B. II, p. 248.
[3] S. B. II, P. 248.
[4] S. B. II, p. 249.

The account, as stated above, remains question-begging for Cudworth has only shown that whatever in fact exists must exist as something, but he has not shown that moral good and evil, justice and injustice are existents. He himself realizes this later on in the essay :

Now the Demonstrative Strength of our Cause lying plainly in this, That it is not possible that any thing should Be without a Nature, and the Natures or Essences of all things being Immutable, *therefore upon Supposition that there is any thing Really Just or Unjust, Due or unlawful, there must of necessity be something so both Naturally and Immutably, which no Law, Decree, Will nor Custom can alter.*[5]

Accordingly, his account still requires that he establish the reality of moral good and evil, justice and injustice. In order to do so Cudworth maintains that good and evil, justice and injustice are not empirical features of objects, discerned by the senses, but are discerned by a vital principle in the soul through which we "have a natural Determination in them [us] to do some things, and to avoid others ..." [6] Thus, the soul apprehends and acts on its conception of morality. And the reality of its moral conceptions is argued for through the fact that mind is superior to senseless matter so that those things which belong to it cannot be treated as unreal :

... since Mind and Intellect are a higher, more real and substantial Thing than senseless Body and Matter, and what hath far the more Vigour, Activity and Entity in it, Modifications of Mind and Intellect, such as Justice and Morality, must of Necessity be more real and substantial Things, than the Modifications of meer senseless Matter, such as Hard and Soft, Thick and Thin, Hot and Cold, and the like are.[7]

II. SAMUEL CLARKE

(A) Fitting and unfitting actions

Samuel Clarke, like Cudworth, seeks to show that the wills of men cannot determine what is good or evil, just or unjust, although unlike Cudworth, Clarke does not argue from the notion of a defining characteristic. Rather Clarke begins with the uncontentious claim that "there are Differences of Things; and different Relations, Respects or Propositions, of some things towards others".[8] Now focussing on these different relations and proportions

[5] S. B. II, p. 258.
[6] S. B. II, p. 260.
[7] S. B. II, p. 262.
[8] Samuel Clarke, *A Discourse Concerning the Unchangeable Obligations of Natural Religion, And the Truth and Certainty of the Christian Revelation in The works of Samuel*

which things bear to each other, Clarke maintains that from the different relations "there necessarily arises an agreement or disagreement of some things with others ..." [9] He further maintains that the first claim above "is as evident and undeniable, as that one magnitude or number, is greater, equal to, or smaller than another" and that the second "is likewise as plain as that there is any such thing as Proportion or Disproportion in Geometry and Arithmetick".[10] Turning next to the realm of conduct, Clarke asserts that "there is a Fitness or Suitableness of certain circumstances to certain Persons, and an unsuitableness of others ... [and] ... that from the different relations of different Persons one to another, there necessarily arises a fitness or unfittness of certain manner of Behaviour of some persons towards others ..." [11] Thus Clarke would appear to be holding that just as there are mathematical relations which produce agreements and disagreements between things, so there are certain relations or fitnesses generated through the circumstances of the case and the persons involved which give rise to certain ways of behaving which are labelled fitting or unfitting.[12] On this interpretation of Clarke, morality is reduced to the level of mathematics with the result that moral propositions are regarded as demonstrably certain. The position for which I am going to

Clarke, D. D. Vol. II (London : Printed for John and Paul Knapton in Ludgate Street, MDCCXXXVIII), p. 608. Italics in text omitted. Hereafter cited as Discourse.

[9] Discourse, p. 608. Italics in text omitted.

[10] Discourse, p. 608. Italics in text omitted.

[11] Discourse, p. 608. Italics in text omitted.

[12] Thus the term fitness is treated equivocally by Clarke, meaning either the relation obtaining between circumstances and persons, or the behaviour appropriate to persons in these circumstances. Mrs. Kydd expresses this interpretation very clearly : "We can perhaps express this view more simply in the following way : There are differences in nature between things : some things are unlike others, as, for example, a circle is unlike a square. From these differences we can deduce that certain things agree with others in some respects and disagree in others as a circle agrees with a square in being an extended two-dimensional figure and disagrees in having a round shape and not a square one. And further, Clarke argues, it follows from these agreements and disagreements that the 'application' of some things to others is fitting while to others it is not; as for instance it follows from the disagreement of squares and circles in respect of shape that round pegs are unfittingly applied to square holes and are fittingly applied to round ones. In precisely the same way we can speak of the fittingness and unfittingness of human actions to the circumstances in which they occur and the people affected by them. Thus an act of keeping faith is fittingly applied to a situation if a promise has been made, for there is a natural agreement between this act and the situation". R. M. Kydd, Reason and Conduct in Hume's Treatise (Oxford University Press, London, 1946). Reprinted : Russell and Russell Inc., New York, 1964. p. 17.

argue is that Clarke's ensuing analysis will not support the reduction of morality to mathematics : Clarke's arguments only warrant the claim that there are certain similarities between mathematical reasoning and moral reasoning. Further, the alleged identification of moral with mathematical reasoning is due in large part to the fact that Clarke does not emphasize the differences between the two as much as he elaborates on the similarities. Nevertheless, the inclusion of mathematics is done so only for purposes of analogy.[13]

A convenient way of elaborating my interpretation will be through the examination of a criticism of Clarke as offered by R. M. Kydd. She states that Clarke usually confuses 'rightness' with 'obligation' : "To say that an act is fitting and to say that fitting acts ought to be done is not the same, yet this is a distinction which Clarke to a large extent obscures".[14]

What Mrs. Kydd is ignoring in Clarke's account is his attempted demonstration of the fittingness or rightness of a particular mode of behaviour, and his *subsequent* attempt to show that such behaviour is obligatory. Clarke himself is most emphatic on the connection, rather than identity, existing between fittingness and obligation. Thus in one place he writes :

... these eternal and necessary differences of things make it fit and reasonable for Creatures so to act; they cause it to be their Duty, or lay an Obligation upon them, so to do ...[15]

To look first then at Clarke's attempted demonstration of the fittingness of an action. It is offered against Hobbes whom Clarke considers to have held that there is no real difference "originally, necessarily, and absolutely in the Nature of Things" [16] between good and evil but that appropriate behaviour between men is founded on compact. Clarke argues that if there is no distinction between Good and Evil prior to the making of compacts then 'tis equally as good, just and reasonable' for one man to kill another not only when his own existence is threatened by that other, but also arbitrarily and without provocation. The consequence of this, Clarke maintains, is that people would destroy one another and the effect of this practice, if pursued vigourously, would be the termination of the human race :

[13] This position is hinted at, although not fully argued for, by C. G. Thompson, *The Ethics of William Wollaston*, (Boston, Richard G. Badger, The Gorham Press, 1922) p. 78-81.

[14] Kydd, p. 18.

[15] *Discourse*, p. 608.

[16] *Discourse*, p. 609.

Which being undeniably a great and unsufferable Evil; Mr. Hobbes himself confesses it reasonable, that, to prevent this Evil, Man should Enter into certain Compacts to preserve one another. Now if the destruction of Mankind by each other's Hands, be such an Evil, that, to prevent it, it was fit and reasonable that Men should enter into Compacts to preserve each other; then before any such Compacts, it was manifestly a thing unfit and unreasonable in itself, that Mankind should all destroy one another.[17]

Clarke's argument is actually a *reductio ad absurdum*, for he is saying that if you begin by assuming no distinction between good and evil prior to the making of compacts, you find that Compacts are made to prevent a certain evil. Accordingly, evil and good must be prior to all compacts. But what is it which determines what is good and what is evil? On the view cited earlier which seeks to reduce morality to mathematics this question appears to be unanswerable. Thus Mrs. Kydd writes :

If we reconsider our previous example of agreeing things, round pegs and round holes, it is clear that these can be said to agree in respect of shape, and perhaps also of size, i.e. the relations in which they agree are essentially spatial; but there does not seem to be any recognized philosophical relation in respect of which acts can be said to agree with situations, nor does Clarke show what this relation is.[18]

She further argues that Clarke has failed to see that the notion of fittingness – in the sense that an act fits a certain situation - holds not between two things but between three :

In order to speak sensibly in saying that two things fit, we must specify some respect in which they fit. Things are not merely fitting to other things in themselves, but fitting to them in respect of something third : i.e. things are not merely fitting to, but also fitting for – If we are to agree with Clarke in saying that acts can fit the circumstances in which they occur, we must be able to specify in respect of what, and for what purpose, they are fitting.[19]

And finally, she argues that if Clarke were to admit that acts agree with situations in respect of some end, then a further problem arises since repeatedly Clarke maintains that these fitnesses are 'absolute and in the nature of things' :[20]

But had he admitted this [i.e. that fittingness requires the introduction of some end] he would have been faced with questions he could not well have answered, for once it is assumed that the fittingness of actions holds between acts and

[17] *Discourse*, p. 610.
[18] Kydd, p. 20.
[19] Kydd, p. 20-21.
[20] See, for example, *Discourse*, p. 609.

ends in respect of the latter's fulfilment, it is evident that the fittingness of acts is strictly relative to the ends for which they are fit, and must vary concomitantly with them.[21]

I now propose to show in answering the question raised earlier concerning what it is which determines what is good and what is evil that Clarke's analysis does not require that he show some recognized philosophical relation in respect of which acts agree with situations, since Clarke holds the view outlined by Mrs. Kydd that the condition of fittingness requires that we specify some purpose for which they are fitting. However, I shall also attempt to show that this concession of Clarke's does not commit him to the view that the fittingness of acts is now in conflict with his view that fitnesses are absolute and in the nature of things.

Returning then to the question raised earlier, namely, what it is, according to Clarke, which determines what is good and what is evil, his answer is that it is actions which are in the public benefit which are good, and those which do not promote the public benefit which are evil :

... if the practice of certain things tends to the publick benefit of the World, and the contrary would tend to the publick disadvantage; then those things are not in their own nature indifferent, but were good and reasonable to be practiced before any Law was made, and can only for that very reason be wisely inforced by the Authority of Laws. Only here it is to be observed, that by the publick Benefit must not be understood the interest of any one particular Nation, to the plain injury or prejudice of the rest of Mankind; any more than the interest of one City or Family, in opposition to their Neighbours of the same Country : But those things only are truly good in their own Nature, which either tend to the universal benefit and welfare of all Men, or at least are not destructive of it.[22]

... in Men's dealing and conversing one with another, 'tis undeniably more fit, absolutely and in the Nature of the thing itself, that all Men should endeavour to promote the universal good and welfare of All, than that all Men should be continually contriving the ruin and destruction of All.[23]

---

[21] Kydd, p. 21.

[22] *Discourse*, p. 610-611. Italics in text omitted. Although Clarke calls those actions good which 'either tend to the universal benefit and welfare of all men, or at least are not destructive of it', I will, throughout the remainder of this book, emphasize the former disjunct when referring to Clarke's position. I shall do this for the sake of convenience and because Clarke himself emphasizes such actions while largely ignoring those which are not destructive of the public benefit. In one passage, Clarke actually refers to actions which neither further the public advantage nor contribute to its disadvantage as 'trivial' : "... Trivial Actions ... have no way any tendency at all either to the publick welfare or damage". (*Discourse*, p. 611).

[23] *Discourse*, p. 609.

Clarke's position actually is that there are certain things which are always in the interest of the human community – Clarke mentions, 'keeping faith and performing equitable Compacts' [24] – independently of any laws or compacts, and these actions are good and fitting. Other things, on the other hand – here Clarke mentions 'breaking faith, refusing to perform equitable Compacts, cruelly destroying those who have neither directly nor indirectly given any occasion for such treatment' [25] – are never in the interest of the human community, and these actions are absolutely evil and unfitting. Clarke also posits a third category for things he calls 'Indifferent'; that is, they are actions whose tendency to the public benefit or disadvantage is 'either so small or remote, or so obscure and involved' that most people are not able to decide for themselves how to act. Here, then, the various countries make them obligatory through laws. In this regard Clarke mentions 'particular penal laws'.[26]

To hold that Clarke's view of moral good and evil as requiring that some end be specified in regard to which actions can be fitting or unfitting is in conflict with his claim that these fitnesses are 'absolute and in the nature of things' is to misunderstand what it is that Clarke intends to convey by this latter expression. The expression itself is first introduced by Clarke when he is about to attack Hobbes. And the attack on Hobbes centres around Clarke's view that Hobbes (and others Clarke does not mention) "had in earnest asserted and attempted to prove, that there is no natural and unalterable difference between Good and Evil".[27] Clarke then cites his *reductio* which we have already examined as proof of the natural and unalterable difference between good and evil. Clarke continues against all those who hold a view similar to Hobbes on the nature of good and evil :

And in like manner All others, who upon any pretence whatsoever, teach that Good and Evil depend originally on the Constitution of positive Laws, whether Divine or Humane; must unavoidably run into the same absurdity. For if there be no such thing as Good and Evil in the Nature of Things, antecedent to all Laws; then neither can any one Law be better than another; nor any one thing whatever, be more justly established, and inforced by Laws, than the contrary; nor can any reason be given, why any Laws should ever be made at all : But all Laws equally, will be either arbitrary or tyrannical, or frivolous and needless; because the contrary might with equal Reason have been established, if before the making of the Laws, all things had been alike indifferent in their own Nature.[28]

[24] *Discourse*, p. 611.
[25] *Discourse*, p. 611.
[26] *Discourse*, p. 611.
[27] *Discourse*, p. 609.
[28] *Discourse*, p. 610. Italics in text omitted.

On the basis of the arguments mentioned above Clarke concludes : "There are therefore certain necessary and eternal differences of things; and certain consequent fitnesses or unfitnesses of the application of different things or different Relations one to another; not depending on any positive Constitutions, but founded unchangeably in the nature and reason of things, and unavoidably arising from the differences of the things themselves".[29]

It is important to see that throughout Clarke's discussion the view that fitnesses are absolute and in the nature of things is understood in opposition to the view which holds that good and evil are merely conventional notions. Further, the text also reveals that to speak of fitnesses as absolute and in the nature of things requires that the public benefit be introduced as that with respect to which acts are either fitting or unfitting. Thus, immediately after arguing for the absurdity of the Hobbesian view, Clarke introduces the notion of the public benefit.[30] Clarke's view, therefore, is that our actions are not in themselves indifferent and given value through convention; but rather in the light of the public benefit, actions – even before any conventions are made – are either fitting and good, or unfitting and evil. Hence, he speaks of these fitnesses as being 'in the nature of things'. Furthermore, he holds that since moral good and evil are independent of convention, nothing can alter what is good and what is evil, and this includes God; in this sense then they are also 'absolute' :

... as the Addition of certain Numbers, necessarily produce a certain sum; and certain Geometrical or Mechanical Operations, give a constant or unalterable Solution of certain Problems or Propositions : So in moral Matters, there are certain necessary and unalterable Respects of Relations of Things, which have not their Original from arbitrary and positive Constitution, but are of eternal necessity in their own Nature. For example : As in Matters of Sense, the reason why a thing is visible, is not because 'tis Seen; but 'tis therefore Seen, because 'tis visible : So in Matters of Natural Reason and morality, that which is Holy and Good ... is not therefore Holy and Good, because 'tis Commanded to be done : but it is therefore Commanded of God, because 'tis Holy and Good ... Hence God himself, though he has no superiour from whose Will to receive any Law of his Actions; yet disdains not to observe the Rule of Equity and Goodness, as the Law of all his Actions in the Government of the World ... To this Law, the infinite Perfections of his Divine Nature make it necessary for him ... to have constant regard ...[31]

[29] *Discourse*, p. 612.
[30] *Discourse*, p. 610.
[31] *Discourse*, p. 610.

Underlying Clarke's account is his belief that acting for the good of the whole – in God's case the whole being the whole universe, and in ours the whole being the public benefit or general welfare of all men [32] – is and always will be the only reasonable course of action :

Which two Things, viz. negligent and Misunderstanding and Wilful Passions or Lusts, are, as I said, the only Causes which can make a reasonable Creature act contrary to Reason, that is, contrary to the eternal Rules of Justice, Equity, Righteousness and Truth. For, was it not for these inexcusable corruptions and depravations; 'tis impossible but the same Proportions and Fitnesses of things which have so much weight and so much Excellency and Beauty in them, that the All-powerful Creator and Governour of the Universe (who has absolute and uncontroulable Dominion of all things in His own Hands, and is accountable to none for what he does, yet) thinks it no diminution of his Power to make this Reason of Things the unalterable Rule and Law of his own Actions in the Government of the World, and does nothing by mere Will and Arbitrariness; 'tis impossible (Isay) if it was not for inexcusable corruption and depravation, but the same eternal Reason of Things must much more have Weight enough to determine constantly the Wills and Actions of all Subordinate, Finite, Dependent and Accountable Beings.[33]

Clarke's position concerning the role of the public benefit in determining what is good and what is evil is not, therefore, in conflict with his claim that fitnesses are absolute and in the nature of things, inasmuch as he holds that the end which gives merit to actions is not subject to change either by men or by God. Rather, reasonable beings will always acknowledge the welfare of the whole to be that which makes actions fitting. To act contrary to this welfare is to act contrary to Reason, to the order by which the universe exists, and to God.

---

[32] In one place Clarke writes : "... the same necessary and eternal different Relations, that different Things bear one to another; and the same consequent Fitness or Unfitness of the Application of different Things or different Relations one to another, with regard to which the Will of God always and necessarily does determine itself to choose to act only what is agreeable to Justice, Equity, Goodness and Truth in order to the Welfare of the whole Universe; ought likewise constantly to determine the Wills of all subordinate rational Beings, to govern all their Actions by the same Rules, for the Good of the Public in their respective Stations" (*Discourse*, p. 596, Italics in text omitted).

It is important to notice here that in speaking of the rules of Justice, Equity, Goodness and Truth, Clarke means those rules which contribute to the welfare of the whole. See also Discourse, p. 612, p. 613. From now on, whenever Clarke refers to these rules of Justice, Equity, Goodness and Truth, the view will be taken that these rules contribute to the welfare either of the whole universe – in God's case – or to the public benefit – in reference to man.

[33] *Discourse*, p. 613. Italics in text omitted.

Wherefore, all rational creatures, whose wills are not constantly and regularly determined, and their Actions governed, by right Reason and the necessary differences of Good and Evil, according to the eternal and invariable Rules of Justice, Equity, Goodness and Truth; but suffer themselves to be swayed by unaccountable arbitrary Humours, and rash Passions, by Lusts, Vanity and Pride; by private interest, or present sensual Pleasures; These, setting up their own unreasonable Self-Will in opposition to the Nature and Reason of Things, endeavour (as much as in them lies) to make things to be what they are not, and cannot be. Which is the highest Presumption and greatest Insolence, as well as the greatest Absurdity, imaginable. 'Tis acting contrary to that Understanding, Reason and Judgment, which God has implanted in their Natures ... 'Tis attempting to destroy that Order, by which the Universe subsists. 'Tis offering the highest affront imaginable to the Creator of all things, who made things to be what they are ...[34]

In the light of the above analysis sense can now be made of Clarke's repeated assertion that wilfully doing evil is unreasonable since we are endeavouring 'to make things to be what they are not, and cannot be',[35] and that mistaking right and wrong is 'absurd'.[36] Given that good and evil are independent of all wills and conventions, evil actions can never be made good or fitting : "These setting up their own unreasonable Self-Will in opposition to the Nature and Reason of Things, endeavour (as much as in them lies) to make things be what they are not, and cannot be'.[37] The absurdity involved therefore, is the same absurdity which arises whenever any two fixed natures are mistaken one for the other :

In a word; All wilful wickedness and perversion of Right, is the very same Insolence and Absurdity in Moral Matters; as it would be in Natural Things, for a man to pretend to alter the certain Proportions of Numbers, to take away the Demonstrable Relations and properties of Mathematical Figures; to make Light Darkness, and Darkness Light; or to call Bitter Sweet, and Sweet Bitter.[38]

(B) Fitness and obligation

It is important to notice that throughout Clarke's discussion of things fitting and unfitting no mention has been made of obligation nor has there been any attempt – as Mrs. Kydd maintained – to obscure the distinct claims 'that an act is fitting' with 'that act ought to be done'. How then

[34] *Discourse*, p. 613-614.

[35] See the italicized portions of the previously quoted passage, superscript 27. See also, for example, *Discourse*, p. 613.

[36] "... 'tis ... absurd and blameworthy, to mistake negligently plain Right and Wrong ..." (*Discourse*, p. 613. Italics in text omitted).

[37] *Discourse*, p. 613.

[38] *Discourse*, p. 614.

does Clarke introduce obligation and relate it to the notion of fittingness? A clue to this is found in a passage mentioned earlier in which Clarke says that the eternal and necessary difference of things (i.e. eternal and necessary differences so far as the public benefit is concerned) 'make it fit and reasonable for creatures so to act; they cause it to be their duty, or lay an obligation upon them'. The key notion here is, of course, the causal claim contained in the above to the effect that there is a causal relation between the moral differences of things and duty. Before attempting to determine how Clarke tries to establish such a causal connection, it will be worthwhile to deal with the evidence which Mrs. Kydd cites to show that on occasion Clarke confuses fittingness with obligation. The passage she cites is the following : " 'Tis ... Fit ... that Men should deal one with another according to the known Rules of Justice and Equity".[39] She then continues :

... in saying this he seems to imply not merely that acts of equity would be fitting if they occurred, but also that *ipso facto* they ought to be done. That this is his meaning is borne out by the passage where he argues that '... the mind of man cannot avoid giving its assent to the eternal law of Righteousness, that is, cannot but acknowledge the reasonableness and fitness of men's governing all their actions by the will of right or equity; and also that this assent is a formal obligation upon every man, actually and constantly to conform himself to that rule.[40]

But, in fact, the latter passage she cites does not help to substantiate her case, for in this passage Clarke appears to be making two points, namely, that when made aware of the rule of right we must acknowledge it as fitting and reasonable, and secondly that the assent to the rule of right is a formal obligation to conform to the rule. That is, the rule is fitting and reasonable in itself (hence, our assent to it as such) and our assent to it as fitting and reasonable is itself a formal obligation on us to perform such an action. I submit, therefore, that this passage does not give any indication of a confusion in Clarke between fitness and obligation.

Since Clarke holds that the fitnesses of things are independent of all wills and conventions, he also holds that the obligation to perform fitting acts is independent of all wills and conventions :

... these eternal moral obligations are indeed of themselves incumbent on all rational Beings, even antecedent to the consideration of their being the positive Will and Command of God.[41]

---

[39] *Discourse*, p. 609, Italics in text omitted.
[40] Kydd, p. 18.
[41] *Discourse*, p. 597.

... As this Law of Nature is infinitely superiour to all Authority of Men, and independent upon it; so its obligation, primarily and originally, is antecedent also even to this Consideration of its being the positive Will or Command of God himself.[42]

The obligation to do what is fitting stems from the fact that only what is reasonable is fitting :

For originally and in reality, 'tis as natural and (Morally speaking) necessary, that the Will should be determined in every Action by the Reason of the thing, and the Right of the Case : as 'tis natural and (absolutely speaking) necessary, that the understanding should submit to a demonstrated Truth. And 'tis as absurd and blameworthy, to mistake negligently plain Right and Wrong, that is, to understand the Proportions of things in Morality to be what they are not; or wilfully to act contrary to known Justice and Equity, that is, to will things to be what they are not and cannot be; as it would be absurd and ridiculous for a man in Arithmetical Matters, ignorantly to believe that twice two is not equal to Four ... The only difference is, that assent to a plain speculative Truth, is not in a Man's Power to withhold; but to Act according to the plain Right and Reason of things, this he may, by the natural Liberty of his Will, forbear. But the One he ought to do; and 'tis as much his plain and indispensable Duty; as the other he cannot but do, and 'tis the Necessity of his Nature to do it.[43]

But fitting acts are themselves reasonable, as we saw earlier, only because what is fitting is independent of all conventions and wills, so that wilfully to act against what is known to be fitting is attempting the absurd task of making things what they are not and cannot be. Hence, it is the fitnesses which impose obligations on all rational creatures, since for a rational being to be moral he must act reasonably, that is, he must treat everything as it really is, which, for Clarke means that we must not will and perform actions through which we attempt to make what is unfitting or evil fitting or good.

Summing up, it is the reasonableness of virtue and unreasonableness of vice which impose a duty on all rational creatures to conform their behaviour to do what is fitting. And accordingly, he concludes his discussion by saying that '... it appears thus from the abstract and absolute Reason and nature of things that all rational creatures ought, that is, are obliged to take care that their Wills and Actions be constantly determined and governed by the eternal rule of Right and Equity".[44] Nevertheless, virtue is reasonable only because what is fitting is not subject to alteration. Therefore, the notion of fittingness for Clarke is a primary one and obligation a derivative one with no confusion between the two.

[42] *Discourse*, p. 626. Italics in text omitted.
[43] *Discourse*, p. 613. Italics in text omitted.
[44] *Discourse*, p. 614. Italics in text omitted.

So far we have seen the causal relation which Clarke holds exists between the moral differences of things and what we are obliged to do. His analysis of obligation, however, is offered on two different levels. From 'the abstract and absolute Reason and nature of things' fitting acts have always been obligatory on all rational creatures, because the notion of what is fitting is independent of all wills and conventions. Nevertheless, Clarke does show concern for the problem of how human beings are made aware of their obligations and how these obligations are applied to them. Thus, in continuing with the last passage quoted above Clarke writes :

Further, as it appears thus from the abstract and absolute Reason and nature of things, that all Rational Creatures Ought, that is, are obliged to take care that their Wills and Actions be constantly determined and governed by the eternal rule of Right and Equity : So the certainty and universality of the Obligation is plainly confirmed and the force of it particularly discovered and applied to every Man, by This; that in like manner as no one, who is instructed in Mathematics, can forbear giving his Assent to every Geometrical Demonstration, of which he understands the Terms, either by his own Study, or by having had them explained to him by others; so no man, who either has patience and opportunities to examine and consider things himself, or has the means of being taught and instructed in any tolerable manner by Others, concerning the necessary relations and dependencies of things; can avoid giving his Assent to the fitness and reasonableness of his governing all his Actions by the Law or Rule before mentioned, even though his Practice, through the prevalence of Brutish Lusts, be most absurdly contradictory to that Assent.[45]

Just as in 'the abstract and absolute Reason and nature of things' the reasonableness of fitting acts and unreasonableness of unfitting acts can be seen to impose a duty on all rational creatures to conform their behaviour to the performance of fitting acts, so in the case of finite rational creatures, the assent of reason to do what is fitting both shows us what as rational creatures we ought to do – hence, Clarke's use of the word 'discovered' –, and shows us that these obligations are incumbent upon us – which accounts for Clarke's use of the word 'applied'.

That is to say : By the Reason of his mind, he cannot but be compelled to own and acknowledge, that there is really such an Obligation indispensably incumbent upon him; even at the same time that in the Actions of his Life he is endeavouring to throw it off and despise it.[46]

... the Mind of Man naturally and unavoidably gives its Assent ... to the moral differences of things, and to the fitness and reasonableness of the Obligation of the everlasting Law of Righteousness, whenever fairly and plainly proposed.[47]

[45] *Discourse*, p. 614. Italics in text omitted.
[46] *Discourse*, p. 614. Italics in text omitted.
[47] *Discourse*, p. 615. Italics in text omitted.

For us, then, the assent of reason to what is fitting is the source of obligation :

So far therefore as Men are conscious of what is right and wrong, so far they are under an Obligation to act accordingly.[48]

To know what is fitting and yet not to act accordingly is to stand self-condemned by reason, and this, says Clarke, is the greatest and strongest of all obligations :

For the judgment and Conscience of a Man's own Mind, concerning the Reasonableness and Fitness of the thing, that his Actions should be conformed to such or such a Rule or Law; is the truest and formallest obligation; even more properly and strictly so, than any opinion whatsoever of the Authority of the Giver of a Law, or any Regard he may have to its Sanction by Rewards and Punishments. For whoever acts contrary to this sense and conscience of his own mind, is necessarily self-condemned. And the greatest and strongest of all Obligations is that, which a Man cannot break through without condemning himself.[49]

Throughout Clarke's discussion of fitnesses and obligation he asserts that once people are shown the difference between virtue and vice, that is, what is in the public benefit and what is not, they will give their assent to fitting acts, and will hold themselves bound by them, in the same manner as we must assent to mathematical truths once these have been demonstrated :

... the Mind of Man naturally and unavoidably gives its Assent, as to natural and geometrical Truth, so also to the moral differences of things and to the fitness and reasonableness of the Obligation of the everlasting Law of Righteousness, whenever fairly and plainly proposed.[50]

Furthermore, he holds that if ever rational beings felt obliged to perform actions which were contrary to the type of obligation he maintains we have, namely, to promote the public benefit, then this would be the one serious objection against all that he has said concerning the assent of reason to what is fitting and our obligation to perform such acts. Nevertheless, he denies that there are such beings, and argues that those who do wrong are simply ignorant of what is right, just as there are many who are ignorant of mathematical truths. What such people require in morals as in mathematics, is instruction, "and if they be important Truths, then men have need also to have them frequently inculcated, and strongly inforced upon them.[51]

---

[48] *Discourse*, p. 615. Italics in text omitted.
[49] *Discourse*, p. 614. Italics in text omitted.
[50] *Discourse*, p. 614. Italics in text omitted.
[51] *Discourse*, p. 618. The entire discussion of this point appears on p. 617-618.

(C) Mathematical and moral reasoning

Now, Clarke's repeated references to mathematics when discussing morality have given rise to the view that it is the same kind of reasoning which is involved in both morality and mathematics.[52] And, indeed, there are for Clarke certain important similarities between mathematical and moral reasoning. In the first place, as in mathematics our concern is with truth, so in morality our concern is with the public benefit and the unprejudiced reason of man cannot but assent to truths in both realms. Secondly, as the truths of mathematics are entirely independent of arbitrary decisions and conventions, so in morality the truths concerning virtue and vice are independent of any decision and convention. Nevertheless, mathematical and moral reasonings are unlike insofar as mathematical relations hold between the figures themselves [53] whereas moral relations or fitnesses require the introduction of the public benefit. In mathematics, reason has the concern of discovering the mathematical relations existing between different figures or different aspects of the same figure; in morality, reason has a concern for the public benefit and for whatever will promote this benefit. That moral reason does actually have a concern for the public benefit is made clear by Clarke in several passages. For example,

... in Men's dealing and conversing one with another; 'tis undeniably more Fit, absolutely and in the Nature of the thing itself, that all Men should endeavour to promote the universal good and welfare of All; than that all Men should be continually contriving the ruin and destruction of All ... For a Man endued with Reason to deny the Truth of these Things; is the very same thing, as if a Man that has the use of his Sight, should at the same time that he beholds the Sun, deny that there is any such thing as Light in the World.[54]

This passage clearly shows that reason is not indifferent towards human ends, but rather shows a moral concern for the end itself. The public benefit determines moral good and evil and Clarke maintains that "the Mind of Man naturally and unavoidably gives it Assent ... to the moral differences of things, and to the fitness and reasonableness of the everlasting Law of Righteousness, whenever fairly and plainly proposed",[55] again indicating through the expression 'the moral differences of things' that reason has a concern for the proper end of action, as well as the means of advancing it. Also, Clarke's discussion of the self-condemnation

[52] See ,for example, Kydd, p. 27, and Thompson p. 79-80.

[53] Thus, Clarke speaks of "the Demonstrable Relations and properties of Mathematical Figures". (*Discourse*, p. 614).

[54] *Discourse*, p. 603. Italics in text omitted.

[55] *Discourse*, p. 618.

which ensues upon not performing what we know to be good presupposes that reason has a concern for the end of human action; that is, reason must show a preference between good and evil, for otherwise, it could only be of use in moral matters in pointing out which actions promote certain ends and it might then condemn the agent for not using the proper means to achieve the desired end. But Clarke's point about being self-condemned is not morally neutral, for he holds that we stand self-condemned only when we know what is good or fitting and do not perform that action. Reason, for Clarke, therefore, is not morally indifferent but shows a concern for the public benefit.

In the light of the above, I submit that moral reasoning for Clarke has certain resemblances to mathematical reasoning but also has the important difference from mathematical reasoning insofar as it has a concern for the ends of human action and the means for promoting that end. Thus, the relation of mathematical reasoning to moral reasoning is to be regarded as analogical.

III. WILLIAM WOLLASTON

(A) Actions, propositions, and truth values

Wollaston begins by maintaining that a distinction has to be made between that which can act and that which can be acted upon. In order to act three capacities are required – being capable to distinguish, choose, and act for oneself. Without these capacities a thing can only be considered an instrument, or something acted upon. Further, whoever is able to act is subject to moral appraisal,[56] whereas whatever can only be acted upon is in the state of inert and passive matter and cannot be called morally good or evil.

Now in attempting to determine which acts are right and which are wrong, Wollaston has recourse to an analysis involving actions, propositions, and truth values. He begins with propositions and truth values and by having recourse to a correspondence theory of truth he states that "These propositions are true, which express things as they are : or, truth

---

[56] William Wollaston, *The Religion of Nature Delineated*, (the Fifth Edition, London, Printed for James and John Knapton at the Crown in St. Paul's Church-yard, 1738), p. 8. Hereafter cited as R.N.D. with the page number following. I should like to thank the Royal Institute of Philosophy for permission to reprint material on Wollaston in this chapter which appears in *Philosophy* under the title "Truth, Happiness, and Obligation : The Moral Philosophy of William Wollaston".

is the conformity of those words or signs, by which things are exprest, to the things themselves".[57] True propositions can, of course, be denied by other propositions, but Wollaston extends this to include actions : "A true proposition may be denied, or things may be denied to be what they are, by deeds, as well as by express words or another proposition".[58] At first sight this view seems far-fetched and lends itself to the position that what Wollaston is saying is that all acts are assertions. Thus, Mrs. Kydd writes that Wollaston holds

the strange view that all acts are assertions; when I steal a horse I assert that the horse is mine; when I live beyond my means I assert that I have more money than I in fact possess; when I refuse to give alms to a beggar I deny he is in need.[59]

The examples which Mrs. Kydd cites in the above passage do not, in fact, support her claim that for Wollaston 'all acts are assertions'. Rather, they only show that all acts are acts of 'asserting' propositions. She herself notices this for immediately after the preceding passage quoted above, she writes that for Wollaston 'all acts assert propositions'. Nevertheless, at the end of her present discussion she concludes, rather surprisingly, that Wollaston confused 'asserting' with 'assertion' : "... he confused 'asserting' with 'assertion', and although he said that acts are propositions he did not ever try to show that acts are actually assertions, but only that they are acts of asserting".[60] Mrs. Kydd cites no passage in which Wollaston actually states that 'acts are propositions' or that 'acts are assertions', and accordingly she is far from convincing in attributing this view to him. The closest Wollaston ever comes to the view that acts are propositions is in a passage wherein an act is spoken of as "the very proposition itself in practice".[61] Nevertheless, I will show that this does not support the view that all acts are propositions.

What, then, is the relationship between acts and propositions? In the first passage relevant to this discussion Wollaston writes :

There are many acts ... such as constitute the character of a man's conduct in life, which have in nature, and would be taken by any indifferent judge to have a signification, and to imply some proposition, as plainly to be understood as if it was declared in words : and therefore if what such acts declare to be, is not, they must contradict truth, as much as any false proposition or assertion can.[62]

---

[57] R.N.D. p. 8. Italics in text omitted.

[58] R.N.D. p. 8. Italics in text omitted.

[59] Kydd, p. 33.

[60] Kydd, p. 33.

[61] R.N.D. p. 13. Mrs. Kydd has also noticed this passage. (p. 33 of her book) but as I shall go on to show it does not support the view that acts are propositions.

[62] R.N.D. p. 8. Italics in text omitted.

Two problems arise regarding this passage : What evidence does Wollaston provide that actions have signification or meaning, and secondly, what does he mean when he speaks of an act implying some proposition? The only evidence he provides that actions have meaning is that they are understood :

It is certain there is a meaning in many acts and gestures. Everybody understands weeping, laughing, shrugs, frowns, etc.[63]

Or again, speaking of actions he writes : "Now what is to be understood, has a meaning ..." [64]

Concerning the second problem raised, namely, what Wollaston means when he says actions imply propositions, it is best to begin by recalling that for Wollaston whatever is understood has meaning. It is in the light of this fact that Wollaston sees a relationship between actions and propositions, for both actions and propositions have meaning inasmuch as both are understood. Thus, acting and speaking can be regarded as acts of declaring or expressing a certain meaning. That is, just as the activity of speaking has as its product an assertion or proposition which has a certain meaning, so the product of acting is an action which also has a meaning. Wollaston is very careful, however, in distinguishing between actions and propositions. Thus, he says 'that certain acts must contradict truth *as much as any false proposition can*'.[65] It is, I submit, in the light of the fact that Wollaston argues that both actions and assertions or propositions have meaning that we must understand his claim that an act 'is the very proposition itself in practice',[66] for what he is saying is that the same meaning can be possessed by both. As such corresponding to every action there must be a proposition through which the same meaning can be conveyed :

When Popilius Loenas solicited to have Cicero proscribed, and that he might find him out and be his executioner, would not his carriage have sufficiently signified to any one, who was ignorant to the case, that Tully either was some very bad man, and deserved capital punishment; or had some way grievously injured this man; or at least had not saved his life, nor had as much reason to expect his service and good offices upon occasion, as he ever had to expect Tully's? ... It is certain he acted as if those things had been true, which were not true,

---

[63] R.N.D. p. 8.

[64] R.N.D. p. 9.

[65] R.N.D. p. 8.

[66] The entire passage reads as follows : If that proposition, which is false, be wrong, that act which *implies* such a proposition, or is founded on it, cannot be right : because it is the very proposition itself in practice". (R.N.D. p. 13).

and as if those had not been true, which were true (in this consisted the fault of his ingratitude) : and if he in words had said they were true or not true, he had done no more than talk as if they were so : why then should not to act as if they were true or not true, when they were otherwise, contradict truth as much as to say they were so, when they were not so? [67]

I lay this down then as a fundamental maxim, that whoever acts as if things were so, doth by his acts declare, that they are so, or not so; as plainly as he could by words ...[68]

Whenever someone acts his act can be viewed as acting *as if* something is or is not the case. The proposition or assertion corresponding to an action is to be obtained from the clause following the words 'as if'. And this, I suggest, is what Wollaston is getting at when he states that 'actions imply some proposition' in virtue of their possessing a signification. In other words, what Wollaston is maintaining is that the meaning involved in any action requires nothing less than an assertion or proposition if it is to be adequately unpacked :

... if [someone] should by some solemn promise, oath, or other act, undertake to do some certain thing before such a time, and he voluntarily omits to do it, he would behave himself as if there had been no such promise or engagement; which is equal to denying there was any ...[69]

The only propositions relevant to unpacking an action in regard to a moral situation are those which indicate how someone is acting with respect to certain states of affairs. A proposition will be true if what it states corresponds to what is, and a proposition will be false if what it states does not correspond to what is. Furthermore, since actions have meaning, and since whatever has meaning can be true or false, it follows that actions themselves can be true or false :

The thing is the very same still, if into the place of words be substituted actions ... What is to be understood, has a meaning : and what has a meaning, may be either true or false, which is as much as can be said of any verbal sentence.[70]

An action will be true if through it we act as if something is (or is not) the case and it is (or is not) the case, and an action will be false, if through it we act as if something is (or is not) the case and it is not (or is) the case. It is obvious that for every true action the proposition corresponding to

---

[67] R.N.D. p. 9. Italics in text omitted.
[68] R.N.D. p. 13. Italics in text omitted.
[69] R.N.D. p. 16. Italics in text omitted.
[70] R.N.D. p. 9. Italics in text omitted.

it is also true, and for every false action the proposition corresponding to it is also false.

An example will now be appropriate. Wollaston writes :

If A should enter into a compact with B, by which he promises and engages never to do some certain thing, and after this he does that thing : in this case it must be granted, that his act interferes with his promise, and is contrary to it. Now it cannot interfere with his promise, but it must also interfere with the truth of that proposition, which says there was such a promise made, or that there is such a compact subsisting. If this proposition be true, A made such a certain agreement with B, it would be denied by this, A never made any agreement with B ... If then the behaviour of A be consistent with the agreement mentioned in the former proposition, that proposition is as much denied by A's behaviour, as it can be by the latter, or any other proposition. Or thus, if one proposition imports or contains that which is contrary to what is contained in another, it is said to contradict this other ... Just so if one act imports that which is contrary to the import of another, it contradicts this other, and denies its existence.[71]

In this example we can see Wollaston holding that actions have signification or meaning, that when we act we act as if something is or is not the case, that for each action there corresponds a proposition, and that because of the signification of actions whereby they acquire truth value one action can be said to be contradictory to another just as one proposition can be contradictory to another.

The analysis put forward above can also be of use in clearing up the mistaken notion that Wollaston holds that actions which declare false propositions are self-contradictory. Mrs. Kydd writes : "Even if we were to admit that acts assert propositions, we would still be at a loss to know why those which assert false propositions are self-contradictory".[72]

Now Wollaston is not saying that actions which are evil are self-contradictory. Rather, he holds that just as actions are propositional, so states of affairs are propositional, with the result that for every state of affairs there corresponds a proposition or set of propositions which describe that state of affairs. If I steal a horse, for example, my acting as if the horse is not that of another man contradicts the proposition that the horse is that of another man. Consequently, my action contradicts a proposition, but my action is not self-contradictory, since I am not both asserting and denying the same proposition :

I lay this down then as a fundamental maxim, That whoever acts as if things were so, or not so, doth by his acts declare, that they are so, or not so ... And

[71] R.N.D. p. 10. Italics in text omitted.
[72] Kydd, p. 32.

if things are otherwise, his acts contradict those propositions, which assert them to be as they are.[73]

Before proceeding to examine the manner in which Wollaston uses the preceding material in developing a theory of morals, some further word should be offered in order to complete what has been said. The impression might have been given that Wollaston holds the naive view that for any given state of affairs, or any action, the same propositions are always to be taken into account in deciding whether the action contradicts the state of affairs. In fact, however, this is not his position. Wollaston holds that states of affairs are variously describable, depending on the properties, respect, and circumstances we emphasize. Through our actions we may contradict some of these properties, respects, and circumstances (all of which, of course, are propositional). Therefore, in deciding whether an action contradicts a state of affairs it must be decided which properties, respects and circumstances are contradicted by the action, while acknowledging that with respect to other properties, respects or circumstances, no contradiction is present between the action and the state of affairs.[74]

(B) Truth and happiness

How, then, does Wollaston generate a theory of right and wrong from the above considerations? In answering this question he begins by setting out the following proposition : "No act (whether word or deed) of any being, to whom moral good and evil are imputable, that interferes with any true proposition, or denies any thing to be as it is, can be right".[75]

Further on, Wollaston reiterates this position : "And indeed it is true, that whatever will bear to be tried by right reason, is right; and that which

---

[73] R.N.D. p. 13. Italics in text omitted.

[74] "If a man steals a horse, and rides away upon him, he may be said indeed by riding him to use him as a horse, but not as the horse of another man, who gave him no license to do this. He does not therefore consider him as being what he is, unless he takes in the respect he bears to his true owner. But it is not necessary perhaps to consider what he is in respect of his color, shape, or age : because the thief's riding away with him may neither affirm nor deny him to be of any particular color, etc. I say, therefore, that those, and all those properties, respects, and circumstances, which may be contradicted by practice, are to be taken into consideration. For otherwise the thing to be considered is but imperfectly surveyd; and the whole compass of it being not taken in, it is taken not as being what it is, but as what it is in part only, and in other respects perhaps as being what it is not". (R.N.D. p. 18-19. Italics in text omitted).

[75] R.N.D. p. 13. Italics in text omitted.

is condemned by it, wrong".[76] In the light of passages such as these Mrs. Kydd affirms that for Wollaston the word 'right' is synonymous with 'true' :

In so far as he [Wollaston] uses the word 'right' he uses it as synonymous with true; in the sense in which we say 'That's right' meaning 'That's the case'. He is of course only able to apply 'right' in this sense to acts because he holds the very odd theory that acts can be true.[77]

Although I do not wish to deny Mrs. Kydd's position I intend to show that the text bears out that Wollaston is somewhat more complex in his account of right and wrong action than Mrs. Kydd's analysis indicates, for his position will require that he introduce the topic of 'happiness'. In order to establish my case, I shall begin by examining how Wollaston seeks to establish that 'no act, either of word or deed, of any being to whom moral good and evil are imputable that interferes with any true proposition, or denies any thing to be as it is, can be right'.

Wollaston sets out five different reasons for regarding the above statement as true,[78] although as we shall see, they are not of equal weight. He begins by stating that if a false proposition is wrong then that act which implies it cannot be right. However, this in effect begs the question at issue since what we want established is that actions implying false propositions are wrong.[79] Secondly, he says that whereas a true proposition expresses things as they are determined and established by the nature of the things themselves, a false proposition interferes with nature and is unnatural or wrong in nature. This also will not do for two reasons. Firstly, some areas of morals, for example, promise-keeping, exist more by convention than by nature, so that to have recourse to what is natural and unnatural is to exclude from the moral sphere much that we want included. Secondly, to speak of some things as 'wrong in nature' is not the interesting sense of 'wrong' which is required in morals, and can, of course, lead to the absurd position that no activity can be 'right in nature' except perhaps the contemplation of nature.[80]

The third reason advanced by Wollaston for holding to the proposition in question concerns the fact that whatever is in the world is due either to the fact that God causes it or that God permits it, so that "to own things to be as they are is to own what He causes, or at least permits ... and this

---

[76] R.N.D. p. 23.

[77] Kydd, p. 32.

[78] R.N.D. p. 13-15.

[79] Wollaston gives no indication that this problem is present.

[80] Again, Wollaston sees none of this.

is to take things as He gives them ... and to submit to His will, revealed in the books of nature".[81] Accordingly, every voluntary infraction of truth is impiety. Although the preceding is included by Wollaston it is not at all clear that even he intends to give it much weight, since in all other places when discussing the distinction between good and evil, Wollaston ignores the preceding and claims that what is good is always in accordance with reason, and what is evil is not. This matter is first introduced in the fourth reason offered by Wollaston, and it is to it that we now turn.

In his fourth reason Wollaston asserts that "Things cannot be denied to be what they are, in any instance or manner whatsoever, without contradicting axioms and truths eternal".[82] Examples offered are 'every thing is what it is', and 'that which is done, cannot be undone'. Furthering this discussion in his fifth reason he states that to treat things as being what they are not is absurd. It is like taking bitter for sweet, or darkness for light. But, now, in the next paragraph Wollaston moves from what is absurd to what is bad :

To talk to a post, or otherwise treat it if it was a man, would surely be reckoned an absurdity ... because this is to treat it as being what it is not. And why should not the converse be reckoned as bad; that is, to treat a man as a post.[83]

It is only by finding the connecting link between the absurd and the bad that Wollaston's position can be made intelligible. And this link is, I suggest, tied in with his view on happiness, a topic so central to his position that he devotes an entire section to it, which begins with a clear statement of its close connection with his views on truth :

That, which demands to be next considered, is *happiness*; as being in itself most considerable; as abetting the cause of truth; and as being indeed so nearly allied to it, that they cannot well be parted. We cannot pay the respects due to one, unless we regard the other. Happiness must not be denied to be what it is : and it is by the practice of truth that we aim at that happiness, which is true.[84]

Now, we have seen that Wollaston holds that to treat a man as a post is bad since it is to treat him as what he is not. And he continues by saying that we are treating him as what he is not because we regard him "as if he had no sense, and felt no injuries, which he doth feel; as if to him pain and sorrow were not pain; happiness not happiness".[85] To treat a man as

[81] R.N.D. p. 14. Italics in text omitted.
[82] R.N.D. p. 14. Italics in text omitted.
[83] R.N.D. p. 15. Italics in text omitted.
[84] R.N.D. p. 31.
[85] R.N.D. p. 15.

a post, then, is tantamount to denying that happiness is happiness. Why is this so? Wollaston's full answer is provided in two separate passages :

Again, there are some ends, which the nature of things and truth require us to aim at, and at which therefore if we do not aim, nature and truth are denied. If a man does not desire to prevent evils and to be happy, he denies both his own nature and the definition of happiness to be what they are.[86]

To make itself happy is a duty, which every being, in proportion to its capacity, owes to itself; and that which every intelligent being may be supposed to aim at, in general ... And hence it follows, that, We cannot act with respect to either ourselves, or other men, as being what we and they are, unless both are considered as beings susceptive of happiness and unhappiness and naturally desirous of the one and averse to the other.[87]

Since it is natural for us to seek happiness, for anyone to act so as to instill unhappiness in someone else is to deny what he is, and accordingly to regard him as being desirous of unhappiness.[88] For Wollaston, then, something is good if it is conducive to happiness, and evil if it is not.

I said earlier that Wollaston holds that what is good is always in accordance with reason, and what is evil is not.[89] But now in the light of his identification of what is conducive to happiness and what is good, he faces the problem of showing that whatever is in accordance with reason is also conducive to happiness. And here we find Wollaston holding that the pre-established harmony between reason (or truth) and happiness is guaranteed by God :

As the truth and ultimate happiness of no being can be produced by any thing, that interferes with truth, and denies the nature of things : so neither can the practice of truth make any being ultimately unhappy. For that, which contradicts nature and truth, opposes the will of the Author of nature, and to suppose, that an inferior being may in opposition to His will break through the constitution

[86] R.N.D. p. 16. Italics in text omitted.

[87] R.N.D. p. 38. Italics in text omitted.

[88] This view does, of course, stand in great need of elaboration, since it would be difficult, for example, to justify incarcerating someone for a misdeed if this would not lead to his happiness. Wollaston is, in fact, aware of such objections and deals with some of them. See *ibid.* p. 25-31. Essentially his view concerning all such objections is that a man must be regarded from various perspectives and consequently, each relevant perspective must be taken into account when deciding how to treat someone. His treatment of specific objections need not concern us here.

[89] For Wollaston the words 'good' and 'right' on the one hand, and 'evil' and 'wrong' on the other are identical : "Moral good and evil are coincident with right and wrong. For that cannot be good, which is wrong; nor that evil which is right" (R.N.D. p. 20. Italics in text omitted).

of things, and by so doing make himself happy, is to suppose that being more potent than the Author of nature ... which is absurd.[90]

Through this pre-established harmony between the regard for truth and the way to happiness Wollaston is able to justify the passage quoted earlier wherein he claimed that in the case of morality truth and happiness "cannot be parted", that "we cannot pay the respects due to one unless we regard the other".[91] Thus, at the end of the section on happiness he writes :

The way to happiness and the practice of truth incur the one into the other. For no being can be styled happy, that is not ultimately so ... [and] ... nothing can produce the ultimate happiness of any being, which interferes with truth : and therefore whatever doth produce that, must be some thing which is consistent and coincident with this.

Two things then (but such as are met together and embrace each other), which are to be religiously regarded in all our conduct, are truth (of which in the preceding sect.) and happiness (that is, such pleasures, as accompany, or follow the practice of truth, or are not inconsistent with it : of which I have been treating in this).[92]

In addition to the close connection between truth and happiness which is affirmed in the above passage, the latter is also important insofar as it emphasizes the complementary character of that section (Section I) in which truth is regarded as a criterion of right action, and that (Section II) in which happiness is accorded the same status : To allow that truth is the criterion of right action is nothing more than to seek to promote both our own happiness and that of our fellows, and to allow happiness as the criterion of right action is nothing more than to allow our actions to be tried by right reason. Accordingly, either can be employed as a criterion of right action without charging that Wollaston is guilty of an inconsistency.

Wollaston regards happiness as a function of pleasure. Nevertheless in at least one passage in Section I he shows awareness of some of the problems involved in the identification of pleasure with the good.[93] For example, since different people experience pleasure from different things, the morality of actions will vary, being considered good by some and bad by others, and this is something he does not want to allow. Also, Wollaston fears that through the identification of good with pleasure, 'men will be apt to sink into gross voluptuousness'. He concludes this discussion with a note that the good can be identified not with all pleasures, but 'only such pleasure as is true, or happiness.'[94]

[90] R.N.D. p. 38. Italics in text omitted.
[91] See superscript 84.
[92] R.N.D. p. 40. Italics in text omitted.
[93] R.N.D. p. 24.
[94] R.N.D. 24.

Wollaston distinguishes true pleasures from false ones. He does this by dealing with pleasure and pain exclusively in quantitative terms (he gives no hint of seeing that pleasures may be distinguished qualitatively as well) and asserts that pleasure may be compared with pain so that the degree of pleasure may either equal, exceed, or be less than the degree of pain experienced. (He also shows no awareness of the difficulties involved in attempting such calculations.) Now, if the degree of pleasure equals the degree of pain, they destroy each other, whereas when one exceeds the other, the excess yields the true quantity of pleasure or pain. Accordingly, "*the true quantity of pleasure* differs not from that *quantity of true pleasure*; or it is so much of that kind of pleasure, which is *true* (clear of all discounts and future payments)".[95] Furthermore, happiness is identified with the true quantity of pleasure, that is, a person can be regarded as happy to the extent that the totality of his pleasures exceeds that of his pains. Wollaston maintains that those pleasures are to be pursued concerning which reason can find no ground against pursuing them :

Those pleasures are true, and to be reckond into our happiness, against which there lies no reason. For when there is no reason against any pleasure, there is always one for it, *included in the term*. So when there is no reason for undergoing pain (or venturing it), there is one against it.[96]

Several points must be made about this passage. Firstly, when Wollaston speaks of reasons against pursuing a pleasure, he must mean that to pursue it would contravene some truth, especially with regard either to my happiness or that of others. Secondly, the pre-established harmony mentioned earlier which God ensures can now be seen more clearly for what God is intended to guarantee is that by acting in accordance with reason I can never be acting against my own self-interest, that is, in the long run my pleasures must outweigh my pains. Thirdly, the italicized portion of the above passage is not without significance. Wollaston holds that when there is no reason against any pleasure there is always one for it, included in the term, that is, in the term 'pleasure'. The question, however, is why this is so. And the answer, I submit, can be determined through reference to what was said in two passages cited earlier (see superscripts 86 and 87) in which Wollaston stated that to make oneself happy is a duty. If this is the case, and further, if happiness is reckoned in terms of true pleasure, it follows that we have a duty to pursue what will lead to true pleasure. The only thing for Wollaston which could lead to unhappiness is to pursue pleasures against which there is a reason.

[95] R.N.D. p. 36.
[96] R.N.D. p. 40. Italics in text omitted, italics in quotation added.

(C) Truth, Happiness and Obligation

The last point to be discussed is Wollaston's theory of obligation. R. David Broiles writes : "Reason also provides a motive for the agent to do what is right, for in seeing that an action is right, we are forced to acknowledge it as our duty".[97] Similarly, Mrs. Kydd asserts that Wollaston took the view that men are obliged "not merely to avoid falsehood but to assert truth".[98] Now, if my interpretation of Wollaston is correct insofar as I argued that Wollaston speaks of both reason (or truth) and happiness as criteria of right action, then it should follow that both reason and happiness can account for what we ought to do, and further, Wollaston should hold that obligations founded upon one are identical to obligations founded on the other. If both of these claims can be substantiated then it will be seen that Broiles and Kydd are not fully explicating Wollaston's theory of obligation, and speak of it in a misleading manner by entirely neglecting his views on happiness.

We have already seen that Wollaston does want to found a theory of obligation on the fact that each person has a duty to make himself happy[99], and it is significant that this view of obligation has recourse to his doctrine of true action. Thus he says that 'we cannot act with respect to either our selves, or other men, as being what we and they are, unless both are considered as beings susceptive of happiness and unhappiness, and naturally dseirous of the one and averse to the other'. Wollaston also founds a theory of obligation on his doctrine of true and false actions.

By religion I mean nothing else but an obligation to do ... what ought not to be omitted, and to forbear what ought not to be done. So there must be religion, if there are things, of which some ought not to be done, some not to be omitted. But that there are such, appears from what has been said concerning moral good and evil : because that, which to omit would be evil, and which therefore being done would be good or well done, ought certainly by the terms to be done; and so that, which being done would be evil ... ought most undoubtedly not to be done. And then since there is religion, which follows from the distinction between moral good and evil; since this distinction is founded in the respect which men's acts bear to truth; and since no proposition can be true, which expresses things otherwise than as they are in nature : since things are so, there must be religion, which is founded in nature, and may upon that account be most properly and truly called the religion of nature or natural religion; the great law of which

[97] R. D. Broiles, *The Moral Philosophy of David Hume* (Martinus Nijhoff, The Hague, 1964), p. 13-14. It should be noted that Broiles offers no passages from Wollaston to confirm his view.

[98] Kydd, p. 22. Mrs. Kydd also does not offer any passages to confirm her view.

[99] Quotation 87.

religion, the laws of nature or rather ... of the Author of nature is that every intelligent, active, and free being should so behave himself as by no act to contradict truth; or that he should treat everything as being what it is.[100]

What remains to be done is to establish that for Wollaston the obligations founded on happiness are identical to those founded on reason. And in a passage at the end of his discussion on happiness he makes this point very clearly :

And as that religion, which arises from the distinction between moral good and evil, was called natural, because founded upon truth and the natures of things : so perhaps may that too, which proposes happiness for its end, in as much as it proceeds upon that difference, which there is between true pleasure and pain, which are physical (or natural) good and evil. And since both these unite so amicably, and are at last the same, here is one religion which may be called natural upon two accounts.[101]

Accordingly, both reason and happiness can be employed as criteria of actions which we either ought or ought not to perform since each criterion involves the other and leads to the same obligations as the other.

[100] R.N.D. p. 25-26. Italics in text omitted.
[101] R.N.D. p. 40. Italics in text omitted.

CHAPTER V

HUME CONTRA THE RATIONALISTS

I. INTRODUCTION

I have now examined certain elements of Hume's epistemology – most notably, his theory of perceptions, and his view of the different types of reason : demonstrative, causal, and distinctions of reason – and, in addition, I have provided an analysis of the moral theories of Cudworth, Clarke, and Wollaston, theories which Hume argues are defective in one way or another. What now remains to be done is to examine Hume's anti-rationalist approach in ethics both in order to assess his various criticisms and with a view to understanding the roles of the various types of reason in his own ethical theory.

Hume's moral theory actually begins in Book III of the *Treatise* although much of the material for that theory is presented in Book II (especially Book II, Part III, Section iii). Book III begins by Hume informing us that philosophical reasoning (in fact, all abstruse reasoning) is at a disadvantage since the arguments presented require a great effort of mind in order to affect us, and consequently, when we leave our studies, this reasoning has no lingering effect. From this point of view all philosophizing resembles the enterprise of the sceptic since the arguments he advances are also such as require great effort of mind and become ineffective outside the study. Nevertheless, Hume argues that what distinguishes 'the present system of philosophy' is the fact that an inquiry into morality will make his previous speculations 'more real and solid'. The reason given is that all that has been stated previously has a bearing on his moral theory, and as such the interest which we have with morality gives a greater reality to his previous speculations on the understanding.[1] He maintains further that it is only

[1] "Morality is a subject that interests us above all others ... and 'tis evident, that this concern must make our speculations appear more real and solid, than where the subject is, in a great measure, indifferent to us". (T. 455).

because of this advantage that he is inquiring into morality. There are two important points here, the first being that Hume's complete answer to the sceptic necessarily involves an inquiry into morality. Only through the latter can the arguments and conclusions of philosophy be made to have any impact.[2] The sceptic's view, as we have seen, is the very antithesis of this since his a is philosophy of inactivity. Secondly, the opening part of the third book of the *Treatise* reminds us of the close connection which Hume asserts exists between the first two books and the third.

In our discussion of Hume's predecessors we have seen that each in some way attempts to argue against the sceptical position which maintains the denial of the reality of moral distinctions. In the *Enquiry Concerning the Principles of Morals*, Hume also shows himself to be concerned with the problem of answering the sceptic :

... it has readily been inferred by sceptics, both ancient and modern, that all moral distinctions arise from education, and were, at first, invented, and afterwards encouraged, by the art of politicians, in order to render men tractable, and subdue their natural ferocity and selfishness, which incapacitate them for society.[3]

Hume's answer to this is to maintain that education, although a powerful device, could not be the source of all moral distinctions :

Had nature made no such distinction, founded on the original constitution of the mind, the words *honourable* and *shameful, lovely and odious, noble and despicable*, had never had place in any language; nor could politicians, had they invented these terms, ever have been able to render them intelligible, or make them convey any idea to the audience. So that nothing can be more superficial than this paradox of the sceptics ...[4]

The refutation of the sceptic does, of course, rest on Hume's view concerning impressions and ideas, for Hume is arguing that moral educaton is unable to convey the impressions required for our having moral ideas, and since there can be no meaning without ideas, it follows that moral education cannot account for the meaning of moral terms. As a result, moral education cannot account for the manner in which we come to make moral distinctions.[5]

---

[2] In another passage Hume writes : "It seems, then, that nature has pointed out a mixed kind of life as most suitable to the human race ... Indulge your passion or science, says she, but let your science be human, and such as may have a direct reference to action and society". (E. 9).

[3] E. 214. See also E. 169-170.

[4] E. 214.

[5] Beyond this argument based on education Hume treats all further claims which deny 'the reality of moral distinctions' as pyrrhonistic and consequently of never having

Once involved with Hume's doctrine of impressions and ideas, we should expect Hume to raise the question as to where to find the impression or impressions which correspond to the ideas we have of morality. Instead of this, however, he raises the following question :

Now as perceptions resolve themselves into two kinds, viz. impressions and ideas, this distinction gives rise to a question, with which we shall open up our present inquiry concerning morals, Whether 'tis by means of our ideas or impressions we distinguish betwixt vice and virtue, and pronounce an action blameable or praiseworthy? [6]

The material presented on Hume in the preceding chapters can now be used to clarify this question.

In the first place, my analysis of impressions and ideas has shown that ideas for Hume are accountable through two different sources, namely, either by being causally connected with a precedent impression or by being derived through a comparison of other ideas. Thus the fact that Hume admits that we have moral ideas does not by itself commit him to the view that these ideas are derived from certain correspondent impressions. They could be derived from reasoning through a comparison of ideas. The central problem to be resolved, therefore, with respect to Hume's opening question is whether our moral ideas are traceable to impressions or to reasoning through a comparison of ideas. The fact that attempts were made to defend both positions indicates that the issue for Hume is not decidable through introspection but rather only by careful and exact experiments.

Secondly, we have seen that impressions are regarded as those perceptions which constitute our matters of fact, whereas ideas are those perceptions whose content is traceable to other perceptions. Accordingly, although Hume has not denied the reality of moral distinctions, it does not follow

---

a lasting influence on anyone : "Those who have denied the reality of moral distinctions, may be ranked among the disingenuous disputants; nor is it conceivable, that any human creature could ever seriously believe that all characters and actions were alike entitled to the affection and regard of everyone. The difference, which nature has placed between one man and another, is so wide ... that, where the opposite extremes come at once under our apprehension, there is no scepticism so scrupulous, and scarce any assurance so determined, as absolutely to deny all distinction between them. Let a man's insensibility be ever so great, he must often be touched with the images of Right and Wrong; and let his prejudices be ever so obstinate, he must observe, that others are susceptible of like impressions. The only way, therefore, of converting an antagonist of this kind, is to leave him to himself. For, finding that nobody keeps up the controversy with him, it is probable he will, at last, of himself, from mere weariness, come over to the side of common sense and reason". (E. 169-170).

[6] T. 456. Italics in the text omitted.

from this that he thereby regards moral characteristics as matters of fact. This is something which must be argued for rather than merely accepted. Further, if moral distinctions are matters of fact, then such distinctions cannot ultimately be based on demonstrative reasoning, the reason being, as we have seen, that although the conclusions of demonstrative reasoning are applicable to existences, the conclusions themselves are ideas. However, if moral distinctions are matters of fact, then awareness of such distinctions might be based on causal reasoning, since in the case of causal inference we infer matters of fact. By this Hume does not mean that *what* is inferred is a matter of fact, since what is inferred is an idea and ideas are not matters of fact. However, whenever an idea is inferred causally, we believe that the impression or fact corresponding to that idea will exist. It might, therefore, be the case that causal reasoning can be employed in order to become aware of moral perceptions.[7]

All of the above, however, are connected with Hume's attack on the so-called rationalists in ethics – especially Clarke and Wollaston – and it is to this attack that we now turn.

II. CRITIQUE OF WOLLASTON

His initial argument against Wollaston reads as follows :

(a) Reason is the discovery of truth and falsehood. (b) Truth or falsehood consists in an agreement or disagreement either to the *real* relations of ideas, or to *real* existence and matter of fact. (c) Whatever, therefore, is not susceptible of this agreement or disagreement, is incapable of being true or false, and can never be the object of our reason. (d) Now 'tis evident our passions, volitions, and actions, are not susceptible of any such agreement or disagreement; being original facts and realities, compleat in themselves, and implying no reference to other passions, volitions, and actions. (e) 'Tis impossible, therefore, they can be pronounced either true or false, and be either contrary or conformable to reason.[8]

This argument involves considerable discussion and it will be convenient to discuss it sentence by sentence. For this purpose I have included the letters (a) through (e) although they do not appear in the text.

[7] Both points made in this paragraph are summed up by Hume in the following passage : "If thought and understanding were along capable of fixing the boundaries of right and wrong, the character of virtuous and vicious either must lie in some relations of objects, or must be a matter of fact, which is discovered by our reasoning ... the operations of the human understanding divide themselves into two kinds, the comparing of ideas, and the inferring of matter of fact; were virtue discover'd by the understanding; it must be an object of one of these operations ..." (T. 463).
[8] T. 458.

Beginning then with (a) it is clear that Wollaston would agree with Hume that reason is that faculty through which truth or falsehood is discovered. (Wollaston also allows for the employment of the senses in cases where reason is unable to operate, but this can be left aside here.) The disagreement does not even begin with (b). Hume, as we have seen, adopts a correspondence theory of truth. Wollaston also adopts a correspondence theory of truth whereby truth and falsity are determined by correspondence with fact. We can then allow that both Hume and Wollaston hold similar theories of truth insofar as each emphasizes the notion of correspondence. Even (c) should produce no point of disagreement since for consistency Wollaston must hold that whatever is not susceptible of a correspondence with facts cannot be true or false and can never be the object of reason. The real disagreement between them begins with (d) and carries through to (e).

In (d) Hume argues that passions, volitions and actions can have no correspondence either with relations of ideas or with matters of fact, the reason being that these are 'original facts and realities, compleat in themselves, and implying no reference to other passions, volitions, and actions'. A similar claim is made by Hume in Book II when he states :

A passion is an original existence, or, if you will, modification of existence, and contains not any representative quality, which renders it a copy of any other existence. When I am angry, I am actually possesst with the passion, and in that emotion have no more a reference to any other object, than when I am thirsty, or sick, or more than five foot high. 'Tis impossible, therefore, that this passion can be oppos'd by, or be contradictory to truth and reason; since this contradiction consists in the disagreement of ideas, consider'd as copies, with those objects, which they represent.[9]

The first point to notice is that in this passage Hume has recourse to the paradigmatic character of our impressions and the fact that our impressions constitute our facts and thereby maintains that passions, volitions, and actions are original facts and realities. With this much I have no quarrel. Now, insofar as passions, volitions, and actions are paradigmatic, we can also agree with Hume's point that they contain no representative quality which makes them copies of any other existence. Nevertheless, in order for Hume to establish his case that passions, volitions, and actions cannot be true or false he must give reasons for holding that something (A) can agree with something else (B) if and only if (A) is a copy of (B). It is not enough for Hume to say that actions cannot agree with other states

---

[9] T. 415.

of affairs simply because actions are not copies of any other states of affairs : he must show that only ideas can agree or disagree with matters of fact in a sense relevant to ascriptions of truth values, and that only ideas possess the propositional character which enables statements about them to be either true or false. Wollaston has argued that there is a sense in which actions do have reference to states of affairs and can be said to be in agreement or disagreement with them inasmuch as actions have meaning, so that whenever we act we act as if something is or is not the case. Thus Wollaston argues that actions are propositional with the result that the action and the proposition corresponding to it will be true if they agree with the facts and false if they do not. If Hume is to answer Wollaston then he must challenge Wollaston's theory of meaning insofar as it extends to actions and this he does not do in the argument under consideration.

Although Hume does not address this matter of the propositional character of actions in the argument we are examining, he does not ignore it altogether. Rather, he turns to it in his next argument. We will examine it after completing our present discussion.

We have seen that what Hume fails to do in this first argument is to challenge Wollaston's theory of meaning whereby Wollaston tries to show that actions can be true or false. As such (e), the conclusion of the argument, is also not applicable to Wollaston. All that Hume's argument establishes is that to the extent that actions are not copies of any other states of affairs they cannot either agree or disagree with them and therefore cannot be true or false. However, he has not shown that this is the only sense of agreement and disagreement with states of affairs which is relevant to ascriptions of truth values.

Hume ends his discussion of this first argument by stating that "it proves *directly*, that actions do not derive their merit from a conformity to reason, nor their blame from a contrariety to it".[10] We can, of course, accept this conclusion in the light of the argument which Hume has presented, but it must be pointed out that even the statement of the conclusion does not do justice to Wollaston's position. It is true that certain remarks made by Wollaston lend themselves to such an interpretation.[11] However, my own analysis has shown that Wollaston's position is not fully explicated until a proper understanding is obtained of the role of pleasure in his moral theory and of the pre-established harmony between truth and happiness.

[10] T. 458.
[11] For example, "No act (whether word or deed) of any being, to whom moral good and evil are imputable, that interferes with any true proposition, or denies anything to be as it is, can be right". (S. B. II, p. 364).

Consequently, Hume's argument is unacceptable as an argument against Wollaston *both* in the premises which he offers (or more precisely premise (d) which, as we say, is the central point of dispute between Hume and Wollaston) *and* in the conclusion he tries to establish.[12]

I have already mentioned that Hume offers a second argument in which he attempts to deal with the relationship between actions and assertions or judgments. Hume begins this new argument by saying :

But perhaps it may be said, that tho' no will or action can be immediately contradictory to reason, yet we may find such a contradiction in some of the attendants of the action. The action may cause a judgment, or may be *obliquely* caus'd by one ... and by an abusive way of speaking ... the same contrariety may, upon that account, be ascrib'd to the action.[13]

Speaking first of those judgments which may cause an action he asserts :

... reason, in a strict and philosophical sense, can have an influence on our conduct only after two ways : Either when it excites a passion by informing us of the existence of something which is a proper object of it; or when it discovers the connexion of causes and effects, so as to afford us means of exerting any passion.[14]

Hume, of course, recognizes that either of these kinds of judgments can be false. However, he concludes by saying that whenever such judgments are false they are not the source of immorality : "I am more to be lamented than blam'd if I am mistaken with regard to the influence of objects in producing pain or pleasure, or if I knew not the proper means of satisfying my desires".[15]

A full understanding of this argument requires looking beyond it to a passage in which Hume accounts for desire and aversion :

'Tis easy to observe, that the passions ... are founded on pain and pleasure, and that in order to produce an affection of any kind, 'tis only requisite to present some good or evil. Upon the removal of pain and pleasure there immediately follows a removal of ... desire and aversion ... The mind by an *original* instinct tends to unite itself with the good, and to avoid the evil, tho' they be conceiv'd merely in idea, and be considered to exist in any future period of time ... Beside

---

[12] Hume says that that argument also shows that "as reason can never immediately prevent or produce any action by contradicting or approving of it, it cannot be the source of moral good and evil, which are found to have that influence". However, if my criticisms of Hume's argument are correct, then he has not shown that reason cannot be the source of moral good and evil since he has not shown that reason cannot contradict or approve of actions.

[13] T. 459.

[14] T. 459.

[15] T. 459-460.

good and evil, or in other words, pain and pleasure, the direct passions frequently arise from a natural impulse ...[16]

We can see, therefore, that for Hume the ends of human action are unjustifiable, and as a result reasoning can only be used to acquire the end, rather than to justify it.[17]

The interesting aspect of this argument for us is that if my interpretation of Wollaston is correct much of what Hume says he would agree with, and further, the essential area of disagreement between Hume and Wollaston is not all raised by this argument.

We have seen Hume discuss the fact that the mind naturally tends to unite with what is pleasurable, and to shun what is painful. As a result, Hume contends that reason can either tell us what brings these effects about, and how to acquire or avoid them. Now, Wollaston's theory seems much in line with this position. Each of us seeks happiness or true pleasure and reason is employed in order to acquire it :

A careful observation of truth, the way to happiness, and the practice of reason are in the issue the same thing. For of the two last, each falls in with the first, and therefore each with other. And so, at last, natural religion is grounded upon this triple and strict alliance or union of *truth, happiness,* and *reason*; all in the same interest, and conspiring by the same methods, to advance and perfect human nature : and its truest definition is, *The pursuit of happiness by the practice of reason and truth.*[18]

The above shows where Wollaston is essentially in agreement with Hume, namely, insofar as reason can point out objects leading to pleasure and inform us as to how such objects can be obtained. But what Hume neglects in this discussion is the Wollastonian doctrine of 'acting as if' and the propositional character of actions, thereby leaving unresolved a key area of disagreement between himself and Wollaston regarding the role of reason in influencing conduct.

Hume's argument also merits attention insofar as he states that falsity in judgment extends not beyond a mistake of fact and, as such, cannot be regarded as the source of immorality :

---

[16] T. 439. See also T. 574.

[17] This is what Hume means in the following passage : "It appears evident that the ultimate ends of human actions can never in any case, be accounted for by reason, but recommend themselves entirely to the sentiments ... Ask a man why he uses exercise, he will answer, because he desires to keep his health. If you then inquire, why he desires health, he will readily reply, because sickness is painful. If you push your inquiries farther, and desire a reason why he hates pain, it is impossible he can ever give any. This is an ultimate end ..." (E. 293).

[18] R.N.D. p. 52.

A fruit, for instance, that is really disagreeable, appears to me at a distance, and thro'mistake I fancy it to be pleasant and delicious. Here is one error; I choose certain means of reaching this fruit, which are not proper for my end. Here is a second error; nor is there any third one, which can ever possibly enter into our reasonings concerning actions. I ask, therefore, if a man, in this situation, and guilty of these two errors, is to be regarded as vicious and criminal, however unavoidable they might have been? [19]

Hume's point here is clear, namely, Wollaston holds that an action is to be regarded as moral if and only if the judgments attending the action are true and immoral if and only if the attendant judgments are false; and yet the false judgments we find attending our actions do not render our actions immoral; therefore, it is not the case that an action is to be regarded as moral if and only if the judgments attending the action are true. Hume himself adds that such false judgments cannot be regarded as criminal or morally wrong since they are "perfectly involuntary".[20] What will suffice to show that this argument can in no way be considered a successful criticism of Wollaston's theory will be to elicit passages in which Wollaston himself recognizes that such false judgments are not the source of immorality.

There are many passages which are relevant in this regard. For example, in one place Wollaston writes :

It must be confest there is a *difficulty* as to the means, by which we are to consult our own preservation and happiness; to know what those are, and what they are with respect to us. For our abilities and opportunities are not equal : some labor under disadvantages invincible : and our ignorance of the true nature of things, of their operations and effects in such an irregular distempered world, and of those many incidents, that may happen either to further or break our measures, deprive us of certainty in these matters. But still we may judge as well as we can, and do what we can; and the neglect *to do this* will be an omission within the reach of the proposition.[21]

(The proposition to which Wollaston is referring in the last sentence of this quotation is his fifth proposition which reads in part as follows : "... by these [namely, by omissions or neglecting to act] also true propositions may be denied to be true; and then these omissions, by which this is done, must be wrong ..." [22]) This passage shows very clearly that

[19] T. 460.

[20] T. 459.

[21] R.N.D., p. 17. In another place, Wollaston writes in this same regard : "The imputations of moral and evil to beings capable of understanding and acting must be in proportion to their endeavours : or their obligations reach as far as their endeavours may". (*Ibid..*, p. 63).

[22] R.N.D., p. 16.

Wollaston is in agreement with Hume concerning the absence of moral value in mistakes of fact. Wollaston urges that acts generating falsehoods are wrong only if they stem from a being 'to whom moral good and evil are imputable' : "No act (whether word or deed) of any being, to whom moral good and evil are imputable, that interferes with any true proposition, or denies any thing to be as it is, can be right".[23] And, to be a being to whom moral good and evil are imputable one must be capable of distinguishing, choosing and acting for himself :

For that, which cannot distinguish, cannot choose : and that, which has not the opportunity, or liberty of choosing for itself, and acting accordingly, from an internal principle, acts, if it acts at all, under a necessity incumbent *ab extra* ... A being under the above-mentioned inabilities is, as to the morality of its acts, in the state of inert and passive matter ... to which no language or philosophy ever ascribed mores.[24]

Accordingly, to make the errors of which Hume speaks in selecting a fruit is for Wollaston to perform actions which are morally indifferent. In fact, at the very beginning of *The Religion of Nature Delineated* Wollaston asserts that acts can be either good, evil or indifferent : "The foundation of religion lies in that difference between the acts of men, which distinguishes them into *good, evil, indifferent*". Accordingly, the example and argument which Hume offers are both in agreement with Wollaston's moral theory and Hume's example of selecting a fruit which, if eaten, will cause great discomfort cannot be regarded as an effective use of a counter example against Wollaston.

In Hume's discussion of "those judgments which are the effects of our actions" [25] he is thinking of a judgment regarding an action which is made by an observer :

'Tis certain, that an action, on many occasions, may give rise to false conclusions in others ... In this respect my action resembles somewhat a lye or falsehood; ... It causes, however, a mistake and false judgment by accident; and the falsehood of its effect may be ascribed, by some odd figurative way of speaking, to the action itself. But still I can see no pretext of reason for asserting, that the tendency to cause such an error is the first spring or original source of all immorality.[26]

In a footnote Hume furthers his attack on Wollaston beginning with the claim that if error in judgment (or the tendency to cause error in judgment)

[23] R.N.D., p. 13. The reasons for this position were discussed earlier in the fourth chapter.
[24] S. B. II, p. 361-362.
[25] T. 461. Italics omitted.
[26] T. 461.

is the source of all immorality then this must also apply to errors we make in our judgments regarding inanimate objects, and furthermore a concealed action can never be immoral since there is no observer present to pass judgment on it.

Now, it is far from clear that Wollaston ever attributed the importance to an observer which Hume thinks he does. It is true that in various passages Wollaston speaks of an observer (either as an indifferent judge [27] or spectator [28]). However, a careful reading of these and other passages shows that Wollaston holds that any signification which actions have they have in nature or inalterably :

There are many acts of other kinds, such as constitute the character of a man's conduct in life, which have *in nature*, and would be taken by any indifferent judge to have a signification, and to imply some proposition ...[29]

It may not be improperly observed by the way, that the *significancy* here attributed to men's acts, proceeds not always from nature, but sometimes from custom and agreement among people, as that of words and sounds mostly doth ... But acts ... such as I chiefly here intend, have an *unalterable* signification, and can by no agreement or force ever be made to express the contrary to it.[30]

Accordingly, the role of the observer is not at all as pivotal for Wollaston's view as Hume believes. Wollaston holds that an impartial observer should be able to uncover the meaning which an action possesses, but the signification is fixed and the moral worth of the action is determined even if the act is not properly understood or observed by a spectator. Wollaston does not regard any error or false conclusion on the part of the observer as the source of immorality. Immorality is due to what the agent does and is not due to an interpretation placed on the action.

In the last paragraph of the footnote we are considering [31] Hume raises a question concerning the relationship between a regard to truth and being motivated to act. Proceeding on the mistaken assumption that Wollaston sees the role of the observer as pivotal, Hume asks : "... who ever thought

[27] S. B. II, p. 362.

[28] S. B. II, p. 363.

[29] S. B. II, p. 362. My italics.

[30] R.N.D., p. 12. Mrs. Kydd also appears to miss Wollaston's point. She writes : "... Wollaston's contention [is] that the criterion by which we discover what it is that an act asserts is not the intention of the agent but the conclusions which the spectator draws from it." (p. 33).

[31] We can omit from our discussion most of the remainder of this footnote since it is largely predicated on Hume's mistaken notion concerning the role of the observer in Wollaston's moral theory.

of forbearing any action, because others might possibly draw false conclusions from it? Or, who ever perform'd any, that he might give rise to true conclusions?" Underlying this question is Hume's belief that a regard to truth *per se* can never be a motive to action, and as a result, reason which is the faculty concerned with and able to discover truth, cannot be a motive to action. Accordingly, in concluding his attack on Wollaston Hume writes : "Thus, upon the whole, 'tis impossible, that the distinction betwixt good and evil, can be made by reason; since that distinction has an influence upon our actions, of which reason is incapable".[32]

Again here, however, Hume is mistaken. For Wollaston the end of human action is happiness : "To make itself happy is a duty, which every being, in proportion to its capacity, owes to itself; and that, which every intelligent being may be supposed to aim at, in general ..." [33] Also, it is only by acting in accordance with truth that I ensure my own happiness : "Happiness must not be denied to be what it is : and it is by the practice of truth that we aim at happiness, which is true".[34] Accordingly, for Wollaston, the original motive for acting in accordance with truth is the fact that only in this way do I contribute to my own happiness. Further, given that for Wollaston happiness is determined in terms of true pleasure, it follows that the original motive to act in accordance with truth is the prospect of pleasure which is true. Nowhere does Wollaston argue that reason alone or a regard to truth *per se* can be a motive to act.

III. CRITIQUE OF CLARKE

From here, Hume turns his criticism against Clarke and his followers and undertakes an examination of the notion of immutable fitnesses and unfitnesses : "But to be more particular, and to shew, that those eternal immutable fitnesses and unfitnesses of things cannot be defended by sound philosophy, we may weigh the following considerations".[35]

The first such consideration stems from his notion of reason. Since reason can only be employed in order to compare ideas and infer matters of fact, if morality were within the province of reason, then virtue and vice must either consist in some relation or some impression or matter of fact. Now, granting that demonstrative reasoning cannot be extended to impres-

---

[32] T. 462.
[33] S.B. II, p. 381.
[34] S.B. II, p. 254. See also superscript 18.
[35] T. 463.

sions, it follows that if morality is demonstrable, it must consist in some relation between ideas. Hume now has recourse to his own view of knowledge in the strict sense and argues that the only relations relevant here are resemblance, contrariety, degrees in quality, and proportions in quantity and number. However, such a position leads to an absurd position : "For as you make the very essence of morality lie in the relations, and as there is no one of these relations but what is applicable, not only to an irrational, but to an inanimate object; it follows, that even such objects must be susceptible of merit and demerit".[36]

The status accorded Hume's attack against Clarke in this and other passages by most commentators is well summarized in the following passage :

If Hume failed to see how Clarke's view could be developed and made consistent, this was certainly in part Clarke's fault, for his view, as he stated it, was susceptible to all Hume's criticisms.[37]

I now propose to show that this view is fundamentally mistaken as a result of a misunderstanding of the essential points in Clarke's position.

Hume's first point against Clarke, as we saw above, seeks to reduce Clarke's position to absurdity by arguing that all four relations involved in knowledge claims have application beyond the realm of human actions. Now, Hume's criticism rests on the view that Clarke himself never really worked out a theory of moral relations, and consequently Hume is, as it were, filling in the missing steps with his own theory of relations.[38] However, Hume is in error here, for Clarke had already argued that morality is determined by how actions are related to the public benefit and not simply in terms of how they are related to each other. It may be true that with respect to one another the only demonstrable relations between actions are the four Hume mentions. However, once the public benefit is introduced Hume's discussion seems entirely out of place, since actions can be related to the public benefit in a way in which inanimate objects cannot be. Clarke himself is partially responsible for the misunderstanding for in certain early passages he speaks of fitnesses as obtaining between people without any mention of the public interest.[39] My discussion in the previous

---

[36] T. 464.

[37] Kydd, p. 49.

[38] On this point Mrs. Kydd writes : "... Clarke and his followers did not substantiate their claim. For they showed neither that the relation of moral rightness is *a priori*, nor in what it consists". (p. 49).

[39] See, for example, S.B. II, p. 4.

chapter has shown, however, that the fitnesses in behaviour between people are determined by what is in the public benefit. In one passage, Hume comes close to seeing Clarke's point. Hume writes in a footnote :

... we may observe, that those who assert, that morality is demonstrable, do not say, that morality lies in the relations, and that the relations are distinguishable by reason. They only say, that reason can discover such an action, in such relations, to be virtuous, and such another vicious.[40]

It seems that Clarke does want to hold this position, viz. that actions are virtuous or vicious, and not relations, and that he holds that these actions are virtuous or vicious insofar as they are related to the public benefit. But now it is important to see that for Clarke's theory there is no need to introduce special moral relations. Rather, morality, for Clarke, is determined by how actions are *causally* related to the public benefit. Clarke's discussion throughout is based on causal langugage.[41] As a result of this, Hume's next point against Clarke is off the topic. For Hume challenges Clarke to show what relation, other than the four he has outlined, could give rise to the notion of morality.[42]

Although this challenge of Hume's is off the point, nevertheless, it will still be of some value to pursue what Hume has to say here.

In the first place, Hume argues that those who hold that morality consists in some relation must show that these same relations cannot be applicable either to internal actions of the mind or to external objects :

For as morality is supposed to attend certain relations, if these relations cou'd belong to internal actions consider'd singly, it wou'd follow, that we might be guilty of crimes in ourselves ... And in like manner, if these moral relations cou'd be apply'd to external objects, it wou'd follow, that even inanimate beings wou'd be susceptible of moral beauty and deformity.[43]

In the light of our discussion it is clear that Hume has not grasped Clarke's essential point about actions being moral or immoral for in this passage

---

[40] T. 464 n.

[41] A key passage in this regard is the following one : "For if the practice of certain things tends to the publick benefit of the World, and the contrary would tend to the publick disadvantage, then those things are not in their own nature indifferent, but were good and reasonable to be practised before any Law was made". (S.B. II, p. 8). See also S.B. II, p. 23-27.

[42] "Shou'd it be asserted, that the sense of morality consists in the discovery of some relation, distinct from these, and that our enumeration was not compleat, when we comprehended all demonstrable relations under four general heads : To this I know not what to reply, till some one be so good as to point out to me this new relation". (T. 464).

[43] T. 465.

Hume is still concentrating on the relations obtaining between things *simpliciter*, and, of course, so long as he does this, he will have scored a victory. But it is important to notice this is not a victory against Clarke. Clarke maintains that morality does not require special relations, but rather application of the relation of causality between actions and the public benefit. Accordingly, moral rightness for Clarke results from nothing but particular applications of causality.

A second condition which Hume sets down for Clarke is the following. Whereas Hume's first point discussed above sets down a prime condition which moral relations must meet, this second point focusses on the effects which contemplation of such relations is said to have on us :

... 'tis not only suppos'd, that these relations, being eternal and immutable, are the same, when consider'd by every rational creature, but their *effects* are also suppos'd to be necessarily the same; and 'tis concluded they have no less, or rather a greater, influence in directing the will of the deity, than in governing the rational and virtuous of our own species.[44]

But now Hume raises his objection :

These two particulars are evidently distinct. 'Tis one thing to know virtue, and another to conform the will to it. In order, therefore, to prove, that the measures of right and wrong are eternal laws, *obligatory* on every rational mind, 'tis not sufficient to shew the relations upon which they are founded : We must also point out the connexion betwixt the relation and the will; and must prove that this connexion is so necessary, that in every well-disposed mind, it must take place and have its influence; tho' the difference betwixt these minds be in other respects immense and infinite. Now besides what I have already prov'd, that even in human nature no relation can ever alone produce any action ... it has been shown, in treating of the understanding, that there is no connexion of cause and effect, such as this is suppos'd to be which is discoverable otherwise than by experience ... we cannot prove a priori, that these relations, if they really existed and were perceiv'd, would be universally forcible and obligatory.[45]

This objection is quite complex and consequently it calls for closer attention. Hume is saying that Clarke maintains (1) that moral relations are the same for all rational creatures (he has in mind man and the deity) and (2) they have the same influence on the wills of all rational beings. But (1) and (2) are two different propositions : (1) regards our apprehension of moral relations, while (2) concerns the obligation which these relations place us under, obligation being considered in terms of ability to influence the will to act. Now, since (1) and (2) are different propositions, different

[44] T. 465.
[45] T. 465-466.

arguments are needed to justify them. We have aleady seen what Hume regards as a necessary condition for any argument which will justify (1). But now in order to justify (2) we must show that a necessary connection exists between these relations and the will so that every well-disposed mind will be affected by them. Causal arguments, however, are not *a priori* arguments. Accordingly, the necessary connection required in order to show that such eternal fitnesses are universally forcible can never be provided.

When commentators discuss this argument it is held that the objection which Hume raises stems from his own view of obligation [46] which is developed later in the third book of the *Treatise*. In fact, however, this is not correct since the objection simply develops a point which Hume believes Clarke makes. Thus, early in this passage Hume remarks that *it is supposed* that these alleged relations when once apprehended will invariably direct the will of all rational beings. The objection then seeks to show what is required to confirm this supposition and why such confirmation is impossible.

Now that the nature and source of Hume's criticism has been unpacked, we will turn to Clarke to see what he held on the relationship between the eternal fitnesses and the will. (That Hume misunderstood Clarke's notion of fitnesses is irrelevant to the point I wish to make here, since my attention now is on the relation between the eternal fitnesses and the will rather than on the nature of the fitnesses themselves.)

What will suffice to show Hume's error in assessing Clarke will be to prove that Clarke himself recognizes that ' 'tis one thing to know virtue, and another to conform the will to it', since if Clarke recognizes this then he cannot hold – at least he cannot consistently hold – that there is a necessary connection between the apprehension of these fitnesses and the will. If so, then Hume's challenge that Clarke establish the necessary connection between these fitnesses and the will is without force.

That Clarke does recognize the difference between knowing virtue and conforming the will to it is evident in many passages. For example, he writes :

... Assent to a plain speculative Truth, is not in a Man's Power to withhold, but to Act according to the plain Right and Reason of things, this he may, by the natural Liberty of his Will, forbear.[47]

---

[46] See, for example, Broiles, p. 83; and Kydd, p. 54.
[47] S.B. II, p. 14.

In another place Clarke concerns himself with cases where the practice of virtue does not appear in accordance with self-interest :

... the practice of Vice, is accompanied with great Temptations and allurements of Pleasure and Profit, and the practice of Virtue is often threatened with great Calamities, Losses, and sometimes even with Death itself. And this alters the Question, and destroys the practice of that which appears so reasonable in the whole Speculation, and introduces a necessity of Rewards and Punishments. For though Virtue is unquestionably worthy to be chosen for its own sake, even without any expectation of Reward, yet it does not follow that it is therefore intirely Self-sufficient, and able to support a Man ... without any prospect of future Recompense.[48]

Accordingly, Hume is wrong when he regards Clarke as maintaining that there is a necessary connection between the apprehension of the eternal fitnesses and the will.[49] Clarke is very much concerned with the fact that knowing what is right need not always move us to act if we think that such actions conflict with our own self-interest. The only connection which Clarke is prepared to maintain is one between the eternal fitnesses and reason,[50] and from this connection we have seen him argue that the eternal fitnesses are obligatory upon all rational beings. At no time does he argue for a necessary connection between these fitnesses and the will. In fact, Clarke is bothered by the knowledge that the will need not follow the assent of reason, since for him this means that God has put men under a necessity of approving certain actions and yet in many cases has not provided any support or incentive to practising virtue. Clarke concludes that this problem can be resolved and morality made supportable in practice only through the belief in 'a future State of rewards and punishments.'[51] I conclude, therefore, that Clarke himself recognizes that ' 'tis one thing to know virtue and another to conform the will to it' and as a result Hume's objection is without any force.

---

[48] S.B. II, p. 35.

[49] Mrs. Kydd is also mistaken on this point. She writes that Clarke held "that there is an absolute *a priori* necessity of willing fitting acts" (p. 82), although she is unable to produce any passage to substantiate this claim.

[50] "Now the Observation which every one cannot but make in this Matter, is This : that Virtue and true Goodness, Righteousness and Equity are things so truly noble and excellent, so lovely and venerable in themselves, and do so necessarily approve themselves to the Reason and consciences of Men ..." (S.B. II, p. 20). See also S.B. II, p. 16.

[51] The entire passage reads as follows : "Men never will generally and indeed 'tis not very reasonably to be expected they should, part with all the Comforts of Life, and even Life itself, without expectation of any future Recompense. So that, if we suppose no future State of Rewards, it will follow that God has endued Men with such Faculties,

Although the objection as stated by Hume in no way damages Clarke's moral theory, it might be said that in the light of my own discussion of Clarke, Hume's objection can, with certain changes, be directed against Clarke's moral theory. That is, I have argued that Clarke holds that once we are shown the difference between right and wrong our reason will give its assent to those actions which are right. However, it might now be said that it is incumbent upon Clarke to prove that the effects of these fitnesses are the same on the reasoning faculties of all individuals for only in this way can Clarke establish that these fitnesses are obligatory. Clarke actually anticipated this objection and he argues that the onus is on the critic to point to anyone who is both rational and considerate and yet whose reason does not assent to the eternal fitnesses as discussed by Clarke, that is, to actions which are in the public benefit.[52] Clarke's position then is not that his own position is proveable *a priori* and therefore necessarily, but only that these fitnesses can be regarded as binding so long as they are accompanied by the assent of reason. He himself, however, does not doubt that rational creatures will always assent to fitting actions when once they are clearly apprehended, in the same way that he does not doubt that rational creatures will assent to mathematical truths when once they are clearly apprehended.

With this I have concluded all I wish to say about Section I of Book III of the *Treatise* insofar as Hume is concerned with what he regards as the rationalists' claim concerning the role of demonstrative reasoning in

---

as put them under a necessity of approving and chusing Virtue in the Judgment of their own Minds, and yet has not given them wherewith to support themselves in the suitable and constant Practice of it. The Consideration of which inexplicable Difficulty, ought to have led the Philosophers to a firm belief and expectation of a future State of Rewards and Punishments, without which their whole scheme of Morality cannot be supported". (S.B. II, p. 36).

[52] "Were there upon Earth a Nation of rational and considerate Persons, whose Notions concerning moral Obligations, and concerning the Nature and Force of them, were universally and directly contrary to what I have hitherto represented, this would be indeed a weighty Objection. But Ignorance and Stupidity are no Arguments against the Certainty of any thing. There are many Nations and People almost totally ignorant of the plainest Mathematical Truths ... And yet these Truths are such, to which the Mind cannot but give its assent necessarily and unavoidably, so soon as they are distinctly proposed to it. All that this Objection proves therefore, supposing the Matter of it to be true, is only this; not, that the mind of man can ever dissent from the rule of Right [but only] that Men have great need to be taught and instructed in some very plain and easy, as well as certain Truths, and, if they be important Truths, that then men have need also to have them frequently inculcated, and strongly inforced upon them". (S.B. II, p. 21-22).

morals.[53] And I have attempted to show that this section of the *Treatise* is largely mistaken in the criticisms it raises inasmuch as Hume has misunderstood the rationalists' claims. Nevertheless, throughout this section we have seen Hume develop arguments which depend upon his own analysis of perceptions and relations.

Throughout our discussion of both Wollaston and Clarke, I have tried to establish that both men hold that it is not reason alone which provides the motive to perform virtuous actions. For Wollaston the motive is provided by the prospect of happiness through the performance of virtuous actions, while for Clarke the motive is provided through the prospect of some future recompense either in this life or in a future state. Both men, however, maintain – although each in their own way – that moral distinctions are discernible only through reason.

But Clarke and Wollaston go further than this and hold that not only is reason able to discern the difference between good and evil, it is also the source of the rules and precepts which ought to govern our behaviour. Thus Clarke repeatedly refers to our acting "contrary to Reason, that is, contrary to the eternal Rules of Justice, Equity, Righteousness, and Truth",[54] and Wollaston asserts that "To be governed by reason is the general law imposed by the Author of nature upon them, whose uppermost faculty is reason ... It is plain, that reason is of a commanding nature : it injoins this, condemns that, only allows some other things ..."[55]

Now, Hume's own moral theory is based on the belief that reason alone can never influence actions directly and for this reason it cannot be the source of moral distinctions :

Since morals, therefore, have an influence on the actions and affections, it follows that they cannot be derived from reason; and that because reason alone, as we have already prov'd, can never have any such influence. Morals excite passions, and produce or prevent actions. Reason of itself is utterly impotent in this particular. The rules of morality, therefore, are not conclusions of our reason.[56]

Concerning this topic R. D. Broiles writes :

[53] Hume actually carries his discussion further through the use of examples and argues that whatever relations we discover are also applicable to inanimate objects and lower animals. My discussion of Clarke shows this all to be of no consequence to Clarke's position since what Hume invariably omits from his discussion of Clarke's moral theory is the relation of actions to the public benefit. Accordingly, we need not concern ourselves with the arguments which Hume puts forward.

[54] S.B. II, p. 13.

[55] R.N.D., p. 51. Italics omitted.

[56] T. 457.

Hume is correct that reason never causes actions, but he is not correct in what he means by this and the conclusions he draws from it. There is something odd in speaking of reason causing actions. In answer to the question "What caused him to do that?" one would be a bit puzzled at the reply "Reason caused him to do that" ... We don't speak of reason as causing the agent to act.[57]

Broiles continues by maintaining that reason dictates the actions that ought to be taken, but it does not cause actions :

The whole issue, whether reason can or cannot cause actions is a pseudo issue. No one ever supposed it did. Certainly philosophers have held that reason can influence our moral decisions and that we ought to do what reason dictates. But this is not the same as saying that reason causes actions.[58]

Each of the passages quoted deserves some attention. Broiles is correct when he asserts in the first passage quoted that speaking of reason as a cause is odd. Also, at least so far as the moral theories of Wollaston and Clarke are concerned (Broiles speaks of all moralists, but I am unable to make such a sweeping claim) the issue as to whether reason can cause an action is a pseudo issue since we saw that neither held that it alone could cause actions.

Insofar as Hume holds the argument as Broiles interprets it, then all that Broiles says is correct. Nevertheless, Hume is not holding the view which Broiles attributes to him. In the passage from Hume under consideration it is important to see that Hume's discussion is focussed on the rules of morality, and that the term 'morals' in the first and second sentence is regarded as synonymous with 'the rules of morality' in the last sentence. Accordingly, in the first sentence Hume is asserting that moral rules have an influence on actions and affections and therefore moral rules cannot be derived from reason. As such Hume's essential argument here which is found in the last three sentences should be read : 'The rules of morality excite passions, and produce or prevent actions', 'The conclusions of reason do not excite passions and produce or prevent actions', therefore 'The rules of morality are not conclusions of our reason'.

One final point here about Broiles' position. In the second passage quoted earlier from Broiles' book, we saw him maintain that although reason cannot cause actions it can dictate the actions which ought to be taken. Now, if Hume is holding the interpretation of his argument which I put forward above then what he is holding is that no conclusion of reason can be inculcated to move us to act. Of course, this is precisely what Clarke

---

[57] Broiles, p. 77.
[58] *Ibid.*, p. 78-79.

and Wollaston argue can be done, that is, reason can provide a rule or precept upon which we can be made to act by the prospect of pleasure or happiness. Hume's point then is that the conclusions of reason do not relate *directly* [59] to actions. Accordingly, reason alone cannot dictate which action should be performed :

If morality had naturally no influence on human passions and actions, 'twere in vain to take such pains to inculcate it ...; Philosophy is commonly divided into *speculative* and *practical*; and as morality is always comprehended under the latter division, 'tis supposed to influence our passions and actions, and to go beyond the calm and indolent judgments of the understanding. [60]

Thus, when Hume says (two paragraphs later) that 'an active principle can never be founded on an inactive; and if reason be inactive in itself, it must remain so in all its shapes and appearances' the active principle referred to is the moral rule or precept and the inactive is a conclusion of reason.

Although Hume misunderstood many of the essential points raised by Clarke and Wollaston, the heart of the controversy has yet to be unfolded, since what Hume must establish against both thinkers is that reason is incapable of practical moral judgments. Hume's argument for this position is contained in Book II, Part III, Section iii, and it is to this section that we now turn.

---

[59] Just how they do relate to actions and affections will be examined in the ensuing chapters.
[60] T. 457.

CHAPTER VI

REASON AND THE WILL

I. INTRODUCTION

An important step toward establishing Hume's moral theory is found in Book II, Part III, Section iii of the *Treatise* where Hume discusses the influencing motives of the will. However, this is largely unintelligible without some understanding of the preceding sections in Part III which deal with the will, and accordingly, something must first be said of Hume's account of the will.

Hume defines the will as "the internal impression we feel and are conscious of, when we knowingly give rise to any new motion of our body, or new perception of our mind".[1] His main concern with the will is whether the will can be self-determined or whether it is causally determined in all its actions. From his analysis of causality Hume concluded that two things were necessary for the ascription of necessity in the case of the operations of external bodies, namely, constant conjunction, and the inference of the mind from the appearance of one to the thought of the other. From this he concludes that wherever these two elements are found we must acknowledge a like necessity. And Hume argues these two elements are to be found with regard to the relation existing between our motives, tempers and circumstances and the actions we perform. In the case of constant conjunction he argues that "... actions have a constant union and connexion with the situation and temper of the agent, [and] however we may in words refuse to acknowledge the necessity we really allow the thing".[2] Concerning the inferences we draw Hume argues that

There is no philosopher, whose judgment is so riveted to this fantastical system of liberty, as not to acknowledge the force of *moral evidence*, and both in specu-

[1] T. 399.
[2] T. 403.

lation and practice proceed upon it, as upon a reasonable foundation. Now moral evidence is nothing but a conclusion concerning the actions of men, deriv'd from the consideration of their motives, temper and situation.[3]

We must therefore attribute the same necessity to human actions as we do to external objects.[4] It follows from this that necessity is something which an observer to an action finds rather than something present in the agent himself :

The necessity of any action, whether of matter or of the mind, is not properly a quality in the agent, but in any thinking or intelligent being, who may consider the action, and consists in the determination of his thought to infer its existence from some preceding objects ...[5]

The analysis of the influencing motives of the will must, therefore, take place from the observer's standpoint and cannot rely on the testimony of the subject.

II. THE ALLEGED COMBAT BETWEEN REASON AND PASSION

The section on the influencing motives of the will takes on the task of clarifying the material discussed on the will. For the conclusion of Hume's discussion on the will is "that all actions of the will have particular causes" and now it remains "to explain what these causes are, and how they operate".[6] The only two contenders for this role which Hume discusses are reason and passion : "Nothing is more usual in philosophy, and even in common life, than to talk of the combat of passion and reason, to give the preference to reason, and to assert that men are only so far virtuous as they conform themselves to its dictates".[7] Now Hume claims that he will show up the fallacy of holding that there is such a combat between reason and passion : "In order to shew the fallacy of all this philosophy, I shall endeavour to prove *first*, that reason alone can never be a motive to any action of the will; and *secondly* that it can never oppose passion

---

[3] T. 404.

[4] "Motion in one body in all past instances, that have fallen under our observation, is follow'd upon impulse by motion in another. 'Tis impossible for the mind to penetrate farther. From this constant union it *forms* the idea of cause and effect, and by its influence *feels* the necessity. As there is the same constancy, and the same influence in what we call moral evidence, I ask no more. What remains can only be a dispute of words". (T. 406).

[5] T. 408.

[6] T. 412.

[7] T. 413.

in the direction of the will".[8] In accordance with Hume's discussion at T. 457 wherein reason was regarded as able to produce or prevent actions to the extent that it could yield practical moral judgments, when Hume speaks in the preceding quotation as intending to show that reason can never be a motive to any action of the will he must mean that he intends to show that reason cannot provide practical moral judgments, thereby establishing that reason cannot dictate which action to perform. Again, in the opening paragraph of the section on the influencing motives of the will – or more precisely in the first two sentences – Hume makes it clear that reason or any other faculty can be regarded as a motive of the will if it is able to dictate actions.

(A) Demonstrative reasoning and the will

In his attempt to establish that reason alone can never be a motive to any action of the will, Hume begins with demonstrative reasoning :

As it's proper province is the world of ideas, and as the will always places us in that of realities, demonstration and volition seem, upon that account, to be totally remov'd, from each other.[9]

In the light of our earlier discussion of Hume's analysis of demonstrative reasoning, we can see that in this passage Hume is relying on the fact that the perception of a philosophical relation is always only an idea, whereas volition is concerned with realities or impressions. Accordingly, demonstrative reasoning alone cannot provide a motive for the will to act.

Although demonstrative reasoning has been denied a direct influence on the will, Hume is not prepared to deny it an indirect influence, namely, insofar as "it directs our judgment concerning causes and effects". An example is provided :

Mathematics, indeed, are useful in all mechanical operations, and arithmetic in almost every art and profession : But 'tis not of themselves they have any influence ... A merchant is desirous of knowing the sum total of his accounts with any person : Why? but that he may learn what sum will have the same *effects* in paying his debt, and going to market, as all the particular articles taken together.[10]

In discussing this section it is important to recall the fact that what Hume is attempting to establish is that the conclusions of reason alone cannot

[8] T. 413.
[9] T. 413.
[10] T. 413-414.

excite passions and produce and prevent actions. Now these two are not unrelated since Hume holds that where the truths discovered "beget no desire or aversion, they can have no influence on conduct and behaviour".[11] In the above passage, then, Hume is arguing that the conclusions of demonstrative reasoning alone cannot produce desire or aversion, and that, unless we already feel a certain desire or aversion, demonstrative reasoning is useless in directing conduct.

What Hume does not do in this passage is to fully unpack the role of demonstrative reasoning in directing conduct. Mrs. Kydd [12] attempts to fill in some details to compensate for the brevity of Hume's discussion by arguing that although he selects a mathematical example, he does in fact have in mind all ordinary *a priori* judgments. She then selects examples such as 'deaf men cannot overhear what is said'. She claims that if a man does not like being overheard, but wants to employ a servant, he may hire a deaf man as a servant as a result of his awareness of the judgment 'deaf men cannot eavesdrop'. Although such judgments are important, it is not at all clear to me that Hume has such judgments in mind. We have seen that for Hume knowledge in the strict sense is obtainable not only from the philosophical relation of proportions in quantity or number, but also from the relations of resemblance, degrees in any quality, and contrariety. Accordingly, to make Hume's position as full as possible, we must now see the influence which judgments concerning these relations can have on conduct.

Turning first to resemblance, it is fairly clear what can be said on Hume's behalf. For example, if after having seen an original painting a man is desirous of buying a copy of that painting, his decision or action can be influenced by the resemblance which a print of a certain type bears to the original. Without the desire to obtain a copy of the painting, no print would be obtained. However, once the desire to obtain an accurate print is present, the philosophical relation of resemblance can play an important role.

Since the relation of degrees of any quality functions in much the same way as resemblance, it need not occupy us here.

When Hume first introduces the relation of contrariety he says that "no two ideas are in themselves contrary, except those of existence and non-existence, which are plainly resembling, as implying both of them an idea of an object : tho' the latter excludes the object from all times and

---

[11] E. 172.
[12] Her discussion begins on p. 62 of her book *Reason and Conduct in Hume's Treatise*.

places in which it is supposed not to exist".[13] Now this account of contrariety fits the account I gave of the philosophical relations since contrariety is seen to depend on an inequality existing between two items in virtue of a common property, the common property in this case being the content of the ideas under consideration. Further, the above passage is in agreement with my own discussion of 'actual existence' several chapters earlier wherein I showed that Hume analyzes the thought of actual or external existence in terms of the relations, connections, and durations attributed to the perception.[14] For in the above quotation Hume distinguishes the thought of existence from that of non-existence through the thoughts or ideas of relations and durations which arc attributed to the perception in question. This is what Hume means when he states that non-existence 'excludes the object from all times and places, in which it is supposed not to exist'. To think the non-existence of an object is merely to think it without certain spatial and temporal relations.

In another passage, Hume gives a further insight into what he means by contrariety. It occurs in the second *Enquiry* when he is concerned to show that vice cannot consist in any moral relations akin to the relations discovered in mathematics :

Crime, indeed, consists not in a particular fact, of whose reality we are assured by reason; but it consists in certain *moral relations* discovered by reason, in the same manner as we discover by reason the truths of geometry or algebra. But what are the relations, I ask, of which you here talk? In the case stated above, I see first good-will and good-offices in one person; then ill-will and ill-offices in the other. Between these, there is a relation of *contrariety*. Does the crime consist in that relation? But suppose a person bore me ill-will or did me ill-offices; and I, in return, were indifferent towards him, or did him good-offices. Here is the same relation of *contrariety*; and yet my conduct is often highly laudable.[15]

At first sight, this passage seems inconsistent with his previous account inasmuch as in this account two different objects are involved rather than the same one. However, this inconsistency can be explained away. In the first place, in the above passage when Hume says that 'between these, there is a relation of contrariety' the word 'these' does not refer to the

---

[13] T. 15.

[14] It is important to make this point since Passmore (*Hume's Intentions*, Basic Books Inc., New York, 1968, p. 26-7) notes this passage on contrariety but yet sees it as conflicting with what he calls Hume's official doctrine about existence propositions, namely, that we cannot think of a thing except as existing. If my interpretation of Hume's view on existence and non-existence is correct then there is no such inconsistency.

[15] E. 288.

people but to their actions or conduct. Consequently, there is a basis for a resemblance through the notion of an action. An action, for Hume, is something which is distinguished from the object acting only by a distinction of reason : "By an action we mean ... something, which, properly speaking, is neither distinguishable, nor separable from its substance, and is only conceiv'd by a distinction of reason, or an abstraction".[16] Further, the contrariety is actually traced to the incompatibility between the kinds of actions involved, that is, between actions of good will and action of ill will. Now, if we put together all the elements, I believe that a plausible account can be given of how the above quoted passage can be rendered consistent with Hume's earlier account of contrariety. For, in the earlier account, the emphasis is actually on resemblance, rather than on the resemblance of objects. Thus, when Hume begins his discussion of contrariety he points out that 'no relation of any kind can subsist without some degree of resemblance'. And in Hume's discussion of contrariety in regard to actions of good will and ill will the required resemblance can be found in the product of the distinction of reason, namely, in the notion of an action. The contrariety amidst this resemblance can then be discerned through a contrasting comparison. The action of ill will stands to the action of good will in the same manner as the globe of black marble stands to the globe of white marble in his discussion of distinctions of reason : in both cases, a contrasting [17] comparison is possible. Accordingly, in the case of actions of good and ill will, the essential ingredients for the relation of contrariety, namely, resemblance and contrast, are both present. Thus, when Hume speaks of contrariety as holding between existence and non-existence, these terms can be taken as referring either to objects or to their properties or aspects [18] provided that resemblance and contrast are both present. The philosophical relation of contrariety can then be said to obtain wherever contrasting claims can be made as long as there is a common element upon which the contrast can be made.

Having now cleared up Hume's treatment of the philosophical relation of contrariety we can turn to how it relates to his discussion of the role of demonstrative reasoning in determining actions. And here we should encounter little trouble since it cannot be denied that once we have a certain desire we are very much directed in our actions by contrasting

---

[16] T. 245.

[17] In a footnote in the first *Enquiry*, p. 24, Hume actually uses the word 'contrast' as a synonym for 'contrariety'.

[18] The term 'aspect' is used here in its technical sense as it was introduced in my third chapter when discussing distinctions of reason. Thus, an aspect of a perception

comparisons. To illustrate this we can use Mrs. Kydd's example of the man who does not like being overheard but yet wants to employ a servant. Given that the man has these desires, it is likely that he will be moved to hire a deaf servant through the contrast discerned through a comparison of the two men, the one who hears and the one who doesn't. The difficulty with Mrs. Kydd's account is that she lays stress on the judgment 'deaf men cannot eavesdrop' thereby neglecting entirely Hume's doctrine of the philosophical relations. In fact, she does not even mention, and is perhaps not aware that, her example can be used as an illustration of the role of the philosophical relation of contrariety in directing conduct.

Also, by confining her analysis to analytic statements such as 'deaf men cannot eavesdrop' Mrs. Kydd neglects the fact that the philosophical relation of contrariety or contrast between resembling items is discerned after a certain amount of empirical investigation. For example, given my desire to buy a satisfactory used car, I may not be able to decide between car (a) and car (b) until each is test-driven, even though the cars resemble in that they are the same make and model. It is only after I find that car (a) rides very poorly and car (b) does not that I then select the latter on the basis of my comparison. This, for Hume, constitutes an instance of the philosophical relation of contrariety, and yet it will be neglected so long as attention is confined to statements such as 'deaf men cannot eavesdrop'.

So far we have examined Hume's views concerning the role of demonstrative reasoning in influencing our conduct and we have seen that he maintains the position that demonstrative reasoning can influence our conduct insofar as it is able to direct us to that which can satisfy a desire. Hume also offers a second argument in which he attempts to show that reason – and especially demonstrative reasoning, since Hume regards his rationalist predecessors as holding that it is demonstrative reasoning which can yield rules of conduct – cannot oppose passion in the direction of the will. The argument itself runs as follows :

A passion is an original existence, or, if you will, modification of existence, and contains not any representative quality, which renders it a copy of any other existence or modification. When I am angry, I am actually possesst with the passion, and in that emotion have no more a reference to any other object, than when I am thirsty, or sick, or more than five foot high. 'Tis impossible, therefore, that this passion can be oppos'd by, or be contradictory to truth and reason;

---

is inseparable from it and can be distinguished from the perception only through a distinction of reason.

since this contradiction consists in the disagreement of ideas, consider'd as copies, with these objects, which they represent.[19]

In the last chapter we examined this argument and one similar to it [20] in relation to Wollaston's moral theory. In reintroducing this argument here it will be useful to study it through a comparison with Clarke's moral theory since the latter does speak of the combat of reason and passion.[21]

Toward the end of the last chapter I established that Clarke holds that although a relationship can be established between the awareness of the eternal fitnesses and reason he denies any such invariable connection between reason and the will. As a result of this he holds that it is possible to act contrary to the Understanding. Before analyzing Hume's argument, it is worthwhile to turn to Clarke in order to determine the sense in which he holds that passions can be contrary to reason. Only in the light of this is it possible to assess Hume's argument against Clarke to the effect that there can be no combat between reason and passion.

Clarke often maintains that it is absurd to act against what we know to be fitting :

And 'tis absurd and blameworthy to mistake negligently plain Right and Wrong, that is, to understand the Proportions of things in Morality to be what they are not, or wilfully to act contrary to known Justice and Equity, that is, to will things to be what they are not and cannot be, as it would be absurd and ridiculous for a Man in Arithmetical Matters ignorantly to believe that Twice Two is not equal to Four ...[22]

All wilful wickedness and perversion of right, is the very same insolence and absurdity in moral matters, as it would be in natural things, for a man to pretend to alter certain proportions of numbers ...[23]

Mrs. Kydd interprets Clarke here [24] as intending to convey that some acts are logically impossible, i.e., that there are some acts of which we cannot say that they occur without contradicting ourselves. Although there are certain assertions about acts which are contradictory, for example, I am right now both walking and not walking, I believe it can be shown that

[19] T. 415.

[20] See T. 458.

[21] Wollaston also speaks of the combat of reason and passion : see R.N.D., especially p. 169-179. There is no need, however, to include what he says into the present discussion since the points I want to make regarding Hume's treatment of this topic can be made by attending to Hume and Clarke.

[22] S.B. II, 13.

[23] S.B. II, 15.

[24] See her book, p. 29-30.

Clarke does not have assertions of this kind or form in mind when he speaks of absurdity and contradiction in the above passages. Also, if Clarke does mean that some acts are logically impossible, as Mrs. Kydd holds, then Clarke cannot hold that there can be actions which are contrary to reason since if the description of an action is contradictory, it is logically impossible for that act to occur.[25] Accordingly, on this interpretation Clarke could not hold that reason and passion can conflict since an action not in accordance with reason could not occur.

Now, when Clarke speaks of actions as absurd or contradictory this must be linked to, and understood in terms of, his claim (see first passage quoted above) that in the case of absurd or contradictory actions we are willing things to be what they are not and cannot be. In what sense, then, are we willing things to be what they are not and cannot be? In the two passages quoted Clarke gives no indication that so-called absurd actions cannot be performed; therefore, whatever interpretation the notion of an absurd or contradictory action is to have, it must be consistent with our being able to perform it. In deciding on the sense of willing things to be what they are not and cannot be, our earlier study of Clarke can assist us. For we saw that Clarke holds that actions are good or bad insofar as they either promote the public benefit or do not, and we also saw that the relation which an action bears to the public benefit is not subject to change. Thus, to say, as Clarke does, that certain actions are absurd or contradictory is tantamount to saying that they proceed as if they are fitting and this is something which they are not and can never be. Just as the proportions of numbers are fixed, so actions which are good or bad, fitting or unfitting, are also fixed. We have also seen that reason for Clarke has a concern for the public benefit in moral matters and it assents to precepts which affirm actions which further the public benefit. Such precepts he regards as true. Thus all precepts which do not dictate actions which are in the public benefit must be considered unreasonable and false since they are contrary to reason.

This account shows that Clarke does leave room for the combat of reason and passion, and it thereby refutes Mrs. Kydd's interpretation of Clarke on this point. It is also valuable in showing us the sense of unreasonableness which Clarke maintains, and which must be countered if Hume is to disprove Clarke's claim concerning the combat between reason and passion.

---

[25] Mrs. Kydd does actually interpret Clarke in this way. See, for example, p. 72 of her book.

Hume's argument rests on the distinguishing feature of impressions, namely, that they are paradigmatic, and as such they are, as are all matters of fact, distinct from everything else. Since truth concerns ideas treated as copies, passions cannot be regarded as either true or false. Accordingly, the dictates of passions cannot ever be considered contrary to reason, since the sole concern of the latter is with truth and falsehood.

To the extent that this argument is directed against Clarke's position it is entirely ineffective since the dispute does not centre around whether or not a passion is a copy of something else. The dispute concerns the origin of rules of conduct, and accordingly, if Hume is to refute the Clarkian position he must show that a dictate which runs counter to that originating in a passion can never be provided by reason. To be fair to Clarke, then, further discussion of the alleged combat between reason and passion must be undertaken.

Hume appears to be sensitive to the need for additional argumentation in his next paragraph. For he argues there that since nothing can be contrary to truth or reason unless it has some reference to it, and since only the judgments of the understanding have this reference, it follows that a passion can be contrary to reason only by being accompanied by a false judgment. He then states that there are only two senses in which a passion can be unreasonable : "First, When a passion, such as hope or fear, grief or joy, despair or security, is founded on the supposition of the existence of objects which really do not exist. Secondly, When in exerting any passion in action, we chuse means insufficient for the design'd end, and deceive ourselves in our judgment of causes and effects. Where a passion is neither founded on false suppositions, nor chuses means insufficient for the end, the understanding can neither justify nor condemn it".[26]

This argument also cannot further Hume's position since it is question-begging in that it simply ignores the Clarkian position rather than seeking to refute it. Clarke cannot be refuted by Hume through the latter confining his discussion to two senses in which a passion can be unreasonable, for so long as he does this he either ignores or accepts as false Clarke's notion of the unreasonableness of a passion. As we have seen, Clarke holds that reason has a concern for the public benefit, that it assents to (and dictates) precepts which affirm actions which are in the public benefit, and that such precepts can be regarded as true. To show that Clarke's position is mistaken, therefore, what Hume must do is to show that reason

[26] T. 416.

has no original concern with the public benefit. The question of the combat of reason and passion when directed against Clarke must be understood in the following manner, namely, can that faculty which is capable of yielding both deductive and inductive (or causal) inferences also assent to and dictate precepts which are in the public benefit. Instead of attempting an answer to this question Hume gives his two senses of an unreasonable passion and concludes that reason is indifferent as regards ends :

Where a passion is neither founded on false suppositions, nor chuses means insufficient for the end, the understanding can neither justify nor condemn it. 'Tis not contrary to reason to prefer the destruction of the whole world to the scratching of my finger. 'Tis not contrary to reason for me to chuse my total ruin, to prevent the least uneasiness of an Indian or person wholly unknown to me.[27]

The question to be raised at this point is why Hume begged the question in this argument, at least to the extent that it is directed against Clarke. My analysis of Clarke's moral theory can be of assistance here. In stating his moral theory Clarke uses language which is identical to or closely resembles language which is appropriately applied to reason in its speculative uses. This is especially evident, for example, when Clarke compares morality with mathematics. If as a result of such a practice Clarke is regarded as holding that the speculative and practical operations of reason are identical then Hume's argument against Clarke appears to be well taken. For in such a situation Hume could, for instance, introduce the criteria of truth employed by the speculative use of reason and ask how such criteria can be applied to our passions. However, I have shown that when Clarke speaks of reason in moral matters, he regards reason as capable of an additional capacity beside those of deduction and induction, namely, of having a concern for the public benefit. And it is only insofar as Clarke holds this position with its consequent alterations in the sense of 'truth' that Hume's argument begs the question against Clarke. Throughout his entire discussion of Clarke Hume regards the latter as maintaining that the *operation* of reason is identical in both speculative and practical affairs.[28]

[27] T. 416.
[28] John Laird, *Hume's Philosophy of Human Nature* (Archon Books, 1967), p. 203, also charges Hume with having begged the question. He says that Hume defined reason as a conclusion only of our intellectual faculties, i.e. as not practical, although the rationalists held there was a practical as well as an intellectual employment of reason. However, Laird fails to note that the charge of begging the question is appropriate here

(B) Causal reasoning and the will

Demonstrative or abstract reasoning, as we have seen, Hume considers to be significant in directing conduct to the extent that some end is already desired. If I already have a desire to pay my debts or to buy a good used car, demonstrative reasoning can assist me in achieving my end. Regarding causal reasoning Hume begins in much the same way by referring to the prospect of pleasure and pain from any object, feeling a resulting emotion of aversion or propensity, and employing causal reasoning to either gain the object affording pleasure or avoid the object affording pain :

'Tis obvious that when we have the prospect of pain or pleasure from any object, we feel a consequent emotion of aversion or propensity, and are carry'd to avoid or embrace what will give us this uneasiness or satisfaction. "Tis also obvious, that this emotion rests not here, but making us cast our view on every side, comprehends whatever objects are connected with its original one by the relation of cause and effect. Here then our reasoning takes place to discover the relation; and according as our reasoning varies, our actions receive a subsequent variation.[29]

He insists on pointing out here that " 'tis evident in this case, that the impulse arises not from reason, but is only directed by it. 'Tis from the prospect of pleasure or pain that the aversion or propensity arises towards any object ..." [30]

This argument of Hume's also fails against Clarke insofar as it seeks to show that reason in incapable of dictating actions. In the first place it tends to lose sight of the type of situation for which it is attempting to account, namely, instances in which we believe that there is an opposition between passion and reason. Thus, he provides an argument in which no mention is made of the alleged opposition between passion and reason, and within the argument he asserts that ' 'tis evident that the impulse or dictate does not arise from reason but is only directed by it' – a surprising claim indeed when we look beyond this argument to one of Hume's conclusions three pages later in which we are told that we believe that reason can dictate actions because we confuse the feeling attached to the operation of reason with that of certain calm desires and tendencies. If the feeling associated with reason is in fact similar to the feelings of certain calm desires and tendencies then when Hume is trying to establish

---

only if the practical exployment of reason is regarded by the rationalists as different in its operation from the speculative employment. Also, Laird fails to show in what way the practical employment of reason differs from its speculative employment.

[29] T. 414.
[30] T. 414.

that reason cannot dictate actions his ground for this claim cannot be an assertion of introspective certainty or self-evidence. Toward the end of his argument he has recourse to the same sort of tactic. Thus, he proceeds by saying :

It can never in the least concern us to know, that such objects are causes, and such others effects, if both the causes and effects are indifferent to us. Where the objects themselves do not affect us, their connection can never give them any influence; and *'tis plain, that as reason is nothing but the discovery of this connexion*, it cannot be by its means that the objects are able to affect us.[31]

The portion of this passage which I have italicized is precisely the premise which needs further support, and yet none is provided by Hume.

The only evidence which remains for Hume's position that reason cannot dictate actions, therefore, is his claim that we will not act without some prospect of pleasure or pain which in turn gives rise to the passions of propensity or aversion. Now I have already shown in the previous chapter that Clarke himself holds this position and therefore he would agree with this claim of Hume's. But it is a non sequitur to conclude from this fact alone, as Hume is now seen to do, that any dictate to act must stem only from the passions. Nothing said thus far rules out the possibility of reason dictating which action to take. In order for Hume to secure his case he must show that the following statement is true : Only that which moves us to act can dictate actions. In this way his full argument would be : Only that which moves us to act can dictate actions; only the passions move us to act; therefore, only the passions can dictate actions.

Besides not offering a decisive counter argument to the Clarkian position the passage from the *Treatise* now under examination is misleading in many ways in trying to understand Hume's own position on the relation between causal reasoning and conduct. Accordingly, I shall now attempt to state more precisely the relationship which Hume holds obtains between causal reasoning and conduct.

To begin with, Hume does not hold that the impulse to act stems only from the prospect of 'my' pleasure or pain. Thus, in one passage he writes :

So far from thinking, that men have no affection for anything beyond themselves, I am of the opinion, that tho' it be rare to meet with one, who loves any single person better than himself; yet 'tis as rare to meet with one, in whom all the kind affections, taken together, do not over-ballance all the selfish. Consult common experience ... there are few [masters] that do not bestow the largest part of their fortunes on the pleasures of their wives, and the education of their children ...[32]

[31] T. 414, my italics.
[32] T. 487.

Accordingly, desire and aversion can stem from the prospect of my pleasure or pain or the prospect of the pleasure or pain of someone else. Hume also maintains that desire and aversion can arise through having a pleasure or pain present to the mind :

... pain and pleasure have two ways of making their appearance in the mind; of which the one has effects very different from the other. They may either appear in impression to the actual feeling, or only in idea, as at present when I mention them. 'Tis evident the influence of these upon our actions is far from being equal. Impressions always actuate the soul; and that in the highest degree ...[33]

As a result, desire and aversion can result either from a present pleasure or pain or from the anticipation of pleasure or pain, my own or someone else's. The relation of causal reasoning to conduct must then be determined in the light of this expanded picture of the sources of desire and aversion and not simply in terms of the paragraph at T. 414.

Now, causal reasoning is said by Hume to have two and only two roles to play in the determination of conduct :

It has been observ'd, that reason, in a strict and philosophical sense, can have an influence on our conduct only after two ways : Either when it excites a passion by informing us of the existence of something which is a proper object of it; or when it discovers the connexion of causes and effects, so as to afford us means of exerting any passion.[34]

Of these two roles only the first is in any sense problematic and requires a detailed examination. The second role of causal reasoning mentioned presents us with nothing novel since the same role has already been seen in the case of demonstrative reasoning. That is, given a certain desire, demonstrative reasoning may provide the means of satisfying that desire. And now Hume is saying that given a certain passion or desire causal reasoning may assist us in fulfilling it. For example, if I have the desire to study the Bertrand Russell papers, causal reasoning can be employed to direct me to McMaster University in Hamilton, Ontario, Canada.

As mentioned above, it is the first role Hume assigns to causal reasoning which is somewhat problematic. We have seen Hume's argument that since morals excite passions and produce or prevent actions, and since reason cannot do these things, it follows that moral rules are not conclusions of reason. However, if reason can excite passions it seems as though the second premise of Hume's argument is false. Accordingly, we must examine what Hume means by reason being able to excite passions, and we must

[33] T. 118.
[34] T. 459. See also T. 416.

attempt to reconcile this claim with his claim that reason has no influence on our passions and actions.[35]

I argued earlier that for Hume desire and aversion can come about either from a present pleasure or pain, or from the anticipation of my own or someone else's pleasure or pain. Since we are now concerned with reason exciting a desire, it follows that we need not attend here to the former, that is, to the cases where desire and aversion are caused by a present pleasure or pain, since no causal *inference* would be involved in exciting the desire. Accordingly, if causal reasoning is to excite desire or aversion it must involve cases where desire and aversion arise through the anticipation of my own or someone else's pleasure or pain. Because the latter would involve us in a discussion of the indirect passions it can be left until the next chapter where this matter is taken up.[36] We can then confine our attention here to the case where causal reasoning excites a desire through the anticipation of some pleasure for me.

Hume maintains that all passions depend on the imagination and the manner in which it entertains certain ideas :

... it is by means of thought only that anything operates upon our passions ...[37]

I have already observ'd, that belief is nothing but a lively idea related to a present impression. This vivacity is a requisite circumstance to the exciting all our passions, the calm as well as the violent; nor has a mere fiction of the imagination any considerable influence upon either of them. 'Tis too weak to take hold of the mind, or be attended with emotion.[38]

Thus, the temper of a person or his general disposition depends on the imagination and not just on his passions :

'Tis remarkable, that lively passions commonly attend a lively imagination. In this respect, as well as others, the force of the passion depends as much on the temper of the person, as the nature or situation of the object.[39]

'Tis remarkable, that the imagination and affections have a close union together, and that nothing, which affects the former, can be entirely indifferent to the latter.[40]

---

[35] Mrs. Kydd has also seen that these problems are present (see her book, p. 104 ff). However, my solutions are entirely different from hers.

[36] See the next chapter, footnote 56.

[37] D. Hume's *An Abstract of a Treatise of Human Nature*, 1740 (Reprinted with an Introduction by J. M. Keynes and P. Sraffa, Anchor Books, Hamden, Connecticut, 1965), p. 32.

[38] T. 427.

[39] T. 427.

[40] T. 424.

We must now relate these passages to our present problem of determining what Hume means when he says that reason can excite passions.

In a much too neglected section of the *Treatise* (Book I, Part III, Section x) Hume gives an indication of his meaning when he speaks of the influence of certain ideas on the will. He observes that not every idea of pleasure and pain affects the will :

... did every idea influence our actions, our condition would not be much mended. For such is the unsteadiness and activity of thought, that the images of every thing, especially of goods and evils [i.e. pleasures and pains] are always wandering in the mind; and were it moved by every idle conception of this kind, it would never enjoy a moment's peace and tranquility.[41]

The ideas of pleasures and pains which do affect desire are those which we believe can be brought about to affect us, and one means of making us believe that they can be brought about to affect us is to infer them causally from some present impression of the senses :

Nature has, therefore, chosen a medium, and has neither bestow'd on every idea of good and evil the power of actuating the will, nor has yet entirely excluded them from this influence. Tho' an idle fiction has no efficacy, yet we find by experience, that the ideas of those objects [i.e. the ideas of those goods and evils or pleasures and pains] which we believe are or will be existent, produce in a lesser degree the same effect with those impressions, which are immediately present to the senses and perception. The effect, then, of belief is to raise up a simple idea to an equality with our impressions, and bestow on it a like influence on the passions ... this, then, may both serve as an additional argument for the present system, and give us a notion after what manner our reasonings from causation are able to operate upon the will and passions.[42]

Hume does not intend to hold that causal inferences are the only means of getting an idea of pleasure and pain to affect the will.[43] He only intends that it is one such means.

(We are now in a position to explain why it is that causal reasoning can excite a passion whereas demonstrative reasoning cannot. Demonstrative reasoning is always confined to finding some relation or other between the ideas compared; causal reasoning is employed to associate a present impression with some other idea constantly conjoined with it. Consequently, demonstrative reasoning cannot present the mind with the prospect of pleasure or pain.)

---

[41] T. 119.
[42] T. 119-120.
[43] For some other ways of getting an idea to affect the will, see T. 426-427.

Having shown what Hume means when he speaks of causal inferences exciting passions, we must determine whether this is consistent with his claim that reason has no influence on our passions and action. It is my contention that these two claims are consistent in the light of the meaning which Hume attaches to the words 'activity' and 'inactivity'. It will be recalled from the last chapter that what Hume is trying to show in 'Of the Influencing Motives of the Will' is that reason is incapable of yielding practical judgments. Now, a faculty for Hume is 'active' if it can yield practical judgments, and inactive if it cannot.[44] Hume's examination of the influence of reason has shown that reason can excite a passion, but it also regards reason as incapable of providing a practical judgment enjoining us to seek the object to which the passion is directed. In other words, reason of itself is always indifferent as regards ends. Reason, therefore, remains inactive in Hume's sense, and can never alone influence action.

(C) Only passions can oppose passions

For Hume, then, the role of reason is always directive – it either directs a passion to its proper object, or it directs a passion to the means of acquiring its proper object. It can never, however, provide a practical judgment of its own. Given that it is directive only, Hume concludes that (a) 'the principle which opposes our passion, cannot be the same with reason, and is only call'd so in an improper sense' and (b) 'Reason is, and ought only to be the slave of the passions, and can never pretend to any other office than to serve and obey them'.[45]

As a result of (b) there can be no combat between reason and passion. In those cases where a passion is founded on causal reasoning, if the reasoning is shown to be faulty – that is, if an object believed to afford pleasure is found not to do so – the passion will no longer move us to act. Where a passion is directed to its end through reasoning, if the reasoning is seen to be in error, the passion again will no longer move us to act.

Having eliminated reason as a possible opponent of passion, Hume concludes that any opposition must be between passions themselves :

What we commonly understand by *passion* is a violent and sensible emotion of mind, when any good or evil is presented, or any object, which, by the original

---

[44] T. 457, and my preceding chapter.
[45] T. 415.

formation of our faculties, is fitted to excite appetite. By *reason* we mean affections of the very same kind with the former; but such as operate more calmly, and cause no disorder in the temper : Which tranquility leads us into a mistake concerning them, and causes us to regard them as conclusions only of our intellectual faculties.[46]

[46] T. 437.

CHAPTER VII

REASON AND MORAL CONDUCT

I. HOW MORAL RULES ARE OBTAINED :
THE THREE STAGES IN HUME'S ARGUMENT

We have seen that Hume holds that rules of action cannot be derived from reason although actions can be directed by reason. Reason is concerned with speculative, as opposed to practical judgments, and as such it itself has no concern with the ends of action. At most causal reasoning can direct a passion to its proper object or assist a passion in selecting the proper means to acquire something which is already desired. Demonstrative reasoning is confined to serving the passions only in the latter manner. Since a moral rule or precept is a type of practical judgment, and since reason is incapable of providing such judgments, Hume concludes that a moral rule cannot be derived from reason alone.

How then are moral rules obtained? Hume's argument for this proceeds through three stages. In the first, he discusses the error in obtaining moral rules and precepts "in every system of morality, which I have hitherto met with".[1] This discussion occurs in the famous "is-ought" passage. The second stage examines those perceptions through which moral distinctions are made; and the third stage for Hume results largely through attending to the conclusions arrived at in the first two stages. My procedure will follow Hume's pattern. Accordingly, we shall begin with an examination of the "is-ought" passage.

II. THE FIRST STAGE : THE "IS-OUGHT" PASSAGE

(A) Hume's meaning

The passage itself reads as follows :
I cannot forbear adding to these reasonings an observation, which may, perhaps,

---

[1] T. 469.

be found of some importance. In every system of morality, which I have hitherto met with, I have always remark'd, that the author proceeds for some time in the ordinary way of reasoning, and establishes the being of a God, or makes observations concerning human affairs; when of a sudden I am surpriz'd to find, that instead of the usual copulations of propositions, *is* and *is not*, I meet with no proposition that is not connected with an *ought*, or an *ought not*. This change is imperceptible; but is, however, of the last consequence. For as this *ought*, or *ought not*, expresses some new relation or affirmation, 'tis necessary that it shou'd be observ'd and explain'd; and at the same time that a reason should be given, for what seems altogether inconceivable, how this new relation can be a deduction from others, which are entirely different from it. But as authors do not commonly use this precaution, I shall presume to recommend it to the readers; and am persuaded, that this small attention wou'd subvert all the vulgar systems of morality, and let us see, that the distinction of vice and virtue is not founded merely on the relations of objects, nor is perceiv'd by reason.[2]

It will be helpful in discussing this passage to begin by setting out step by step what Hume is arguing :

1. All previous systems of morality begin by establishing the existence of God, or make observations concerning human affairs.
2. Suddenly, instead of finding propositions connected by 'is' and 'is not', he finds propositions connected with an 'ought' or an 'ought not'.
3. This change in the copula is never taken note of.
4. But it is important to do so.
5. The reason why this change must be noted is because (i) a statement containing the words 'ought' or 'ought not' expresses a new relation or fact, (ii) being new, we must have it pointed out to us and an explanation provided for how it comes to be and (iii) we need information on how this new relation can be deduced from others, which are different in kind from it, since the deduction seems to be logically impossible.
6. By attending to the need for having the perception giving rise to the 'ought-statement' pointed out to us and accounted for and by noting that it is not possible to deduce the 'ought-statement' from other relational statements we can see (i) that all commonly received moral systems are improperly founded, and (ii) that the way we apprehend vice and virtue is not simply through determining relations obtaining between objects, and (iii) that moral distinctions cannot be based on reason.

In reviewing this passage Professor Sparshott [3] maintains that Hume's thesis is a strange one since in the first place Hume gives no examples

---

[2] T. 469. Throughout this chapter I will sometimes for convenience only speak of 'ought-statements'. Whatever is said about these statements, however, should be regarded as applying also to statements containing the words 'ought not' and in general to all moral rules or prescriptions.

[3] Francis E. Sparshott, "Disputed Evaluations", *American Philosophical Quarterly*, Volume 7, Number 2, April 1950, p. 130 ff. Hereafter referred to as A.P.Q.

thereby concealing what fallacy would be committed. Sparshott also argues that Hume's thesis is a strange one because the most likely form for the condemned transition would not be fallacious, namely, a syllogism with two premises with 'is' and a conclusion with 'ought' : arson is forbidden by Jehovah; burning down the White House is arson; ergo, one ought not to burn the White House down. Now, although invalid as it stands, this argument can be validated by turning it into two syllogisms in Barbara. Thus, it now reads :

Everything Jehovah forbids is something one ought not to do.
Jehovah forbids arson.
_____
    Arson is something one ought not to do.
Arson is something one ought not to do.
Burning down the White House is arson.
_____
    Burning down the White House is something one ought not to do.

Sparshott concludes by saying that if this is the sort of argument Hume and his followers had in mind, then one may infer that either they hadn't taken even a one-semester course in logic or that they were not thinking about what they were saying : "The latter alternative is likely : since they had before their minds no actual instances of the alleged pattern of argument they had no occasion to ask whether any fallacy would really have been committed".[4]

Is it true that Hume had no actual instances in mind when writing this paragraph? And if it is true, can any reason be offered for this?

The 'is-ought' passage is placed at the end of Book III, Part I, Section i, in which section Hume attempts to show that moral distinctions are not derived from reason, and he begins the 'is-ought' passage by indicating that what this passage contains is an addition to what he has said. He begins with "I cannot forbear adding to these reasonings an observation ..." indicating that the theme of this section is being preserved. But what then has Hume tried to establish in the preceding pages? Among other things he sought to show that those who assert that vice and virtue consist in relations susceptible of certainty and demonstration run into certain absurdities. For example, whatever relations are selected "there is no one of these relations but what is applicable, not only to irrational, but also to an inanimate object".[5] Also, since animals are susceptible to the same relation as we are, if morality consisted in a deduction from these

[4] A.P.Q., p. 131.
[5] T. 464.

relations, then animals could have duties and obligations even though they cannot deduce them :

... I would fain ask any one, why incest in the human species is criminal, and why the very same action, and the same relations in animals have not the smallest turpitude and deformity ... Animals are susceptible of the same relations, with respect to each other, as the human species, and therefore wou'd also be susceptible of the same morality, if the essence of morality consisted in these relations. Their want of a sufficient degree of reason may hinder them from perceiving the duties and obligations of morality, but can never hinder these duties from existing; since they must antecedently exist, in order to their being perceiv'd. Reason must find them, and can never produce them.[6]

It is significant that this passage occurs on p. 468 of the *Treatise* and the 'is-ought' passage appears on p. 469. The latter passage can then be viewed as a continuation of the absurdities into which the rationalists fall when they maintain that vice and virtue consist in certain relations susceptible of certainty and demonstration. Just as the demonstrative-relational account of vice and virtue yields the absurdity that animals have obligations and duties, so it yields the further absurdity of attempting to derive this obligation or relation through a process of deductive reasoning which is, by the very nature of the deductive process, logically unable to handle the inference. In short, the inference the rationalists want to make is logically impossible.

Hume holds that in demonstrative reasoning, the conclusion contains some new relation which is dependent upon, and inferred from, certain other relations which are already known :

A speculative reasoner concerning triangles or circles considers the several known and given relations of the parts of these figures, and then infers some unknown relation, which is dependent on the former.[7]

Those who hold that duties are demonstrable are then for Hume committed to showing how this new relation of duty can arise from other relations. Now, the only relations which Hume will admit in demonstrative reasoning are the four philosophical relations of resemblance, contrariety, degrees in any quality, and proportions in quantity or number, and in the 'is-ought' passage he argues that it is inconceivable how this relation of duty can arise from these philosophical relations. He also challenges his opponents to show him some other relations from which moral distinctions can be made,[8] although he feels certain that they cannot do it :

[6] T. 468.
[7] E. 289-290.
[8] T. 464.

When it is affirmed that two and three are equal to the half of ten, this relation of equality I understand perfectly... But when you draw thence a comparison to moral relations, I own that I am altogether at a loss to understand you. A moral action, a crime, such as ingratitude, is a complicated object. Does the morality consist in the relation of its parts to each other? How? After what manner? Specify the relation : be more particular and explicit in your propositions, and you will easily see their falsehood.[9]

Applying this discussion to Professor Sparshott's analysis of the 'is-ought' passage, we can conclude firstly that Hume is clearer about what he is saying than Sparshott allows since what lies behind the 'is-ought' passage is Hume's own theory of abstract or demonstrative reasoning, and what Hume is saying is that no 'ought-statement' can be deduced from other statements which express certain philosophical relations. In the light of my analysis of demonstrative reasoning we can now make clear what Hume means by this : Since all relational statements are statements expressing an equality or inequality between things in virtue of a common property, when Hume denies that 'ought-statements' are deducible from other statements expressing philosophical relations, he is holding that 'ought-statements' are not statements expressing such equalities or inequalities. Also, Professor Sparshott's attempted remedy to the faulty reasoning would not solve Hume's problem in this passage. For Sparshott's validation of the original argument he himself cites (arson is forbidden by Jehovah; burning down the White House is arson; ergo, one ought not to burn down the White House) depends in part upon providing an 'ought-statement' as one of the premises thereby ignoring Hume's problem of challenging others to show how they can maintain that obligations are in essence relations discerned through demonstrative reasoning from other relations. Hume is not, in the 'is-ought' passage, saying that all arguments which have an 'ought' in the conclusion are invalid (even though he might have believed it); he is rather saying that *if 'ought-statements' are relational statements then it is inconceivable how they can be derived from other relational statements which do not have the word 'ought'*. Hume's problem is to determine how we apprehend our duties : it is not what valid inferences he can draw from practical moral propositions which embody our duties.

What sorts of arguments might Hume have encountered in his predecessors which would lead him to react to these arguments in the 'is-ought' passage. The context of the 'is-ought' passage makes it clear that Hume is actually concerned with those who draw comparisons between morality and mathematics. Thus, it is thinkers like Clarke that Hume has in mind

[9] E. 288.

inasmuch as Clarke repeatedly draws such comparisons.[10] In an earlier chapter I showed that Clarke did not actually hold that moral rules are demonstrable but only that moral rules are obtained by determining through causal reasoning what is in the public benefit. In this respect the analogy with mathematics is misleading. And it is interesting to note that when Hume begins his discussion of Clarke's position he points out that he has never yet found any Clarkian (or anyone else) who has provided a demonstration in morality :

There has been an opinion very industriously propagated by certain philosophers, that morality is susceptible of demonstration; and tho' no one has ever been able to advance a single step in those demonstrations; yet 'tis taken for granted, that this science may be brought to an equal certainty with geometry or algebra. Upon this supposition, vice and virtue, must consist in some relations ... Let us therefore, begin with examining this hypothesis, and endeavour, if possible, to fix those moral qualities, which have been so long the objects of our fruitless researches. Point out distinctly the relations, which constitute morality or obligation, that we may know wherein they consist, and after what manner we must judge of them.[11]

Thus, it appears true to say, as Professor Sparshott does, that Hume had no actual instances of the alleged argument before his mind. But this is not quite enough, since in the 'is-ought' passage Hume remarks that in every previous system of morality which he has read the author moves from a proof of God's existence or observations concerning human actions to certain 'ought-statements', leading one to believe that one could pick up any book on morals and find instances of the alleged argument. However, I think that this is not Hume's meaning. For Hume is not saying that every previous moralist has *attempted* to deduce an 'ought-statement' from statements about God or about human affairs : All that he says is that "of a sudden I am surpriz'd to find that instead of the usual copulations of propositions *is*, and *is not*, I meet with no proposition that is not connected with an *ought* or an *ought not*". Presumably the only relations which would be relevant to a demonstration of an 'ought-statement' would be those between men and God and between men and other men. Accordingly, what Hume is doing is to challenge the rationalists to show how such a

---

[10] In one place Clarke writes : "... in like manner as no one, who is instructed in Mathematicks, can forbear giving his Assent to every Geometrical Demonstration, of which he understands the Terms ... so no man, who either has patience and opportunities to examine and consider things himself ... concerning the necessary relations and dependencies of things, can avoid giving his Assent to the fitness and reasonableness of his governing all his Actions by the Law or Rule before mentioned ... (S.B. II, p. 15-16).

[11] T. 463.

demonstration is possible, in the light of the fact that his own analysis of demonstrative reasoning shows how such an argument must be composed, namely, with statements expressing certain philosophical relations in the premises, and a statement containing the word 'ought' in the conclusion. As such the 'ought-statement' would be a relational statement also, and Hume asserts it to be logically impossible for 'ought-statements' to be relational statements which are derived from other relational statements which do not contain the word 'ought'.

(B) Hume's own program outlined

In the course of this rather lengthy discussion we have been able to explicate some of what is involved in points (1), (3), (4), and (5) which I set down earlier immediately after quoting the 'is-ought' passage. That is, we have seen why Hume believes that attention must be given to the sentence containing the word 'ought' in the case of those who hold that moral rules are demonstrable in the way the truths of mathematics can be demonstrated. But the passage as I set it out contains more than the above and I will conclude my discussion of this passage by treating the other points Hume makes. This will lead us into the second phase of Hume's analysis, viz. discussion of those perceptions through which Hume holds that moral distinctions are made.

Steps two through four present little difficulty : Step two simply takes note of the fact that the copula is altered from the verb 'to be' to 'ought'; step three points out that no reason is given for how the 'ought-statement' is arrived at; and step four indicates that it is important to do so. It is when we reach step five that we can see not only Hume's complaint against others but also the program he sets for himself.

I have indicated that the fifth step makes three points, the first of which states that "this *ought* or *ought not* expresses some new relation or affirmation" and which I have interpreted as meaning that a statement containing 'ought' or 'ought not' expresses some new relation or fact. I read Hume in this way since the 'is-ought' passage is the concluding paragraph in a section which began with the question of whether it is by means of our ideas or impressions that we distinguish between vice and virtue and with the problem of whether moral rules and precepts can be discerned through ideas or impressions. Thus, when Hume states that the change from 'is-statements' to 'ought-statements' expresses some new relation or affirmation I take him to be reminding us of the alternatives available for obtaining 'ought-statements' : An 'ought-statement' either expresses a new relation obtained by deduction from other relational statements, or it expresses some impression or matter of fact. Also, if the statement is read making the expression 'new relation' and 'affirmation' synonyms, then Hume must be interpreted to mean that 'ought' and 'ought not' do in fact express some relation which Hume would have to explain when he discusses obligation. However, since he only recognizes demonstrative reasoning as the means of inferring relations (causal inferences only enable us to infer matters of fact) Hume would then have to do what he argued is logically impossible, viz. derive an 'ought-statement' from other relational statements which do not contain the word 'ought'. As we shall see, Hume's main thesis concerning 'ought-statements' is that they do not express relations at all, and are not founded solely on demonstrative reasoning. In the light of these considerations, then, I propose that the term 'affirmation' is intended to indicate the only alternative to an 'ought' or 'ought-not statement' expressing some new relation, namely, it must express some impression or matter of fact.

The second point which the fifth step makes is that since the 'ought' or 'ought-not statement' expresses either a new relation or a new fact, we must have either the relation or the fact pointed out to us so that we can have the referent of such statements, and we require an explanation for how this new relation or fact comes to be. The third point in the fifth step rules out deduction as the means of obtaining a statement containing 'ought' or 'ought-not', thereby leaving an impression as the only source of 'ought-statements'. If Hume asked that the rationalists point out the relation giving rise to 'ought-statements', so Hume can be asked to point out the impression giving rise to such statements. Further, if an explanation was demanded by Hume of the rationalists for how this alleged new relation could be deduced, so an explanation can be asked of Hume as to how the impression giving rise to 'ought' and 'ought-not statements' arises. Accordingly, Hume has two tasks before him, namely, to identify the impressions giving rise to moral rules, and to explain how these impressions arise.

The first point made in the sixth step is that attention to the three points in step five shows that all commonly received moral systems are improperly founded. The reason for this is clear, namely, no one has yet accounted for a moral rule even though all commonly received moral systems employ them. It is not only incumbent upon the rationalists to account for 'ought-statements', it is incumbent upon anyone who uses such statements since until this is done such statements are without any referent or explanation.

The last two points in step six state that attention to the three points in step five shows that vice and virtue cannot be relations between objects and they cannot be based on reason, the only faculty which discovers relations. Now these two points are noteworthy since throughout this passage Hume has been talking of moving from statements with the copula 'is' and 'is not' to statements connected by 'ought' and 'ought not', and yet in the last two points in step six he speaks of distinguishing vice and virtue and the fact that the preceding discussion on moral rules can assist us in determining how we distinguish vice and virtue. In other words, Hume is saying that only the faculty capable of distinguishing vice and virtue is capable of yielding moral rules.

Since reason is incapable of distinguishing vice and virtue it follows that this distinction cannot be based on a comparison of ideas, but must stem from certain impressions or matters of fact. Before turning to Hume's analysis of obligation we must first turn to his discussion of those impressions through which we distinguish vice and virtue.

III. THE SECOND STAGE : EXAMINING THE IMPRESSIONS WHICH GIVE RISE TO MORAL DISTINCTIONS

(A) Identifying these impressions

Hume begins his discussion of those impressions through which we distinguish vice and virtue in Section ii of Book III of the *Treatise* :

Thus the course of the argument leads us to conclude, that since vice and virtue are not discoverable merely by reason, or the comparison of ideas, it must be by means of some impression or sentiment they occasion, that we are able to mark the difference betwixt them. Our decisions concerning moral rectitude and depravity are evidently perceptions; and as all perceptions are either impressions or ideas, the exclusion of the one is a convincing argument for the other. Morality, therefore, is more properly felt than judg'd of; tho' this feeling or sentiment is commonly so soft and gentle that we are apt to confound it with an idea ...[12]

Having established that impressions are the only source of moral distinctions, Hume proceeds to ask about the nature of these impressions : "Here we cannot remain long in suspense, but must pronounce the impression arising from virtue, to be agreaeble, and that proceeding from vice to be uneasy".[13]

Hume is not altogether clear about the type of perception we actually have when we pronounce something virtuous or vicious. He does say, as we saw above, that the impression arising from virtue is agreeable and that from vice is uneasy. Nevertheless, many perceptions are agreeable and

[12] T. 470.
[13] T. 470.

many others uneasy which we do not consider as moral perceptions. Accordingly, further refinements are necessary. In the *Treatise* he says that "the distinguishing impressions, by which moral good or evil is known, are nothing but *particular* pains or pleasures".[14] "An action, or sentiment, or character, is virtuous or vicious ... because its view causes pleasure or uneasiness of a particular kind. In giving a reason, therefore, for the pleasure or uneasiness, we sufficiently explain the vice or virtue. To have a sense of virtue is nothing but to *feel* a satisfaction of a particular kind from the contemplation of a character".[15] In the *Enquiry Concerning the Principles of Morals*, on the other hand, Hume tells us that "this sentiment can be no other than a feeling for the happiness of mankind, and a resentment of their misery since these are the different ends which virtue and vice have a tendency to promote".[16] Or again, three pages later he says that "the approbation or blame ... which ensues cannot be the work of the judgment but of the heart; and it is not a speculative proposition or affirmation, but an active feeling or sentiment ... which we unavoidably feel". At the end of the first appendix Hume drops this strictness in regard to this impression and claims that "it is requisite that there should be some sentiment which it touches – some internal taste or feeling, or whatever you please to call it ..." [17]

It should be noticed that the moral sentiment is redefined in the *Enquiry* from whatever meaning it is to have in the *Treatise*. There is no suggestion in the *Treatise* that we have a feeling for the happiness of mankind. In fact, in one passage Hume states that "in general, it may be affirmed, that there is no such passion in human minds, as the love of mankind, merely as such, independent of personal qualities, of services, or of relation to ourself".[18] It is true, Hume claims, that whenever we are in contact with other people, their happiness or misery affects us to some extent, but "this proceeds merely from sympathy, and is no proof of such an universal affection to mankind." If then we are to have a feeling for the happiness of mankind and a resentment of their misery this must come about through sympathy. Just how much assistance sympathy can be is not yet clear since Hume repeatedly maintains that the impressions giving rise to vice and virtue are pleasures and pains of a particular kind, that "when any action, or quality of the mind, pleases us *after a certain manner*, we say it

[14] T. 471.
[15] T. 471.
[16] E. 105.
[17] E. 472.
[18] T. 481.

is virtuous; and when the neglect, or non-performance of it, displeases us *after a like manner*, we say that we lie under an obligation to perform it".[19] Whether sympathy can generate the impressions required and cause them to please or displease us in the proper manner is a matter we will examine later after a general understanding of sympathy itself.

Before beginning our discussion of the moral sentiments in the *Treatise* several other points should be made. In the first place, when Hume speaks of vice and virtue as any action or quality of the mind which pleases or displeases us after a certain manner he makes it clear that by this manner of being pleased or displeased he means that the pleasure of pain must arise without having our own interest in mind :

'Tis only when a character is considered in general, without reference to our particular interest, that it causes such a feeling or sentiment, as denominates it morally good or evil.[20]

Secondly, Hume points out that vice and virtue must give rise to one of the four indirect passions – pride, humility, love, and hatred :

... virtue and vice ... must give rise to one of these four passions; which clearly distinguishes them from the pleasure and pain arising from inanimate objects, that often bear no relation to us : And this is, perhaps, the most considerable effect that virtue and vice have upon the human mind.[21]

In another passage he identifies the moral sentiments with these four indirect passions :

... these two particulars are to be consider'd as equivalent, with regard to our mental qualities, *virtue* and the power of producing love or pride, *vice* and the power of producing humility or hatred. In every case, therefore, we must judge of the one by the other; and may pronounce any *quality* of the mind virtuous, which causes love or pride; and any one vicious, which causes hatred or humility.[22]

Thus, two distinguishing characteristics of the moral sentiments are that they are identified with the passions of love, hatred, pride, and humility, and that when these passions are experienced in a moral situation our own interest cannot be involved. A third requirement for the moral sentiment, as we shall see, is that it be based on an adequate comprehension of the facts and relations involved in the situation.

[19] T. 517.
[20] T. 472.
[21] T. 473.
[22] T. 575.

At first sight, the first two requirements, namely, that of exciting one of pride, humility, love, and hatred, and being disinterested, appear to be incompatible since the four passions always appear to operate in a self-interested manner. The central problem of Hume's causal account of the origin or the moral sentiment then becomes that of reconciling these two seemingly incompatible criteria for the moral sentiment itself. My account of the moral sentiment will terminate with a discussion of this reconciliation.

(B) The origin of moral impressions

Moral distinctions, according to Hume, are based on certain sentiments of pleasure and pain. And his insistence on this point both in the *Treatise* and the second *Enquiry* often leads commentators to think that there can be little, if any, role for reason in the making of moral distinctions. In point of fact, however, this is not Hume's view, since strictly stated his position is only that 'the final sentence' is based on sentiment, but in arriving at this final sentence much reasoning can take place. Early in his analysis in the second *Enquiry* when predicting how his own examination will turn out he writes :

... *reason* and *sentiment* concur in almost all moral determinations and conclusions. The final sentence, it is probable, which pronounces characters and actions amiable or odious ... that which renders morality an active principle and constitutes virtue our happiness, and vice our misery : it is probable, I say, that this final sentence depends on some internal sense or feeling ... But in order to pave the way for such a sentiment, and give a proper discernment of its object, it is often necessary, we find, that much reasoning should precede, that nice distinctions be made, just conclusions drawn, distant comparisons formed, complicated relations examined, and general facts fixed and ascertained.[23]

And in the first Appendix this position is affirmed :

A speculative reasoner concerning triangles or circles considers the several known and given relations of the parts of these figures, and then infers some unknown relation, which is dependent on the former. But in moral deliberations we must be acquainted beforehand with all the objects, and all their relations to each other; and from a comparison of the whole, fix our choice or approbation.[24]

In this respect morality resembles our pronouncements concerning beauty and deformity :

This doctrine will become still more evident, if we compare moral beauty with natural, to which in many particulars it bears so near a resemblance. It is on

[23] E. 173.
[24] E. 289-290.

the proportion, relation, and position of parts, that all natural beauty depends; but it would be absurd thence to infer, that the perception of beauty, like that of truth in geometrical problems, consists wholly in the perception of relations ... In all the sciences, our mind from the known relations investigates the unknown. But in all decisions of taste or external beauty, all the relations are beforehand obvious to the eye; and we thence proceed to feel a sentiment ...[25]

With the need for the employment of reason and the subsequent appearance of the moral sentiment both in aesthetics and morality, it follows that for each situation there is an appropriate or 'proper' sentiment and a proper judgment with the result that moral sentiments and judgments are subject to correction :

... in many orders of beauty, particularly those of the finer arts, it is requisite to employ much reasoning, in order to feel the proper sentiment; and a false relish may frequently be corrected by argument and reflection. There are just grounds to conclude, that moral beauty partakes much of this latter species, and demands the assistance of our intellectual faculties, in order to give it a suitable influence on the human mind.[26]

Several points emerge from this discussion, the first being that it is Hume's view that moral situations can be accurately assessed if based on a proper understanding of the facts and relations involved. For each different moral situation there is a proper sentiment. Throughout the discussion of the influencing motives of the will we saw Hume maintain that reason can only provide a directive role because it is confined to the speculative judgments of the understanding. And it is important to point out that within the context of Hume's moral theory the role of reason remains directive, since reason can merely present the facts and relations of the situation thereby directing the moral sentiments to their proper objects :

In these sentiments then, not in a discovery of relations of any kind, do all moral determinations consist. Before we can pretend to form any decision of this kind, everything must be known and ascertained on the side of the object or action. Nothing remains but to feel, on our part, some sentiment of blame or approbation; whence we pronounce the action criminal or virtuous.[27]

The one alteration which Hume's view makes concerning what he said in the section on the influencing motives of the will concerns demonstrative reasoning. For in that section demonstrative reasoning was confined to assisting a passion in the selection of the proper means to acquire some-

[25] E. 291.
[26] E. 173.
[27] E. 291.

thing already desired. Now, however, it has been assigned a part in directing a passion or sentiment to its proper object, the same role previously assigned by Hume to causal reasoning. Accordingly, in the case of the moral sentiments, both kinds of reasoning can be employed in order to "excite a passion by informing us of the existence of something which is a proper object of it".[28]

Although an adequate understanding of a moral situation should yield the proper moral sentiment, Hume also shows concern for this view because human sentiments are not disinterested, and are variable, whereas we can speak of a proper moral sentiment only where as a result of an adequate understanding of the situation, our sentiments can be disinterested and stabilized. Hence Hume is worried about situations where we have an adequate understanding of a situation and yet may err regarding the proper feeling in that situation. This leads us to a discussion of Hume's concept of sympathy.

Hume maintains that many qualities acquire our approbation because of their tendency to the good of mankind and are consequently regarded as moral virtues. This, for example, is true in the case of justice : "No virtue is more esteem'd than justice, and no vice more detested than injustice ... Now justice is a moral virtue, merely because it has that tendency to the good of mankind".[29] It is also true in the case of most other virtues :

... most of those qualities, which we *naturally* approve of, have actually that tendency, and render a man a proper member of society : While the qualities, which we *naturally* disapprove of, have a contrary tendency ... That many of the natural virtues have this tendency to the good of society, no one can doubt of. Meekness, benificence, charity, generosity, clemency, moderation, equity, bear the greatest figure among the moral qualities, and are commonly denominated the social virtues, to mark their tendency to the good of society.[30]

When discussing personal identity in the first book of the *Treatise* Hume remarked that there are two senses of personal identity : "personal identity as it regards our thought or imagination, and as it regards our passions or the concern we take in ourselves".[31] So far as our passional nature is concerned, therefore, our concern is only with ourselves. If then we are to take a concern in society or the interests of others a new principle is

28 E. 459.
29 T. 577.
30 T. 578.
31 T. 253.

required whereby a concern for others can affect us in much the same way as our concern for ourselves. Hume finds this principle in sympathy :

... moral distinctions arise, in a great measure, from the tendency of qualities and characters to the interests of society, and ... 'tis our concern for that interest, which makes us approve or disapprove them. Now, we have no such extensive concern for society but from sympathy; and consequently 'tis that principle, which takes us so far out of ourselves, as to give us the same pleasure or uneasiness in the characters of others, as if they had a tendency to our own advantage or loss.[32]

Some qualities are called virtuous even though they have no direct tendency to the good of mankind. Such qualities are, for example, temperance, prudence, and assiduity.[33] And regarding such qualities Hume maintains :

Every quality of the mind is denominated virtuous, which gives pleasure by the mere survey; as every quality, which produces pain, is call'd vicious. This pleasure and this pain may arise from four different sources. For we reap a pleasure from the view of a character, which is naturally fitted to be useful to others, or to the person himself, or which is agreeable to others, or to the person himself.[34]

But here, again, the pleasure or pain which I receive from surveying these qualities where my own interest is not involved arises through sympathy :

Virtue is consider'd as means to an end. Means to an end are only valued so far as the end is valued. But the happiness of strangers affects us by sympathy alone. To that principle, therefore, we are to ascribe the sentiment of approbation, which arises from the survey of all the virtues. that are useful to society, or to the person possess'd of them. These form the most considerable part of our morality.[35]

When Hume first introduces sympathy, he speaks of it as "that propensity we have to sympathize with others, and to receive by communication their inclinations and sentiments, however different from, or even contrary to our own".[36] We are told that when any affection is transmitted through sympathy, we first know it only through its effects, and by those external signs in the countenance and conservation which convey an idea of it.[37] He then states that "this idea is presently converted into an impression" so as to "produce an equal emotion, as any original affection".[38] How is

[32] T. 579.
[33] T. 587.
[34] T. 591.
[35] T. 619. See also T. 588, T. 618.
[36] T. 316.
[37] T. 317.
[38] T. 317.

this conversion of an idea into an impression brought about? In his answer Hume has recourse to the impression of self and the natural relations of causality, resemblance, and contiguity :

'Tis evident, that the idea, or rather impression of ourselves is always intimately present with us, and that our consciousness gives us so lively a conception of our own person that 'tis not possible to imagine, that any thing can in this particular go beyond it. Whatever object, therefore, is related to ourselves must be conceived with a like vivacity of conception; and tho' this relation shou'd not be so strong as that of causation, it must still have a considerable influence. Resemblance and contiguity are relations not to be neglected; especially when by an inference from cause and effect, and by the observation of external signs, we are inform'd of the real existence of the object, which is resembling or contiguous.[39]

This account is intended to show that sympathy operates in the case of the passions in a manner parallel to the operation of belief in causal inferences. Hume himself takes note of this :

What is principally remarkable in this whole affair is the strong confirmation these phenomena give to the foregoing system concerning the understanding, and consequently to the present one concerning the passions; since these are analogous to each other ... sympathy is exactly correspondent to the operations of our understanding ...[40]

This account of sympathy raises certain problems. I have been maintaining throughout this book that the distinguishing feature of impressions is that they are paradigmatic, that is, that although impressions are caused, their content is not copied from any other perceptions either directly or through a comparison of ideas. Ideas, on the other hand, are derivative in the sense that their content is traceable either to some impression or to other ideas which are compared thereby yielding the idea in question. Now, however, in Hume's account of sympathy, we find him referring to the conversion of an idea into an impression, thereby challenging this interpretation. Not only is my interpretation of the doctrine of impressions and ideas being challenged through the account of sympathy, but also

---

[39] T. 317-318. Hume never denied that there was an impression of the self; he merely claimed that he could not provide an adequate causal account for it. Also, the impression of the self involved in sympathy is not the self dealt with when he was treating of the understanding. The self involved in sympathy is that self which "regards our passions or the concern we take in ourselves" (T. 253), although when an 'opinion' is infused by sympathy it may be enlivened by the self which "regards our thought or imagination" (T. 253). Hume does not discuss this matter in great enough detail to allow us to treat this matter further.

[40] T. 319-320.

the question with which he began the third book of the *Treatise* would require reinvestigating if he means that the distinction between impressions and ideas is in terms of force and vivacity. For when Hume there asks 'whether 'tis by means of our ideas or impressions we distinguish betwixt vice and virtue, and pronounce an action blameable or praiseworthy' it appears that this question is being raised because there is a difference between impressions and ideas which is more basic than force and vivacity. However, if the criterion of impressions and ideas is one of force and vivacity, then even if reason could yield moral distinctions (which we have seen Hume claim it cannot) this would not by itself establish that the conclusions of reason are ideas and not impressions. The only means of deciding whether the conclusions of reason are impressions or ideas would, on this account, be through introspection, that is, by examining the vivaciousness of the conclusion or perception. Further, even if reason cannot be the source of moral distinctions (as Hume believes his argument shows) this would not by itself establish that moral distinctions are based on impressions, since it may still be the case that moral distinctions are based on our more languid perceptions. Again, here, the issue would be decidable only through introspection. But, being so decidable, it is not at all clear why one answer must be given for all moral distinctions : It may be that some are based on our vivid perceptions or impressions and others on our more languid perceptions or ideas. In short, if the criterion of force and vivacity is being used by Hume when he raises the opening question in the third book of the *Treatise*, the question itself loses much of its potential for forming the basis of a moral theory, since the question it raises is answerable through introspection only, and we are totally baffled by the ensuing discussion in Book III which seeks means other than introspection for answering the question. Also, if the criterion of force and vivacity is being employed by Hume it is difficult to understand what he means when he concludes in Section two of Part one of the Third book of the *Treatise* that "Morality, therefore, is more properly felt than judg'd of; tho' this feeling or sentiment is commonly so soft and gentle, that we are apt to confound it with an idea'. In fact, if the criterion of force and vivacity is being employed, it is difficult, if not impossible, to see why this conclusion is so important. Why should it be significant if we find that morality is based on perceptions of a certain vivaciousness? The text yields no answer. In fact, how would such a finding disprove what Hume takes to be the position of the rationalists such as Clarke? Again, the text provides no answer. We must then return to Hume's account of sympathy in order to determine what Hume means when he speaks of the conversion of an idea into an impression. If the text reveals – which I will try to show it does not – that Hume intends the phrase 'the conversion of an idea into an impression' to be taken literally, then we will have to return to Book III in order to re-examine what Hume could possibly mean by the question with which the third book begins. Since sympathy is regarded by Hume as the chief source of moral distinctions, whatever account we give of sympathy must be such that it throws light on the opening question of the third book of the *Treatise*, and is consistent with the answer he gives to this question in Book III, Part I, Section ii. Also, of course, the analysis of sympathy must aid us in understanding how Hume believes this analysis helps to disprove his interpretation of thinkers like Samuel Clarke.

I shall now attempt to put forward reasons for holding that when Hume speaks of sympathy as involving the conversion of an idea into an impression this must be regarded in a sense other than that in which Hume is taken as meaning that force and vivacity provide the means of distinguishing impressions and ideas.

Hume maintains as we have seen that the operation of sympathy is "exactly correspondent" to the operations of the understanding, and, of course, what he has in mind is the parallel between sympathy and belief. Now belief is analyzed by Hume as "a lively idea related to or associated with a present impression".[41] Thus "when any impression becomes present to us, it not only transports the mind to such ideas as are related to it, but likewise communicates to them a share of its force and vivacity".[42] Hume holds that the natural relation of causality is requisite in order to believe any idea associated with a present impression since only this relation informs us of the *existence* of objects which are not directly perceived. Thus although the natural relations of resemblance and contiguity can enable us to associate ideas, it is only through the natural relation of causality that the idea associated with the impression is believed. An idea believed, Hume remarks, is "more strong, firm, and vivid, than the loose reveries of a castle-builder";[43] belief "is nothing but a more forcible and vivid conception of an idea".[44]

It is important to notice that throughout his discussion of belief Hume maintains that the vivacity given to the inferred idea by the present impression simply provides a more forcible conception of *an idea*. He nowhere states that the vivacity acquired by the idea turns the idea into an

[41] T. 96. Italics omitted.
[42] T. 98. Italics omitted.
[43] T. 97.
[44] T. 107.

impression. Now, if sympathy is exactly correspondent to the operation of belief then here too there should be an inference to an idea through the natural relation of causality and an enlivening of this idea. And this is precisely the position which Hume adopts :

Whatever object ... is related to ourselves must be conceived with a like vivacity of conception, according to the foregoing principles; ... resemblance and contiguity are relations not to be neglected; especially when by an inference from cause and effect, and by the observation of external signs, we are inform'd of the real existence of the object, which is resembling or contiguous.[45]

In fact, in at least one passage Hume actually points out that the idea in sympathy when enlivened remains an idea : "All these relations [namely, cause and effect, resemblance, and contiguity] when united together, convey the impression or consciousness of our own person to the *idea* of the sentiments or passions of others, and makes us conceive *them* [i.e. these ideas] in the strongest possible manner".[46]

A further consideration arises out of the parallel between belief and sympathy. When Hume speaks of an idea believed through a causal inference he makes it clear that except in those cases where the imagination suffers severe disorders [47] we are always able to distinguish between an idea which is believed as a result of its relation to some present impression and impressions of the senses; that is, we are able to distinguish our belief that something will exist from the fact that something does exist. We do not confuse the believed idea with an existent. Through sympathy, Hume asserts, opinions [48] as well as sentiments can be communicated. Accordingly, if in the case of sympathy an idea is converted into an impression, it follows that any opinion so communicated must be confused with or actually identified with the matter of fact corresponding to this opinion inasmuch as our impressions form our matters of fact. In other words, opinions transmitted through sympathy must affect us in the way in which ideas affect us when the imagination suffers from certain disorders.

An examination of sympathy in the light of the role it plays in the case of the passions of pride, humility, love and hatred, will also lend support to the view that Hume does not intend to found the distinction between impressions and ideas on force and vivacity. We must begin this part of our examination with an outline of the causes of these four passions.

[45] T. 317-318. See also T. 575-576.
[46] T. 318, my italics.
[47] T. 123.
[48] T. 319. See also T. 592.

When initiating his study of the passions, Hume asserts that they can be divided into the direct and indirect :

By direct passions I understand such as arise immediately from good or evil, from pain or pleasure. By indirect such as proceed from the same principles, but by the conjunction of other qualities ... under the indirect passions I comprehend pride, humility, ambition, vanity, love, hatred, envy, pity, malice, generosity, with their dependents. And under the direct passion, desire, aversion, grief, joy, hope, fear, despair and security.[49]

Hume begins his study of the passions with the indirect passions of pride and humility.[50] Since the passions of pride and humility are simple, no definition can be given of them. The object of both these passions is the self. Although the self is the object of these passions, it cannot be their cause since "as these passions are directly contrary, and have the same object in common; were their object also their cause; it could never produce any degree of the one passion, but at the same time it must excite an equal degree of the other; which opposition and contrariety must destroy both".[51] Regarding the causes of these passions, Hume distinguishes the quality which operates and the subject on which it is placed. For example, if one were proud of a beautiful house, we can distinguish between the quality which operates on the passion – in this case the beauty – from the subject on which it is placed, in this case the house.

In his next step Hume calls attention to two types of association. The one is the association of ideas which is based on the natural relations of causality, resemblance, and contiguity. The other is an association of impressions, although Hume observes that impressions are only associated by the natural relation of resemblance. These two kinds of association can assist each other "where they both concur in the same object".[52]

Applying this to the production of pride and humility, Hume first makes the following observations. Regarding the qualities of the objects which cause these passions they always produce the sensation of pain and pleasure independently of the passions themselves : "Thus the beauty of our person, of itself, and by its very appearance, gives pleasure, as well as pride; and its deformity, pain as well as humility".[53] The subjects on which these qualities adhere are always either parts of ourselves, or something nearly related to us. On the side of the passions themselves he finds

---

[49] T. 276-277.
[50] T. 227 ff.
[51] T. 278.
[52] T. 284.
[53] T. 285.

that the object of the passion is always the self, and that their sensations "constitute their being and essence. Thus pride is a pleasant sensation, and humility a painful; and upon the removal of the pleasure and pain, there is in reality no pride nor humility".[54] With all this material the production of these passions is accountable :

That cause, which excites the passions is related to the object, which nature has attributed to the passion, the sensation, which the cause separately produces, is related to the sensation of the passion : From this double relation of ideas and impressions, the passion is deriv'd. The one idea is easily converted into its correlative; and the one impression into that, which resembles and corresponds to it.[55]

The indirect passions of love and hatred are accounted for in much the same way except that the object of these passions is always some other thinking being. Thus, again here the cause of the passion is related to the object of the passion, and the sensation which the cause produces is related to the sensation of the passion.[56]

Throughout the *Treatise* Hume adhered to the view that the passions of pride and humility, love and hatred, are produced through a double relation of impressions and ideas, and this includes the two passages already quoted [57] in which Hume identifies these indirect passions with the moral sentiments. Since sympathy plays such a large role in Hume's moral theory, it would be inconsistent of Hume to maintain both that these passions arise through this double association and that they arise through sympathy, whereby an idea is converted into an impression, since

[54] T. 286.

[55] T. 286-287.

[56] Having now seen the manner in which the indirect passions are produced we are in a position to complete a matter introduced in the preceding chapter concerning the role which causal reasoning plays in exciting desire and aversion through the anticipation of someone else's pleasure or pain. To begin with, through causal reasoning I infer that a certain object will produce a certain pleasure or pain. This anticipation of pleasure or pain, as we have seen, produces the direct passions of desire and aversion. But if the object causing the pleasure or pain acquires a relation to some other person then all the ingredients are present for the production of love or hatred. (All of this discussion can be found at T. 574.) The passions of love and hatred, however, "are not compleated within themselves, nor rest in that emotion, which they produce, but carry the mind to something farther. Love is always follow'd by a desire of the happiness of the person belov'd, and an aversion to his misery : As hatred produces a desire of the misery and an aversion to the happiness of the person hated". (T. 367. See also T. 591).

[57] T. 473, T. 574-575. "I say then, that nothing can produce any of these passions without bearing it a double relation, viz. of ideas to the object of the passion, and of sensation to the passion itself". (T. 333).

if the latter is maintained as causing the passion there is no need for the double association. What, then, is the role of sympathy in causing these passions?

I submit that in sympathy as in belief the inferred idea which is enlivened raises up an idea to an equality with our impressions in the sense of giving such ideas a greater influence on the mind than they would otherwise have.[58] Thus through the sympathetic mechanism we are provided with ideas of pleasure and pain which take an adequate hold of the mind for them to replace the requirement discussed above, namely, that for the production of the indirect passions a sensation is required which resembles the sensation of the passion. Without the sympathetic mechanism I could, for example, only love someone who possessed some quality which produced a certain pleasure for me. Through sympathy, however, I am able to feel love for someone even where I have no connection with this person provided that some other person receives a separate pleasure from the mere contemplation of some quality related to this person, and provided that I am able to form a lively idea of the other person's pleasure; or provided the one who possesses this quality is proud of it, since here again, through sympathy I can partake of his pleasure and through the double relation I can experience the passion of love for this person. Regarding this latter point Hume writes in one place :

Upon the whole, there remains nothing, which can give us an esteem (esteem and contempt are species of love and hatred) for power and riches, and a contempt for meanness and poverty except the principle of *sympathy*, by which we enter into the sentiments of the rich and poor, and partake of their pleasures and uneasiness. Riches give satisfaction to their possessor; and this satisfaction is convey'd to the beholder by the imagination, which produces an idea resembling the original in force and vivacity. This agreeable idea or impression is connected with love, which is an agreeable passion. It proceeds from a thinking conscious being, which is the very object of love. From this relation of impressions, and identity of ideas, the passion arises, according to my hypothesis.[59]

Two important matters emerge from this account of the origin of our esteem or love for the wealthy. Firstly, assuming that the wealthy man is proud of his riches if sympathy were nothing but the conversion of an idea into an impression then it would follow that through sympathy I

---

[58] "Wherever we can make an idea approach the impressions in force and vivacity, it will likewise imitate them in its influence on the mind; and *vice versa*, where it imitates them in that influence ... this must proceed from its approaching them in force and vivacity". (T. 119).

[59] T. 362.

would experience the pride which the wealthy man experiences. However, since the object of pride is the self this is impossible since it is not my wealth. Accordingly, it is not his passion which I experience. Rather, I am able to experience through sympathy a lively idea of the pleasure which he receives from his riches. But this pleasure when felt by me produces, not pride, but love or esteem for him. Secondly, it is significant that in this quotation Hume speaks of that perception which is conveyed through sympathy as "this agreeable idea or impression" indicating that what is important here is that the feeling belonging to this perception resembles the feeling intrinsic to the passion of love. Sympathy does not convert an idea into an impression; it enables an idea to have an influence which approaches that of an impression.

If pride in others can produce love in us, it should follow that love or esteem in others for us should through sympathy produce pride in us. And this is precisely Hume's position :

We may observe, that no person is ever prais'd by another for any quality, which wou'd not, if real, produce, of itself, a pride in the person possesst of it. The eulogisms either turn upon his power, or riches, or family, or virtue; all of which are subjects of vanity ... 'Tis certain, then, that if a person consider'd himself in the same light, in which he appears to his admirer, he would first receive a separate pleasure, and afterwards a pride or self-satisfaction ... Now nothing is more natural than for us to embrace the opinions of others in this particular; both from *sympathy*, which renders all their sentiments intimately present to us; and from *reasoning*, which makes us regard their judgment, as a kind of argument for what they affirm.[60]

Again, here, we can see that what is communicated through sympathy is not the love of the other for me, because of some quality which I possess, but only the pleasure which he receives through its contemplation. The lively idea of his pleasure when felt by me is associated with the feeling of pride and through the double relation the passion of pride is produced in me.

In the light of the preceding considerations I conclude that nothing in Hume's account of sympathy shows that force and vivacity is being used by Hume as the basic criterion for distinguishing impressions from ideas. The belief that Hume is employing force and vivacity as the criterion for distinguishing impressions from ideas can arise only through misunderstanding what is inferred through sympathy, and through a total neglect of Hume's point that the indirect passions always require a double impulse in order to arise. Through sympathy we infer the pleasures or

[60] T. 370-371.

pains of others; these are enlivened in our minds through their relation with the self; by being enlivened they have a hold on the mind similar to that of an impression; as such these enlivened ideas can be associated with the sensation of the passion since they resemble them in feeling; and depending upon whether the quality which prompts this lively idea is related to me or to someone else the appropriate indirect passion arises through a double impulse. In his discussion of sympathy Hume is not concerned with undertaking a discussion of the basic distinction between impressions and ideas. His concern in his account of sympathy is to attempt to determine how the concern which we take in ourselves through the impression of the self can be extended so as to make us have some regard or concern for the feelings and well-being of others.

(In completing this part of our analysis it should be pointed out that a similar state of affairs arises at one place in his analysis of causality. Throughout this analysis he argues that the idea inferred through the natural relation of causality is enlivened through its association with a present impression of the senses. However, he once remarks that "not only an impression may give rise to reasoning, but that an idea may also have the same influence; especially upon my principle, that all our ideas are deriv'd from correspondent impressions".[61] The example he uses is that of entertaining an idea the corresponding impression of which has been forgotten, and Hume argues that simply through holding this idea I can conclude or believe that such an impression did once exist. How then are we to account for the vivacity of this conclusion? His answer is through the idea :

For as this idea is not here consider'd as the representation of any absent object, but as a real perception in the mind of which we are intimately conscious, it must be able to bestow on whatever is related to it, the same quality, call it firmness, or solidity or force, or vivacity ... *The idea here supplies the place of an impression, and is entirely the same, so far as regards our present purpose.*[62]

The only point of comparison I wish to draw between sympathy and this account is Hume's concession here that ideas can substitute for impressions and in some instances can affect the mind in a manner similar to impressions.)

Thus, neither the opening question of the third book of the *Treatise* nor Hume's answer to this question should be understood as though Hume is merely trying to determine whether vivacious or languid percep-

[61] T. 105.
[62] T. 106. Italics in text omitted. My own italics added.

tions enable us to make moral distinctions. Hume's concern in a possible role for ideas in making such distinctions centres around his belief that the conclusions of reason are always ideas since the content of such perceptions is traceable to other perceptions through comparison. In this sense then a conclusion of reason can never be an impression. In the event that reason is ruled out as the source of moral distinctions the only remaining alternative is that such distinctions are made through perceptions which, although caused, have a content which is not traceable to other perceptions either directly or through comparison. (Hume, as we saw, interpreted Clarke as maintaining that moral perceptions were deducible through a comparison of ideas.) Such perceptions or impressions are regarded as providing our facts or matters of fact. If there are such facts they must be apprehended in a manner consistent with the ways in which we apprehend impressions. Impressions are divided by Hume into those of sensation or reflection : "Of the first kind are all the impressions of the senses, and all bodily pains and pleasures : Of the second are the passions and other emotions resembling them".[63] Thus when Hume proceeds to identify the impressions giving rise to moral distinctions he looks to these two sources of facts :

Take any action allow'd to be vicious : Wilful murder, for instance. Examine it in all lights and see if you can find that matter of fact, or real existence, which you call *vice* ... The vice entirely escapes you, as long as you consider the objects. You can never find it, till you turn your reflexion into your own breast, and find a sentiment of disapprobation, which arises in you, towards this action. Here is a matter of fact; but 'tis the object of feeling, not of reason. It lies in yourself, not in the object.[64]

(C) How a disinterested standpoint is achieved

Thus far we have seen two areas where Hume maintains that reason enters into the moral evaluations we make. Both demonstrative and causal reasoning are necessary if we are to gain a proper understanding of situations; and the moral sentiment which we feel depends upon causal reasoning since it plays a key role in sympathy and the communication of the pleasures and pains which are required if any of the four indirect passions are to arise. But now, however, we must inquire further since as I have already mentioned, Hume is worried about cases wherein we have an adequate understanding of a situation and yet may err in evaluating

[63] T. 275.
[64] T. 469.

it. This arises because the passions operate more through what affects our own interest than what affects the interests of others. Hume actually discusses three types of cases. The first is the case in which "the good qualities of an enemy are hurtful to us" [65] and we confound feelings arising from interest with those needed to make a moral evaluation of these qualities. Thus, a quality which would ordinarily be assessed as virtuous because of the pleasure it brings to the possessor or others through its usefulness or agreeableness would likely be regarded as vicious if the possessor is my enemy. And here, Hume argues, that by preserving the proper temper and judgment we should be able to see that the sentiments from interest and morals are distinct :

In like manner, tho' 'tis certain a musical voice is nothing but one that naturally gives a particular kind of pleasure; yet 'tis difficult for a man to be sensible, that the voice of an enemy is agreeable, or to allow it to be musical. But a person of a fine ear, who has the command of himself can separate these feelings, and give praise to what deserves it.[66]

In this first case we find that there are distinct sentiments involved which we sometimes fail to distinguish, thereby treating that sentiment arising from interest as though it was an evaluative or moral sentiment. The other two cases to which Hume calls attention differ from this one in that only one sentiment is involved, and it must somehow serve as a source of moral distinctions even though the manner of apprehending it is variable.

In certain instances an act may be both vicious and be directed toward me. On both counts the passion of hatred should arise in me toward the person performing this action since the action will produce pain which resembles the uneasiness intrinsic to hatred, and the quality yielding the pain belongs to some other thinking being which is also the object of hatred. Thus through a double impulse the passion of hatred should be felt by me toward this person. Now, because my own interest is involved the hatred will be felt intensely. Nevertheless, in evaluating this action and the person performing it, I must again have recourse to this feeling of hatred, but I cannot claim that this action is more vicious than it would be if directed toward someone else. Accordingly, in assessing this person I must somehow adopt a disinterested standpoint.[67]

[65] T. 472.
[66] T. 472.
[67] E. 272-273.

In the second area where Hume calls attention to the presence of only one sentiment which must serve as a source of moral distinctions it is his account of sympathy which is to be the source of the problem, for in these cases our own interest is in no way involved :

When any quality, or character, has a tendency to the good of mankind, we are pleas'd with it, and approve it; because it presents the lively idea of pleasure; which idea affects us by sympathy, and is itself a kind of pleasure. But as this sympathy is very variable, it may be thought, that our sentiments of morals must admit of all the same variations. We sympathize more with persons contiguous to us, than with persons remote from us : With our acquaintance, than with strangers : With our countrymen, than with foreigners. But notwithstanding this variation of our sympathy, we give the same approbation to the same moral qualities in *China* as in *England*. They appear equally virtuous, and recommend themselves equally to the esteem of a judicious spectator. The sympathy varies without a variation in our esteem. Our esteem, therefore, proceeds not from sympathy.[68]

In both of the cases mentioned – those where our own interest is involved and where it is not – it is the variability of the moral sentiments which requires that for purposes of accurate evaluation a common or disinterested standpoint be adopted. Hume's solution to how such a disinterested standpoint is adopted is far from clear. He says that the disinterested standpoint is achieved through "that *reason*, which is able to oppose our passion; and which ... [is] ... nothing but a general calm determination of the passions, founded on some distant view or reflexion".[69]

---

[68] T. 580-581.

[69] T. 583. In the passage itself, Hume regards this reason as something which he has already discussed. Thus, he speaks of 'that reason, which is able to oppose our passion; and which *we have found to be* nothing but a general calm determination of the passions, founded on some distant view or reflexion'. I have, in quoting this passage above, omitted the underlined words because to the best of my knowledge Hume has not in any previous section discussed a reason which can oppose passion in the sense of being a calm determination of the passions founded on some distant view or reflexion. In fact, up to now Hume has been arguing that reason cannot oppose the passions and that in such situations what are commonly regarded as the dictates of reason are nothing but the impulses of certain calm passions. Selby-Bigge errs in thinking (T. 686) that the reason mentioned at T. 583 must be the calm passions mentioned at T. 417 when Hume discusses the alleged opposition between reason and passion. The calm passions often oppose the violent passions and Hume points out not that the calm passions can serve as a general calm determination of a passion founded on some distant view or reflexion, but rather that "in general, we may observe, that both these principles operate on the will; and where they are contrary, that either of them prevails, according to the general character or present disposition of the person". (T. 418. Italics in text omitted). Accordingly, if there is to be a general calm determination of the passions founded on some distant view or reflexion this can not be carried out through the calm passions.

When Hume speaks here of 'some distant view or reflexion' he means that in order to standardize the passion I must take into account how the passion would present itself if my own situation were altered : "We blame equally a bad action, which we read of in history, with one perform'd in our neighbourhood t'other day : The meaning of which is, that we know from reflexion, that the former action wou'd excite as strong sentiments of disapprobation as the latter, were it plac'd in the same position".[70] What still remains to be cleared up is what meaning is to be attached to the ordering faculty, that is, to 'that *reason*, which is able to oppose our passion ...' By merely taking into account how a passion would affect me if my position were altered, I am able to see that the passion is variable, but that by itself does not yield a disinterested standpoint : it only provides information concerning other subjective expressions of these passions. Thus, considering the variability of the passion through 'some distant view or reflexion' is a necessary condition for standardizing the sentiment, but not a sufficient one.

Hume points out that this ordering faculty into which we are inquiring does not usually make any impact on the passions themselves :

The intercourse of sentiments ... in society and conversation, makes us form some general inalterable standard, by which we may approve or disapprove of characters and manners. And tho' the *heart* does not always take part with those general notions, or regulate its love or hatred by them, yet are they sufficient for discourse, and serve all our purposes in company, in the pulpit, or the theatre, and in schools.[71]

Accordingly, the ordering faculty we are trying to uncover must be able to operate even when the perceptions themselves are unaffected by the ordering process. Of the senses of reason which Hume discusses we can eliminate demonstrative reasoning as this ordering faculty since it only seeks to apprehend relations existing between ideas. Nor is causal reasoning able to do the ordering since it operates on the basis of past uniformities and is useful only for predicting or retrodicting. Thus, causal reasoning can inform me how I would feel if I altered my present standpoint but it itself cannot be the source of the order I impose on the passion.

I suggest that the only sense of reason which answers to the ordering faculty discussed by Hume is a distinction of reason. In the case of adopting a disinterested standpoint what we must do is to distinguish the content of the passion from its vivacity or manner of presentation.

[70] T. 584.
[71] T. 603.

That is to say, in the case of actions denominated virtuous we must attend to the content of the passions of love or pride while ignoring their vivacity, whereas with vicious acts we must attend to the uneasiness of the passions of hatred or humility while again ignoring their vivacity. This situation is analogous to that discussed by Hume when he introduced the topic of distinctions of reason. There we found that colour and figure are inseparable so that in reality no distinction between them can be made. Nevertheless, given a globe of white marble and a cube of white we can through a distinction of reason establish a philosophical relation or resemblance between these two objects in order to enable us to attend to the colour while ignoring the figure. Similarly, in adopting a disinterested standpoint in morals we find that we must attend to the content of certain passions, that is, their pleasure or uneasiness, while ignoring their manner of presentation or vivacity. In reality this too cannot be done since the vivacity of a passion is not something which we can separate from the content of a passion. Just as colour is always attended with figure, so passions are attended with some vivacity or other. If, then, we are to distinguish the content of a passion from its vivacity, this can only be done through a contrasting comparison. We must, in other words, call to mind other instances of this passion wherein there is a difference in its vivacity, and through a distinction of reason attend to the resemblance of the passions so far as content is concerned and ignore their differences in vivacity. Just as "a person, who desires us to consider the figure [or colour] of a globe of white marble without thinking on its colour [or figure], desires an impossibility",[72] so a person who asks us to consider the content of a passion without attending to its vivacity is asking for an impossibility. Nevertheless, through a distinction of reason both are possible conceptually, and in the case of morality, it is "sufficient for discourse, and serves all our purposes in company, in the pulpit, on the theatre, and in the schools".[73]

We can now see that in the making of moral distinctions reason can enter at three key points : (i) in providing an adequate understanding of the situation to be assessed, (ii) in providing the causal inference vital to the operation of the sympathetic mechanism, and (iii) in providing, through a distinction of reason, the means of ordering our passions so as to enable us to adopt a disinterested standpoint when making moral evaluations. All three play a vital role and show why Hume is willing to speak of a proper sentiment and false relish in morality : Through reason an accuracy

[72] T. 25.
[73] T. 603.

is possible in moral evaluations which is lacking in subjective passional reactions to situations. As Hume himself says in one place :

When a man denominates another his *enemy*, his *rival*, his *antagonist*, his *adversary*, he is understood to speak the language of self-love, and to express sentiments, peculiar to himself, and arising from his particular circumstances and situation. But when he bestows on any man the epithets of *vicious* or *odious* or *depraved*, he then speaks another language, and expresses sentiments, in which he expects all his audience to concur with him. He must here, therefore, depart from his private and particular situation, and must choose a point of view, common to him with others ...[74]

IV. THE THIRD STAGE :
PROVING THAT MORAL RULES CAN ONLY BE OBTAINED
FROM THE MORAL IMPRESSIONS IDENTIFIED IN THE SECOND STAGE

I mentioned at the beginning of this chapter that Hume's analysis of the manner in which moral rules are obtained proceeds through three stages, the third stage relying heavily upon the arguments and conclusions of the first two stages. In the first stage Hume argued that an 'ought-statement' or moral rule expresses either a new relation or a fact, and he attempted to rule out the former on the ground that it is logically impossible to deduce a statement containing the word 'ought' from other relational statements which do not contain it. Since relational statements express an equality or inequality between two ideas in virtue of a common property, Hume is actually arguing than an' ought-statement' is not such a statement of equality or inequality. With the possibility of an 'ought-statement' being reducible to a relational statement being ruled out, he holds that in accordance with his theory of perceptions an 'ought-statement' expresses a new fact, and must have as its referent an impression, since impressions constitute our matters of fact. The first stage also required that impressions giving rise to 'ought-statements' be identified and accounted for causally. The second stage examined those perceptions through which moral distinctions are made, and established that although accurate moral distinctions are dependent upon reason, it is through certain impressions that moral distinctions are actually made. Virtuous actions are those yielding a feeling of pleasure and vicious actions are those which give rise to a feeling of uneasiness. In the *Treatise* Hume argues that the impressions involved in moral distinctions are the indirect passions of pride, humility, love, and hatred.

[74] E. 272.

In the third stage, Hume begins by calling attention to the fact that when we call an action virtuous or vicious the action itself is only considered a sign of a motive, and strictly speaking, it is the motive which we praise or blame :

'Tis evident, that when we praise any actions, we regard only the motives that produced them, and consider the actions as signs or indications of certain principles in the mind and temper. The external performance has no merit. We must look within to find the moral quality ... the ultimate object of our praise and approbation is the motive, that produc'd them.[75]

Since an action is virtuous only if the motive producing the action is virtuous, it follows that the first virtuous motive which bestows merit on any action cannot be a regard to the virtue of that action. Accordingly, "a virtuous motive is requisite to render an action virtuous".[76] Now, what is it which renders a motive virtuous? The second stage of Hume's argument provides the answer to this, namely, a motive is virtuous if through an accurate and disinterested appraisal of the action produced by this motive we feel the passions of pride or love. (Of course, for Hume a motive is vicious if through a similar appraisal of the action produced by this motive we feel humility or hatred.)

Hume holds that if an action is to be my duty then I must be able to perform it. Further, since the will is not self-determining but is determined through the passions which alone provide a motive to act, he maintains that "no action can be requir'd of us as our duty, unless there be implanted in human nature some actuating passion or motive capable of producing the action".[77] But not every action for which there is some actuating passion or motive is considered our duty but only those which stem from virtuous motives. Now since the only actions which can be required as our duty are those which stem from virtuous motives, and since only those motives are virtuous concerning which an accurate disinterested view produces the appropriate pleasurable sentiments, it follows that an action can be regarded as a duty if an accurate disinterested view produces the appropriate pleasurable sentiments. Accordingly, the impressions giving rise to our duty are the very impressions through which moral distinctions are made. Thus, in one place, Hume speaks of "the *moral* obligation, or the sentiment of right and wrong".[78] Upon experiencing a pleasurable

[75] T. 477. See also T. 575.
[76] T. 478.
[77] T. 518.
[78] T. 498.

sentiment in the contemplation of an action we are made aware that a duty – either our own or someone else's, depending upon the circumstances of the situation – has been fulfilled. In the passage just quoted, however, Hume speaks of the moral obligation or the sentiment of right *and wrong*. It remains then to determine the role this latter sentiment plays in determining our duties. The answer is provided in a passage in which Hume writes :

All morality depends on our sentiments; and when any action, or quality of the mind, pleases us *after a certain manner*, we say it is virtuous; and when the neglect, or non-performance of it, displeases us *after a like manner*, we say that we lie under an obligation to perform it.[79]

Accordingly, if to be pleased with an action from a disinterested standpoint is to allow that our duty has been carried out, then to be displeased with an action from a disinterested standpoint is to maintain that our duty has not been carried out. In short, to feel moral approval or disapproval toward an action or its omission is *ipso facto* to feel what duties or obligations are present.

Several important matters emerge from this interpretation of Hume's view of duty and obligation. In the first place, if we recall the 'is-ought' passage we can see that Hume has been able to observe or identify the matter of fact expressed in 'ought-statements', and recalling the second stage of his argument on obligation wherein the origin of the moral sentiments is discussed we can see that he has been able to account for the sentiments giving rise to our duties. This analysis is also important in showing that Hume remains consistent with the claim in the 'is-ought' passage that, due to the nature of demonstrative reasoning, 'ought-statements' cannot be deduced. Obligations for Hume are not deduced, they are felt; and they are felt by those very impressions by which moral distinctions are made. Thus when in Section two of Part one in Book III Hume concludes that "we do not infer a character to be virtuous, because it pleases : But in feeling that it pleases after such a particular manner, we in effect feel that it is virtuous",[80] Hume is actually speaking of our sense of duty or obligation as well as our sense of virtue. Moral distinctions are not arrived at deductively, and neither are moral obligations.

At the beginning of this book mention was made of the fact that Hume sees himself throughout the *Treatise* as an anatomist of human nature, but yet as someone whose results qualify him to give advice to the painter. The last two sentences of the *Treatise* are much to this point :

[79] T. 517.
[80] T. 471.

We must have an exact knowledge of the parts, their situation and connexion, before we can design with any elegance or correctness. And thus the most abstract speculations concerning human nature, however cold and unentertaining, become subservient to *practical morality*; and may render this latter science more correct in its precepts, and more persuasive in its exhortations.[81]

There is for Hume the same relationship between the anatomist and the painter as there is between reason and passion : As reason is the slave of the passions, so abstract speculations are subservient to practical morality, the domain of the political and social painters. Just as passions can be unreasonable when founded on the supposition of the existence of objects which do not exist or when we choose means insufficient for the desired end, so practical morality can be rendered unreasonable when it paints as virtuous or vicious what we can never so regard due to our particular constitutions, or when in an effort to render us virtuous it seeks means which are entirely inappropriate. In both these respects Hume's account of our sense of virtue and obligation will be of great assistance to the painter.

[81] T. 621.

CONCLUSION

In the preceding chapters I have attempted to show how Hume's epistemology is involved in his ethical theory, with particular attention having been paid to his doctrine of impressions and ideas and his three senses of the term 'reason'. Throughout Hume's analysis we find the constant application of his Experimental Method in deciding issues between himself and the rationalists, and in the light of my study some assessment of Hume's method is possible.

The Experimental Method as it is employed in moral philosophy involves having recourse to the impression corresponding to an idea if the latter is rendered obscure through the weak hold which the mind has of it, and of employing 'careful and exact experiments' where the impressions themselves are obscure. Careful and exact experiments are also employed when he wants to study certain mental operations, since many mental operations are found to be obscure when we reflect upon them. In the realm of conduct we have seen Hume argue that both the faculties involved in the determination of our actions,[1] and the impressions involved in making moral distinctions [2] and establishing our duties are not apprehended clearly, with the result that they are often confused with other faculties and perceptions. Thus, in the realm of conduct Hume's Experimental Method consists primarily in 'careful and exact experiments' through which the faculties and perceptions involved can be identified and studied. In each case where careful and exact experiments are employed in studying the mind's powers and qualities, attention is focussed on "those particular effects which result from its different circumstances and situations" [3] in an effort to explain "all effects from the simplest and fewest causes".[4]

[1] T. 417.   [3] T. xxi.
[2] T. 470.   [4] T. xxi.

The first use of the Experimental Method which we studied was in connection with Wollaston's moral theory. In this regard five arguments were studied, and as I showed, none of these is successful against Wollaston. Hume's first argument sought to establish that passions, volitions, and actions could not be true or false since they are not copies of anything and therefore could not be dealt with by reason. Nevertheless, the observations to which Hume has recourse do not establish that reason can only make truth claims in cases where certain perceptions are exact copies of others. To the extent that he confines himself to this sense of truth then his experiment begs the question since it simply rejects any other sense of correspondence or agreement upon which reason is able to make truth claims without providing evidence that reason is restricted to Hume's sense of correspondence. Hume's remaining arguments against Wollaston are noteworthy for our purposes since each employs an observation regarding human nature in an effort to show that Wollaston's version of rationalism cannot be accepted. Thus, the first such argument remarks on two ways in which judgments stemming from reason influence conduct, the second notes that mistakes of fact are never regarded as the source of immorality, the third notes that actions are not deemed virtuous or vicious in terms of whether or not an observer is misled by them, and the last argument makes the observation that a regard to truth *per se* is never a motive to act. Now, my own analysis has shown that Wollaston is entirely in agreement with Hume insofar as his observations are concerned, and that therefore Hume is mistaken in holding that Wollaston's view of reason in morality is inconsistent with the facts to which Hume draws attention. Thus, apart from having misunderstood Wollaston's position, Hume has not seen that the experiments he cites are compatible with at least one version of rationalism in morality.

Regarding Hume's opposition to Clarke I have shown that Hume's observations concerning the employment of demonstrative reasoning and his challenge to Clarke to disclose some further 'moral' relation are of no value in refuting Clarke's version of rationalism since Clarke's rationalism is not based on demonstrative reasoning, but rather on causal reasoning and his claim that reason actually assents to precepts enjoining actions which are in the public benefit. Thus, the essential experiment which Hume required was that in which it could be shown that reason has no original concern with the public benefit, and this he never developed. Further, I have shown that Hume's observation that ' 'tis one thing to know virtue and another to conform the will to it' is not one which adversely affects Clarke's theory since, in effect, he himself recognizes this. Again her'e therefore, in the case of Clarke's moral theory we can conclude that Hume's observations are compatible with Clarke's version of rationalism. Putting the matter generally, we are now able to conclude that to the extent that Hume's arguments are directed against Wollaston and Clarke, the experiments which he cites are not able to confute their views and confirm his own position since the observations which he makes are compatible both with his theory and theirs.

I have also proved (in my sixth chapter) that Hume's arguments against the claim that reason can be practical fail (at least against Clarke) since Hume does not show that reason cannot have a concern with ends, and he has recourse to direct observation in attempting to show what can move us to act in an area where he holds that direct observation is misleading.[5]

Thus, insofar as Hume's Experimental Method is employed against the moral theories of Clarke and Wollaston I conclude that it has been unsuccessful, and therefore it cannot support Hume's view that "the final sentence ... which pronounces characters and actions amiable or odious, praise-worthy or blameable; that which stamps on them the mark of honour or infamy, approbation or censure; that which renders morality an active principle ... depends on some internal sense or feeling".[6]

[5] T. 414, T. 417.
[6] E. 173.

BIBLIOGRAPHY

BOOKS

Aiken, H. D., *Hume's Moral and Political Philosophy*. New York : Hafner Publishing Co., 1948. Reprinted : New York : Hafner Publishing Co., 1966.

Anderson, R. F., *Hume's First Principles*. University of Nebraska Press, 1966.

Basson, A. H., *David Hume*. Harmondsworth, Middlesex : Penguin Books, 1958.

Broiles, R. D., *The Moral Philosophy of David Hume*. The Hague : Martinus Nijhoff, 1964.

Capaldi, N., *Judgment and Sentiment in Hume's Moral Theory*. Ann Arbor, Michigan : University Microfilms, A Xerox Company, 1965.

Chappell, V. C. (ed.), *Hume : A Collection of Critical Essays*. Garden City, New York : Anchor Books, 1966.

Church, R. W., *Hume's Theory of the Understanding*. London : Allen and Unwin, 1935.

Clarke, Samuel, *A Discourse Concerning the Unchangeable Obligations of Natural Religion, and The Truth and Certainty of the Christian Revelation* in *The Works of Samuel Clarke*, D. D. Vol. II. London : Printed for John and Paul Knapton in Ludgate Street, MDCCXXXVIII.

Glathe, A. B., *Hume's Theory of the Passions and of Morals*. Berkeley : University of California Press, 1950.

Hume, David, *An Abstract of a Treatise of Human Nature*. Reprinted (from the 1740 copy) with an Introduction by J. M. Keynes and P. Sraffa. Hamden, Connecticut : Archon Books, 1965. Reprint of the 1740 copy owned by J. M. Keynes was first republished in 1938 by the Cambridge University Press. This work was originally published anonymously as *An Abstract of a book lately published, entituled, A Treatise of Human Nature, etc. wherein the Chief Argument of that Book is farther illustrated and explained*. London : Printed for C. Borbet at Addison's Head, over-against H. Dunstan's Church in Fleetstreet, 1740. In the introduction to the Keynes and Sraffa reprint, convincing evidence is offered to establish that Hume himself is the author of this work.

Hume, David, *Dialogiues Concerning Natural Religion*. Edited by Norman Kemp Smith. Oxford : The Clarendon Press, 1935. Reprinted : New York : Library of Liberal Arts, 1947.

—, *Enquiries Concerning the Human Understanding and Concerning the Principles of Morals*. Selby-Bigge edition. Oxford : Clarendon Press, 1894.

—, *A Treatise of Human Nature*. Selby-Bigge edition. Oxford : Clarendon Press, 1888.

Huxley, T. H., *Hume with Helps to the Study of Berkeley. Essays*. London : Macmillan, 1886. Reprinted : New York : Greenwood Press, 1968.

Kydd, R. M., *Reason and Conduct in Hume's Treatise*. London : Oxford University Press, 1946. Reprinted : New York : Russell and Russell Inc., 1964.

Laird, J., *Hume's Philosophy of Human Nature*. London : Methuen, 1932. Reprinted : Archon Books, 1967.

Macnabb, D. G. C., *David Hume : His Theory of Knowledge and Morality*. London : Hutchinson's University Library, 1951. Reprinted : Oxford : Basil Blackwell, 1966.

Passmore, J. A., *Hume's Intentions*. Cambridge : University Press, 1952.

Pears, D. (ed.), *David Hume, A Symposium*. London : Macmillan and Company Ltd., 1963. Reprinted : New York : Macmillan, St. Martin's Press, 1966.

Raphael, D. D. (ed.), *British Moralists*. 1650-1800 (2 vols.) Oxford : Clarendon Press, 1969.

Selby-Bigge, L. A. (ed.), *British Moralists*. (2 vols.) Oxford : Clarendon Press, 1897. Reprinted : New York : Library of Liberal Arts, 1964.

Smith, N. K., *The Philosophy of David Hume*. London : Macmillan, 1941. Reprinted : New York : Macmillan, St. Martin's Press, 1960.

Stewart, J. B., *The Moral and Political Philosophy of David Hume*. New York : Columbia University Press, 1963.

Thompson, C. G., *The Ethics of William Wollaston*. Boston : Richard G. Badger, The Gorham Press, 1922.

Wollaston, W., *The Religion of Nature Delineated*. The Sixth Edition. London : Printed for John and Paul Knapton at the Crown in Ludgate Street, MDCCXXXVIII.

Zabeeh, F., *Hume : Precursor of Modern Empiricism*. The Hague : Martinus Nijhoff, 1960.

ARTICLES

Atkinson, R. F., "Hume on 'Is' and 'Ought', A Reply to Mr. MacIntyre", *The Philosophical Review*, Vol. LXX (1961). Reprinted in *Hume : A Collection of Critical Essays*, edited by V. C. Chappell, New York : Anchor Books (1966), p. 265-277.

Johnson, O. A., "Begging the Question", *Dialogue*, Vol. VI, No. 2 (1967), p. 135-150.

MacIntyre, A. C., "Hume on 'Is' and 'Ought' ", *The Philosophical Review*, Vol. LXVIII (1959). Reprinted in *Hume : A Collection of Critical Essays*, edited by V. C. Chappell, New York : Anchor Books (1966), p. 240-264.

McGilvray, E. B., "Altruism in Hume's Treatise", *Philosophical Review*, Vol. 12 (1903), p. 272-284.

Price, K. B., "Does Hume's Theory of Knowledge Determine His Ethical Theory?", *Journal of Philosophy*, Vol. 47 (1950), p. 425-434.

Sparshott, F. E., "Disputed Evaluations", *American Philosophical Quarterly*, Vol. 7, No. 2 (April, 1970), p. 131-142.

Wand, B., "Hume's Account of Obligation", *The Philosophical Quarterly*, Vol· VI (1956). Reprinted in *Hume : A Collection of Critical Essays*, edited by V. C. Chappell, New York : Anchor Books (1966), p. 308-334.

INDEX

Abstract Ideas : 51.

Accurate and Abstruse Philosophy : 1; also called Metaphysics, 5; its reference to human behaviour, 5; Method of, 6-10; justification of the method 10-17; as the study of human nature it is confined to impressions of reflection, 33.

Active faculty : for Hume, 137.

Anderson, R.F. 48, and elsewhere through to 70.

Aspect : See Distinctions of Reason.

Association of Ideas : 21-23.

Aversion : see Desire and Aversion.

Beauty and Deformity : for Hume, morality resembles our pronouncements concerning beauty and deformity, 150-151.

Broiles, R. David : 98, 115n, 118-119.

Butler, Ronald J., 41 n.

Calm Desires and Tendencies : we confuse their feeling with feeling attached to the operation of reason, 132.

Capaldi, N. 37, 38, 39.

Causation (in Hume) : a natural relation 22; a source of philosophical relation 24; one of three sense of reason, 41-42; its reference to the will, 121-122; causal reasoning and the will, 132-137; only two roles to play in the determination of conduct, 134; causal inferences constitute one way of getting an idea of pleasure or pain to affect the will, 136; why causal reasoning can excite a passion and demonstrative reasoning cannot, 136; it can direct a passion to its proper object or assist à passion in selecting the proper means to acquire something already desired, 139; its role in sympathy, 157.

Clarke, Samuel : 73-87; Hume's critique of, 111-118; how passions can be contrary to reason, 128-129; Hume's unsucessful critique of Clarke's thesis of the combat between reason and passion, 130-131; reason is able to discern the difference between good and evil, and it is the source of the rules and precepts which ought to govern our behaviour, 118; 143-144; use of Hume's Experimental Method against Clarke, 173-174.

Colour : inseparable from figure, see Distinctions of Reason.

Comparison : necessary for philosophical relations, 24.

Contiguity : a natural relation 21; its role in sympathy, 157.

Contrariety : a source of philosophical relation 24; how it can influence our conduct, 124-127.

Truth:

A. *In Hume's Philosophy* : two kinds of, 40-41; a regard for truth can never be a motive to act, 110-111; if truths discovered beget no desire or aversion, they can have no influence on conduct, 124.

B. *In Wollaston's Philosophy* : connection with actions and propositions in the philosophy of William Wollaston, 87-92; connection with happiness in Wollaston's philosophy, 92-97; connection with happiness and obligation in Wollaston's philosophy, 98-99.

Vice and Virtue : for Hume, only the faculty capable of distinguishing vice and virtue is capable of yielding moral rules, 147; Hume's discussion of those impressions through which we distinguish vice and virtue, 147-171.

Wollaston, William : 87-99; Hume's critique of, 103-111; reason is able to discern the difference between good and evil, and it is the source of the rules and precepts which ought to gover or behaviour, 118; use of Hume's Experimental Method against Wollaston, 173.

Zabeeh, F. 57 n.